CAMBRIDGE
UNIVERSITY PRESS

Chemistry

for Cambridge International AS & A Level

EXAM PREPARATION AND PRACTICE

Carl Thirsk & Kristy Turner

Contents

A Level

There are extra digital questions for this title found online at Cambridge GO.
For more information on how to access and use your digital resource, please see inside the front cover.

> How to use this series

This suite of resources supports students and teachers following the Cambridge International AS & A Level Chemistry syllabus (9701). All of the components in the series are designed to work together and help students develop the necessary knowledge and skills for this subject. With clear language and style, they are designed for international students.

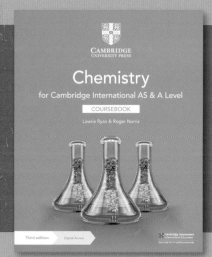

The coursebook provides comprehensive support for the full Cambridge International Chemistry syllabus (9701). It includes exercises that develop problem-solving skills, practical activities to help students develop investigative skills, and real world examples of scientific principles. With clear language and style, the coursebook is designed for international learners.

The teacher's resource supports and enhances the projects, questions and practical activities in the coursebook. This resource includes detailed lesson ideas, as well as answers and exemplar data for all questions and activities in the coursebook and workbook. The practical teacher's guide, included with this resource, provides support for the practical activities and experiments in the practical workbook.

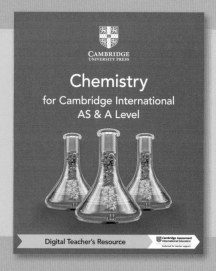

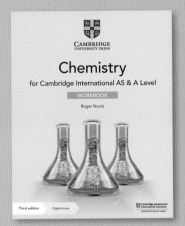

The workbook contains over 100 extra activities that help students build on what they have learned in the coursebook. Students can practise their experimentation, analysis and evaluation skills through exercises testing problem-solving and data handling, while activities also support students' planning and investigative skills.

Hands-on investigations provide opportunities to develop key scientific skills, including planning investigations, identifying equipment, creating hypotheses, recording results, and analysing and evaluating data.

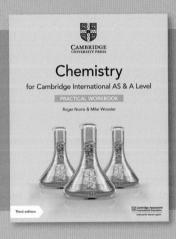

The Exam Preparation and Practice resource provides dedicated support for learners in preparing for their final assessments. Hundreds of questions in the book and accompanying digital resource will help learners to check that they understand, and can recall, syllabus concepts. To help learners to show what they know in an exam context, a specially developed framework of exam skills with corresponding questions, and past paper question practice, is also included. Self-assessment and reflection features support learners to identify any areas that need further practice. This resource should be used alongside the coursebook, throughout the course of study, so learners can most effectively increase their confidence and readiness for their exams.

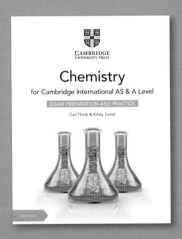

> How to use this book

This book will help you to check that you **know** the content of the syllabus and practise how to **show** this understanding in an exam. It will also help you be cognitively prepared and in the **flow**, ready for your exam. Research has shown that it is important that you do all three of these things, so we have designed the Know, Show, Flow approach to help you prepare effectively for exams.

| Know | You will need to consolidate and then recall a lot of syllabus content. |

| Show | You should demonstrate your knowledge in the context of a Cambridge exam. |

| Flow | You should be cognitively engaged and ready to learn. This means reducing test anxiety. |

Exam skills checklist

Category	Exam skill
Understanding the question	Recognise different question types
	Understand command words
	Mark scheme awareness
Providing an appropriate response	Understand connections between concepts
	Keep to time
	Know what a good answer looks like
Developing supportive behaviours	Reflect on progress
	Manage test anxiety

This **Exam skills checklist** helps you to develop the awareness, behaviours and habits that will support you when revising and preparing for your exams. For more exam skills advice, including understanding command words and managing your time effectively, please go to the **Exam skills chapter**.

Know

The full syllabus content of your AS & A Level Chemistry course is covered in your Cambridge coursebook. This book will provide you with different types of questions to support you as you prepare for your exams. You will answer **Knowledge recall questions** that are designed to make sure you understand a topic, and **Recall and connect questions** to help you recall past learning and connect different concepts.

KNOWLEDGE FOCUS

Knowledge focus boxes summarise the topics that you will answer questions on in each chapter of this book. You can refer back to your Cambridge coursebook to remind yourself of the full detail of the syllabus content.

Knowledge recall questions

Testing yourself is a good way to check that your understanding is secure. These questions will help you to recall the core knowledge you have acquired during your course, and highlight any areas where you may need more practice. They are indicated with a blue bar with a gap, at the side of the page. We recommend that you answer the Knowledge recall questions just after you have covered the relevant topic in class, and then return to them at a later point to check you have properly understood the content.

≪ RECALL AND CONNECT ≪

To consolidate your learning, you need to test your memory frequently. These questions will test that you remember what you learned in previous chapters, in addition to what you are practising in the current chapter.

UNDERSTAND THESE TERMS

These list the important vocabulary that you should understand for each chapter. Definitions are provided in the glossary of your Cambridge coursebook.

Show

Exam questions test specific knowledge, skills and understanding. You need to be prepared so that you have the best opportunity to show what you know in the time you have during the exam. In addition to practising recall of the syllabus content, it is important to build your exam skills throughout the year.

EXAM SKILLS FOCUS

This feature outlines the exam skills you will practise in each chapter, alongside the Knowledge focus. They are drawn from the core set of eight exam skills, listed in the exam skills checklist. You will practise specific exam skills, such as understanding command words, within each chapter. More general exam skills, such as managing test anxiety, are covered in the Exam skills chapter.

Exam skills questions

These questions will help you to develop your exam skills and demonstrate your understanding. To help you become familiar with exam-style questioning, many of these questions follow the style and use the language of real exam questions, and have allocated marks. They are indicated with a solid red bar at the side of the page.

Looking at sample answers to past paper questions helps you to understand what to aim for.

The **Exam practice** sections in this resource contain example student responses and examiner-style commentary showing how the answer could be improved (both written by the authors).

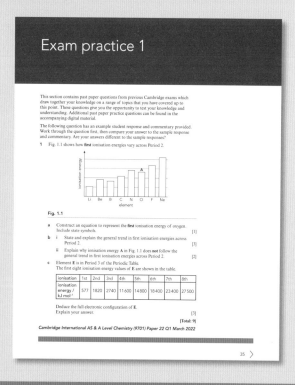

Flow

Preparing for exams can be stressful. One of the approaches recommended by educational psychologists to help with this stress is to improve behaviours around exam preparation. This involves testing yourself in manageable chunks, accompanied by self-evaluation. You should avoid cramming and build in more preparation time. This book is structured to help you do this.

Increasing your ability to recognise the signs of exam-related stress and working through some techniques for how to cope with it will help to make your exam preparation manageable.

REFLECTION

This feature asks you to think about the approach that you take to your exam preparation, and how you might improve this in the future. Reflecting on how you plan, monitor and evaluate your revision and preparation will help you to do your best in your exams.

SELF-ASSESSMENT CHECKLIST

These checklists return to the Learning intentions from your coursebook, as well as the Exam skills focus boxes from each chapter. Checking in on how confident you feel in each of these areas will help you to focus your exam preparation. The 'Show it' prompts will allow you to test your rating. You should revisit any areas that you rate 'Needs more work' or 'Almost there'.

Now I can:	Show it	Needs more work	Almost there	Confident to move on

Increasing your ability to recognise the signs of exam-related stress and working through some techniques for how to cope with it will help to make your exam preparation manageable. The **Exam skills chapter** will support you with this.

Digital support

Extra self-assessment questions for all chapters can be found online at Cambridge GO. For more information on how to access and use your digital resource, please see inside the front cover.

You will find **Answers** for all of the questions in the book on the 'supporting resources' area of the Cambridge GO platform.

Multiple choice questions

These ask you to select the correct answer to a question from four options. These are auto-marked and feedback is provided.

Flip card questions

These present a question on one screen, and suggested answers on the reverse.

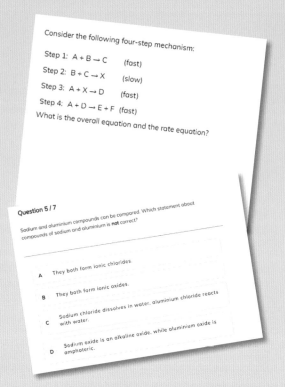

Syllabus Assessment Objectives for AS & A Level Chemistry

You should be familiar with the Assessment Objectives from the syllabus, as the examiner will be looking for evidence of these requirements in your responses and allocating marks accordingly.

The Assessment Objectives for this syllabus are:

Assessment Objective	AS Level weighting	A Level weighting
AO1: Knowledge and Understanding	30%	25%
AO2: Application	30%	25%
AO3: Analysis	20%	25%
AO4: Evaluation	20%	25%

Exam skills

by Lucy Parsons

What's the point of this book?

Most students make one really basic mistake when they're preparing for exams. What is it? It's focusing far too much on learning 'stuff' – that's facts, figures, ideas, information – and not nearly enough time practising exam skills.

The students who work really, really hard but are disappointed with their results are nearly always students who focus on memorising stuff. They think to themselves, 'I'll do practice papers once I've revised everything.' The trouble is, they start doing practice papers too late to really develop and improve how they communicate what they know.

What could they do differently?

When your final exam script is assessed, it should contain specific language, information and thinking skills in your answers. If you read a question in an exam and you have no idea what you need to do to give a good answer, the likelihood is that your answer won't be as brilliant as it could be. That means your grade won't reflect the hard work you've put into revising for the exam.

There are different types of questions used in exams to assess different skills. You need to know how to recognise these question types and understand what you need to show in your answers.

So, how do you understand what to do in each question type?

That's what this book is all about. But first a little background.

Meet Benjamin Bloom

The psychologist Benjamin Bloom developed a way of classifying and valuing different skills we use when we learn, such as analysis and recalling information. We call these thinking skills. It's known as Bloom's Taxonomy and it's what most exam questions are based around.

If you understand Bloom's Taxonomy, you can understand what any type of question requires you to do. So, what does it look like?

Bloom's Taxonomy of thinking skills

The key things to take away from this diagram are:

- Knowledge and understanding are known as lower-level thinking skills. They are less difficult than the other thinking skills. Exam questions that just test you on what you know are usually worth the lowest number of marks.

- All the other thinking skills are worth higher numbers of marks in exam questions. These questions need you to have some foundational knowledge and understanding but are far more about how you think than what you know. They involve:

  - Taking what you know and using it in unfamiliar situations (application).
  - Going deeper into information to discover relationships, motives, causes, patterns and connections (analysis).
  - Using what you know and think to create something new – whether that's an essay, long-answer exam question, a solution to a maths problem, or a piece of art (synthesis).
  - Assessing the value of something, e.g. the reliability of the results of a scientific experiment (evaluation).

In this introductory chapter, you'll be shown how to develop the skills that enable you to communicate what you know and how you think. This will help you achieve to the best of your abilities. In the rest of the book, you'll have a chance to practise these exam skills by understanding how questions work and understanding what you need to show in your answers.

Every time you pick up this book and do a few questions, you're getting closer to achieving your dream results. So, let's get started!

Exam preparation and revision skills

What is revision?

If you think about it, the word 'revision' has two parts to it:

- re – which means 'again'

- vision – which is about seeing.

So, revision is literally about 'seeing again'. This means you're looking at something that you've already learned.

Typically, a teacher will teach you something in class. You may then do some questions on it, write about it in some way, or even do a presentation. You might then have an end-of-topic test sometime later. To prepare for this test, you need to 'look again' or revise what you were originally taught.

Step 1: Making knowledge stick

Every time you come back to something you've learned or revised you're improving your understanding and memory of that particular piece of knowledge. This is called **spaced retrieval**. This is how human memory works. If you don't use a piece of knowledge by recalling it, you lose it.

Everything we learn has to be physically stored in our brains by creating neural connections – joining brain cells together. The more often we 'retrieve' or recall a particular piece of knowledge, the stronger the neural connection gets. It's like lifting weights – the more often you lift, the stronger you get.

However, if you don't use a piece of knowledge for a long time, your brain wants to recycle the brain cells and use them for another purpose. The neural connections get weaker until they finally break, and the memory has gone. This is why it's really important to return often to things that you've learned in the past.

Great ways of doing this in your revision include:

- Testing yourself using flip cards – use the ones available in the digital resources for this book.

- Testing yourself (or getting someone else to test you) using questions you've created about the topic.

- Checking your recall of previous topics by answering the Recall and connect questions in this book.

- Blurting – writing everything you can remember about a topic on a piece of paper in one colour. Then, checking what you missed out and filling it in with another colour. You can do this over and over again until you feel confident that you remember everything.

- Answering practice questions – use the ones in this book.

- Getting a good night's sleep to help consolidate your learning.

> **The importance of sleep and creating long-term memory**
>
> When you go to sleep at night, your brain goes through an important process of taking information from your short-term memory and storing it in your long-term memory.
>
> This means that getting a good night's sleep is a very important part of revision. If you don't get enough good quality sleep, you'll actually be making your revision much, much harder.

Step 2: Developing your exam skills

We've already talked about the importance of exam skills, and how many students neglect them because they're worried about covering all the knowledge.

What actually works best is developing your exam skills at the same time as learning the knowledge.

What does this look like in your studies?

- Learning something at school and your teacher setting you questions from this book or from past papers. This tests your recall as well as developing your exam skills.

- Choosing a topic to revise, learning the content and then choosing some questions from this book to test yourself at the same time as developing your exam skills.

The reason why practising your exam skills is so important is that it helps you to get good at communicating what you know and what you think. The more often you do that, the more fluent you'll become in showing what you know in your answers.

Step 3: Getting feedback

The final step is to get feedback on your work.

If you're testing yourself, the feedback is what you got wrong or what you forgot. This means you then need to go back to those things to remind yourself or improve your understanding. Then, you can test yourself again and get more feedback. You can also congratulate yourself for the things you got right – it's important to celebrate any success, big or small.

If you're doing past paper questions or the practice questions in this book, you will need to mark your work. Marking your work is one of the most important things you can do to improve. It's possible to make significant improvements in your marks in a very short space of time when you start marking your work.

Why is marking your own work so powerful? It's because it teaches you to identify the strengths and weaknesses of your own work. When you look at the mark scheme and see how it's structured, you will understand what is needed in your answers to get the results you want.

This doesn't just apply to the knowledge you demonstrate in your answers. It also applies to the language you use and whether it's appropriately subject-specific, the structure of your answer, how you present it on the page and many other factors. Understanding, practising and improving on these things are transformative for your results.

The most important thing about revision

The most important way to make your revision successful is to make it active.

Sometimes, students say they're revising when they sit staring at their textbook or notes for hours at a time. However, this is a really ineffective way to revise because it's passive. In order to make knowledge and skills stick, you need to be doing something like the suggestions in the following diagram. That's why testing yourself and pushing yourself to answer questions that test higher-level thinking skills are so effective. At times, you might actually be able to feel the physical changes happening in your brain as you develop this new knowledge and these new skills. That doesn't come about without effort.

The important thing to remember is that while active revision feels much more like hard work than passive revision, you don't actually need to do nearly as much of it. That's because you remember knowledge and skills when you use active revision. When you use passive revision, it is much, much harder for the knowledge and skills to stick in your memory.

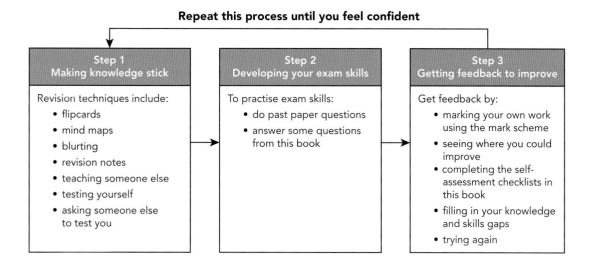

Repeat this process until you feel confident

Step 1 Making knowledge stick	Step 2 Developing your exam skills	Step 3 Getting feedback to improve
Revision techniques include: • flipcards • mind maps • blurting • revision notes • teaching someone else • testing yourself • asking someone else to test you	To practise exam skills: • do past paper questions • answer some questions from this book	Get feedback by: • marking your own work using the mark scheme • seeing where you could improve • completing the self-assessment checklists in this book • filling in your knowledge and skills gaps • trying again

How to improve your exam skills

This book helps you to improve in eight different areas of exam skills, which are divided across three categories. These skills are highlighted in this book in the Exam skills focus at the start of each chapter and developed throughout the book using targeted questions, advice and reflections.

1 **Understand the questions: what are you being asked to do?**

- Know your question types.
- Understand command words.
- Work with mark scheme awareness.

2 **How to answer questions brilliantly**

- Understand connections between concepts.
- Keep to time.
- Know what a good answer looks like.

3 **Give yourself the best chance of success**

- Reflect on progress.
- Know how to manage test anxiety.

Understand the questions: what are you being asked to do?

Know your question types

In any exam, there will be a range of different question types. These different question types will test different types of thinking skills from Bloom's Taxonomy.

It is very important that you learn to recognise different question types. If you do lots of past papers, over time you will begin to recognise the structure of the paper for each of your subjects. You will know which types of questions may come first and which ones are more likely to come at the end of the paper. You can also complete past paper questions in the Exam practice sections in this book for additional practice.

You will also recognise the differences between questions worth a lower number of marks and questions worth more marks. The key differences are:

- how much you will need to write in your answer

- how sophisticated your answer needs to be in terms of the detail you give and the depth of thinking you show.

Types of questions

1   Multiple choice questions

Multiple choice questions are generally worth smaller numbers of marks. You will be given several possible answers to the question, and you will have to work out which one is correct using your knowledge and skills.

There is a chance of you getting the right answer with multiple choice questions even if you don't know the answer. This is why you must **always give an answer for multiple choice questions** as it means there is a chance you will earn the mark.

Multiple choice questions are often harder than they appear. The possible answers can be very similar to each other. This means you must be confident in how you work out answers or have a high level of understanding to tell the difference between the possible answers.

Being confident in your subject knowledge and doing lots of practice multiple choice questions will set you up for success. Use the resources in this book and the accompanying online resources to build your confidence.

This example of a multiple choice question is worth one mark. You can see that all the answers have one part in common with at least one other answer. For example, palisade cells is included in three of the possible answers. That's why you have to really know the detail of your content knowledge to do well with multiple choice questions.

Which two types of cells are found in plant leaves?

    A   Palisade mesophyll and stomata

    B   Palisade mesophyll and root hair

    C   Stomata and chloroplast

    D   Chloroplast and palisade mesophyll

2 Questions requiring longer-form answers

Questions requiring longer-form answers need you to write out your answer yourself.

With these questions, take careful note of how many marks are available and how much space you've been given for your answer. These two things will give you a good idea about how much you should say and how much time you should spend on the question.

A rough rule to follow is to write one sentence, or make one point, for each mark that is available. You will get better and better at these longer-form questions the more you practise them.

In this example of a history question, you can see it is worth four marks. It is not asking for an explanation, just for you to list Lloyd George's aims. Therefore, you need to make four correct points in order to get full marks.

What were Lloyd George's aims during negotiations leading to the Treaty of Versailles? [4]

3 Essay questions

Essay questions are the longest questions you will be asked to answer in an exam. They examine the higher-order thinking skills from Bloom's Taxonomy such as analysis, synthesis and evaluation.

To do well in essay questions, you need to talk about what you know, giving your opinion, comparing one concept or example to another, and evaluating your own ideas or the ones you're discussing in your answer.

You also need to have a strong structure and logical argument that guides the reader through your thought process. This usually means having an introduction, some main body paragraphs that discuss one point at a time, and a conclusion.

Essay questions are usually level-marked. This means that you don't get one mark per point you make. Instead, you're given marks for the quality of the ideas you're sharing as well as how well you present those ideas through the subject-specific language you use and the structure of your essay.

Practising essays and becoming familiar with the mark scheme is the only way to get really good at them.

Understand command words

What are command words?

Command words are the most important words in every exam question. This is because command words tell you what you need to do in your answer. Do you remember Bloom's Taxonomy? Command words tell you which thinking skill you need to demonstrate in the answer to each question.

Two very common command words are **describe** and **explain**.

When you see the command word 'describe' in a question, you're being asked to show lower-order thinking skills like knowledge and understanding. The question will either be worth fewer marks, or you will need to make more points if it is worth more marks.

The command word 'explain' is asking you to show higher-order thinking skills. When you see the command word 'explain', you need to be able to say how or why something happens.

You need to understand all of the relevant command words for the subjects you are taking. Ask your teacher where to find them if you are not sure. It's best not to try to memorise the list of command words, but to become familiar with what command words are asking for by doing lots of practice questions and marking your own work.

How to work with command words

When you first see an exam question, read it through once. Then, read it through again and identify the command word(s). Underline the command word(s) to make it clear to yourself which they are every time you refer back to the question.

You may also want to identify the **content** words in the question and underline them with a different colour. Content words tell you which area of knowledge you need to draw on to answer the question.

In this example, command words are shown in red and content words in blue:

1 a Explain **four** reasons why governments might support business start-ups. [8]

Adapted from Cambridge IGCSE Business Studies (0450)
Q1a Paper 21 June 2022

Marking your own work using the mark scheme will help you get even better at understanding command words and knowing how to give good answers for each.

Work with mark scheme awareness

The most transformative thing that any student can do to improve their marks is to work with mark schemes. This means using mark schemes to mark your own work at every opportunity.

Many students are very nervous about marking their own work as they do not feel experienced or qualified enough. However, being brave enough to try to mark your own work and taking the time to get good at it will improve your marks hugely.

Why marking your own work makes such a big difference

Marking your own work can help you to improve your answers in the following ways:

1 Answering the question

Having a deep and detailed understanding of what is required by the question enables you to answer the question more clearly and more accurately.

It can also help you to give the required information using fewer words and in less time, as you can avoid including unrelated points or topics in your answer.

2 Using subject-specific vocabulary

Every subject has subject-specific vocabulary. This includes technical terms for objects or concepts in a subject, such as mitosis and meiosis in biology. It also includes how you talk about the subject, using appropriate vocabulary that may differ from everyday language. For example, in any science subject you might be asked to describe the trend on a graph.

Your answer could say it 'goes up fast' or your answer could say it 'increases rapidly'. You would not get marks for saying 'it goes up fast', but you would for saying it 'increases rapidly'. This is the difference between everyday language and formal scientific language.

When you answer lots of practice questions, you become fluent in the language specific to your subject.

3 Knowing how much to write

It's very common for students to either write too much or too little to answer questions. Becoming familiar with the mark schemes for many different questions will help you to gain a better understanding of how much you need to write in order to get a good mark.

4 Structuring your answer

There are often clues in questions about how to structure your answer. However, mark schemes give you an even stronger idea of the structure you should use in your answers.

For example, if a question says:

'Describe and explain two reasons why…'

You can give a clear answer by:

- Describing reason 1
- Explaining reason 1
- Describing reason 2
- Explaining reason 2

Having a very clear structure will also make it easier to identify where you have earned marks. This means that you're more likely to be awarded the number of marks you deserve.

5 Keeping to time

Answering the question, using subject-specific vocabulary, knowing how much to write and giving a clear structure to your answer will all help you to keep to time in an exam. You will not waste time by writing too much for any answer. Therefore, you will have sufficient time to give a good answer to every question.

How to answer exam questions brilliantly

Understand connections between concepts

One of the higher-level thinking skills in Bloom's Taxonomy is **synthesis**. Synthesis means making connections between different areas of knowledge. You may have heard about synoptic links. Making synoptic links is the same as showing the thinking skill of synthesis.

Exam questions that ask you to show your synthesis skills are usually worth the highest number of marks on an exam paper. To write good answers to these questions, you need to spend time thinking about the links between the topics you've studied **before** you arrive in your exam. A great way of doing this is using mind maps.

How to create a mind map

To create a mind map:

1 Use a large piece of paper and several different coloured pens.

2 Write the name of your subject in the middle. Then, write the key topic areas evenly spaced around the edge, each with a different colour.

3 Then, around each topic area, start to write the detail of what you can remember. If you find something that is connected with something you studied in another topic, you can draw a line linking the two things together.

This is a good way of practising your retrieval of information as well as linking topics together.

Answering synoptic exam questions

You will recognise questions that require you to make links between concepts because they have a higher number of marks. You will have practised them using this book and the accompanying resources.

To answer a synoptic exam question:

1 **Identify the command and content words.** You are more likely to find command words like **discuss** and **explain** in these questions. They might also have phrases like 'the connection between'.

2 **Make a plan for your answer.** It is worth taking a short amount of time to think about what you're going to write in your answer. Think carefully about what information you're going to put in, the links between the different pieces of information and how you're going to structure your answer to make your ideas clear.

3 **Use linking words and phrases in your answer.** For example, 'therefore', 'because', due to', 'since' or 'this means that'.

Here is an example of an English Literature exam question that requires you to make synoptic links in your answer.

1 Discuss Carol Ann Duffy's exploration of childhood in her poetry.
Refer to two poems in your answer. [25]

Content words are shown in blue; command words are shown in red.

This question is asking you to explore the theme of childhood in Duffy's poetry. You need to choose two of her poems to refer to in your answer. This means you need a good knowledge of her poetry, and to be familiar with her exploration of childhood, so that you can easily select two poems that will give you plenty to say in your answer.

Keep to time

Managing your time in exams is really important. Some students do not achieve to the best of their abilities because they run out of time to answer all the questions. However, if you manage your time well, you will be able to attempt every question on the exam paper.

Why is it important to attempt all the questions on an exam paper?

If you attempt every question on a paper, you have the best chance of achieving the highest mark you are capable of.

Students who manage their time poorly in exams will often spend far too long on some questions and not even attempt others. Most students are unlikely to get full marks on many questions, but you will get zero marks for the questions you don't answer. You can maximise your marks by giving an answer to every question.

Minutes per mark

The most important way to keep to time is knowing how many minutes you can spend on each mark.

For example, if your exam paper has 90 marks available and you have 90 minutes, you know there is 1 mark per minute.

Therefore, if you have a 5 mark question, you should spend five minutes on it.

Sometimes, you can give a good answer in less time than you have budgeted using the minutes per mark technique. If this happens, you will have more time to spend on questions that use higher-order thinking skills, or more time on checking your work.

How to get faster at answering exam questions

The best way to get faster at answering exam questions is to do lots of practice. You should practise each question type that will be in your exam, marking your own work, so that you know precisely how that question works and what is required by the question. Use the questions in this book to get better and better at answering each question type.

Use the 'Slow, Slow, Quick' technique to get faster.

Take your time answering questions when you first start practising them. You may answer them with the support of the coursebook, your notes or the mark scheme. These things will support you with your content knowledge, the language you use in your answer and the structure of your answer.

Every time you practise this question type, you will get more confident and faster. You will become experienced with this question type, so that it is easy for you to recall the subject knowledge and write it down using the correct language and a good structure.

Calculating marks per minute

Use this calculation to work out how long you have for each mark:

Total time in the exam / Number of marks available = Minutes per mark

Calculate how long you have for a question worth more than one mark like this:

Minutes per mark × Marks available for this question = Number of minutes for this question

What about time to check your work?

It is a very good idea to check your work at the end of an exam. You need to work out if this is feasible with the minutes per mark available to you. If you're always rushing to finish the questions, you shouldn't budget checking time. However, if you usually have time to spare, then you can budget checking time.

To include checking time in your minutes per mark calculation:

(Total time in the exam – Checking time) / Number of marks available = Minutes per mark

Know what a good answer looks like

It is much easier to give a good answer if you know what a good answer looks like.

Use these methods to know what a good answer looks like.

1 **Sample answers** – you can find sample answers in these places:

- from your teacher
- written by your friends or other members of your class
- in this book.

2 **Look at mark schemes** – mark schemes are full of information about what you should include in your answers. Get familiar with mark schemes to gain a better understanding of the type of things a good answer would contain.

3 **Feedback from your teacher** – if you are finding it difficult to improve your exam skills for a particular type of question, ask your teacher for detailed feedback. You should also look at their comments on your work in detail.

Give yourself the best chance of success

Reflection on progress

As you prepare for your exam, it's important to reflect on your progress. Taking time to think about what you're doing well and what could be improved brings more focus to your revision. Reflecting on progress also helps you to continuously improve your knowledge and exam skills.

How do you reflect on progress?

Use the 'Reflection' feature in this book to help you reflect on your progress during your exam preparation. Then, at the end of each revision session, take a few minutes to think about the following:

	What went well? What would you do the same next time?	What didn't go well? What would you do differently next time?
Your subject knowledge		
How you revised your subject knowledge – did you use active retrieval techniques?		
Your use of subject-specific and academic language		
Understanding the question by identifying command words and content words		
Giving a clear structure to your answer		
Keeping to time		
Marking your own work		

Remember to check for silly mistakes – things like missing out the units after you carefully calculated your answer.

Use the mark scheme to mark your own work. Every time you mark your own work, you will be recognising the good and bad aspects of your work, so that you can progressively give better answers over time.

When do you need to come back to this topic or skill?

Earlier in this section of the book, we talked about revision skills and the importance of spaced retrieval. When you reflect on your progress, you need to think about how soon you need to return to the topic or skill you've just been focusing on.

For example, if you were really disappointed with your subject knowledge, it would be a good idea to do some more active retrieval and practice questions on this topic tomorrow. However, if you did really well you can feel confident you know this topic and come back to it again in three weeks' or a month's time.

The same goes for exam skills. If you were disappointed with how you answered the question, you should look at some sample answers and try this type of question again soon. However, if you did well, you can move on to other types of exam questions.

Improving your memory of subject knowledge

Sometimes students slip back into using passive revision techniques, such as only reading the coursebook or their notes, rather than also using active revision techniques, like testing themselves using flip cards or blurting.

You can avoid this mistake by observing how well your learning is working as you revise. You should be thinking to yourself, 'Am I remembering this? Am I understanding this? Is this revision working?'

If the answer to any of those questions is 'no', then you need to change what you're doing to revise this particular topic. For example, if you don't understand, you could look up your topic in a different textbook in the school library to see if a different explanation helps. Or you could see if you can find a video online that brings the idea to life.

You are in control

When you're studying for exams it's easy to think that your teachers are in charge. However, you have to remember that you are studying for your exams and the results you get will be yours and no one else's.

That means you have to take responsibility for all your exam preparation. You have the power to change how you're preparing if what you're doing isn't working. You also have control over what you revise and when: you can make sure you focus on your weaker topics and skills to improve your achievement in the subject.

This isn't always easy to do. Sometimes you have to find an inner ability that you have not used before. But, if you are determined enough to do well, you can find what it takes to focus, improve and keep going.

What is test anxiety?

Do you get worried or anxious about exams? Does your worry or anxiety impact how well you do in tests and exams?

Test anxiety is part of your natural stress response.

The stress response evolved in animals and humans many thousands of years ago to help keep them alive. Let's look at an example.

The stress response in the wild

Imagine an impala grazing in the grasslands of East Africa. It's happily and calmly eating grass in its herd in what we would call the parasympathetic state of rest and repair.

Then the impala sees a lion. The impala suddenly panics because its life is in danger. This state of panic is also known as the stressed or sympathetic state. The sympathetic state presents itself in three forms: flight, fight and freeze.

The impala starts to run away from the lion. Running away is known as the flight stress response.

The impala might not be fast enough to run away from the lion. The lion catches it but has a loose grip. The impala struggles to try to get away. This struggle is the fight stress response.

However, the lion gets an even stronger grip on the impala. Now the only chance of the impala surviving is playing dead. The impala goes limp, its heart rate and breathing slow. This is called the freeze stress response. The lion believes that it has killed the impala so it drops the impala to the ground. Now the impala can switch back into the flight response and run away.

The impala is now safe – the different stages of the stress response have saved its life.

What has the impala got to do with your exams?

When you feel test anxiety, you have the same physiological stress responses as an impala being hunted by a lion. Unfortunately, the human nervous system cannot tell the difference between a life-threatening situation, such as being chased by a lion, and the stress of taking an exam.

If you understand how the stress response works in the human nervous system, you will be able to learn techniques to reduce test anxiety.

The role of the vagus nerve in test anxiety

The vagus nerve is the part of your nervous system that determines your stress response. Vagus means 'wandering' in Latin, so the vagus nerve is also known as the 'wandering nerve'. The vagus nerve wanders from your brain, down each side of your body, to nearly all your organs, including your lungs, heart, kidneys, liver, digestive system and bladder.

If you are in a stressful situation, like an exam, your vagus nerve sends a message to all these different organs to activate their stress response. Here are some common examples:

- **Heart** beats faster.

- **Kidneys** produce more adrenaline so that you can run, making you fidgety and distracted.

- **Digestive system** and **bladder** want to eliminate all waste products so that energy can be used for fight or flight.

If you want to feel calmer about your revision and exams, you need to do two things to help you move into the parasympathetic, or rest and repair, state:

1 Work with your vagus nerve to send messages of safety through your body.

2 Change your perception of the test so that you see it as safe and not dangerous.

How to cope with test anxiety

1 Be well prepared

Good preparation is the most important part of managing test anxiety. The better your preparation, the more confident you will be. If you are confident, you will not perceive the test or exam as dangerous, so the sympathetic nervous system responses of fight, flight and freeze are less likely to happen.

This book is all about helping you to be well prepared and building your confidence in your knowledge and ability to answer exam questions well. Working through the knowledge recall questions will help you to become more confident in your knowledge of the subject. The practice questions and exam skills questions will help you to become more confident in communicating your knowledge in an exam.

To be well prepared, look at the advice in the rest of this chapter and use it as you work through the questions in this book.

2 Work with your vagus nerve

The easiest way to work with your vagus nerve to tell it that you're in a safe situation is through your breathing. This means breathing deeply into the bottom of your lungs, so that your stomach expands, and then breathing out for longer than you breathed in. You can do this with counting.

Breathe in deeply, expanding your abdomen, for the count of four; breathe out, drawing your navel back towards your spine, for the count of five, six or seven. Repeat this at least three times. However, you can do it for as long as it takes for you to feel calm.

The important thing is that you breathe out for longer than you breathe in. This is because when you breathe in, your heart rate increases slightly, and when you breathe out, your heart rate decreases slightly. If you're spending more time breathing out overall, you will be decreasing your heart rate over time.

3 Feel it

Anxiety is an uncomfortable, difficult thing to feel. That means that many people try to run away from anxious feelings. However, this means the stress just gets stored in your body for you to feel later.

When you feel anxious, follow these four steps:

1 Pause.

2 Place one hand on your heart and one hand on your stomach.

3 Notice what you're feeling.

4 Stay with your feelings.

What you will find is that if you are willing to experience what you feel for a minute or two, the feeling of anxiety will usually pass very quickly.

4   Write or talk it out

If your thoughts are moving very quickly, it is often better to get them out of your mind and on to paper.

You could take a few minutes to write down everything that comes through your mind, then rip up your paper and throw it away. If you don't like writing, you can speak aloud alone or to someone you trust.

Other ways to break the stress cycle

Exercise and movement	Being friendly	Laughter
• Run or walk. • Dance. • Lift weights. • Yoga. Anything that involves moving your body is helpful.	• Chat to someone in your study break. • Talk to the cashier when you buy your lunch.	• Watch or listen to a funny show on TV or online. • Talk with someone who makes you laugh. • Look at photos of fun times.
Have a hug	**Releasing emotions**	**Creativity**
• Hug a friend or relative. • Cuddle a pet e.g. a cat. Hug for 20 seconds or until you feel calm and relaxed.	It is healthy to release negative or sad emotions. Crying is often a quick way to get rid of these difficult feelings so if you feel like you need to cry, allow it.	• Paint, draw or sketch. • Sew, knit or crochet. • Cook, build something.

If you have long-term symptoms of anxiety, it is important to tell someone you trust and ask for help.

Your perfect revision session

1 Intention

What do you want to achieve from this revision session?
- Choose an area of knowledge or an exam skill that you want to focus on
- Choose some questions from this book to test yourself that focus on this **knowledge area** or **skill**
- Gather any other resources that you will need e.g. pen. paper, flashcards, text book

2 Focus

Set your focus for the session
- **Remove distractions** from your study area e.g. leave your phone in another room
- Write down on a piece of paper or sticky note the **knowledge area** or **skill** you're intending to focus on
- Close your eyes and take three dep belly breaths, with the inhale longer than the exhale

3 Revision

Revise your knowledge and understanding
- **To improve your knowledge and understanding** of this topic use your text book, notes or flashcards
- **To improve exam skills** look at previous answers, teacher feedback, the mark scheme, model answers or examiners' reports

4 Practice

Answer exam style questions
- Use the questions in this book, or in additional online resources, **to practice your exam skills**
- If the exam is soon, do this in timed conditions without the support of the textbook or your notes
- If the exam is a long way away you can use your notes and resources to help you

5 Feedback

Mark your answers
- Use the mark scheme to markk your work
- This is your opportunity to learn to think like the examiner

6 Next steps

What have you learned about your progress from this revision session? What do you need to next?
- What did you do well? Feel good about these things, and know it's safe to set these things aside for a while
- What do you need to work on? How are you going to improve? Make a plan to get better at the things you didn't do well or didn't know

7 Rest

Take a break
- Do something completely different to rest: get up, move, do something creative or practical
- Rest is as important as studying as it gives your brain a chance to integrate your learning

1 Atomic structure

A key part of exam success is understanding what questions are asking for. Command words are specific instructions to answer a question in a certain way. You must follow those instructions carefully, otherwise your answers may be incomplete or inaccurate. In this chapter you will practise your understanding of the command word 'explain'.

Explain	set out purposes or reasons/make the relationships between things obvious/provide why and/or how, and support with relevant evidence

You must also pay attention to other instructions given in questions, for example, where you are asked to give answers to calculations to *three* significant figures or draw organic compounds using *skeletal* formula. Giving your answer to two significant figures, or using displayed formula, would not be awarded marks.

1.1 Elements and atoms

1 The names of some elements have interesting or unusual origins, which do not always fit with their symbols. Using a Periodic Table, give the names and symbols of the following elements based on the descriptions provided in the table.

Description	Element name	Symbol
The name of this element comes from the Greek words meaning 'water generator'.		
This vital element is named after the Latin word meaning 'charcoal'.		
The symbol for this reactive element comes from the Greek word *natrium*, meaning 'natural soda', a type of salt.		
This foul-smelling element is named from the Greek word *bromos*, which means 'stench'.		
The symbol for this metal is derived from its Latin name, *plumbum*.		
The symbol for this metal comes from its Latin name, *argentum*, which describes its appearance.		
This poisonous element is named from the Greek *anti + monachos*, which means 'monk killer'.		
This dense metal has a symbol that comes from the German words *wolf rahm*, meaning 'wolf soot'.		
This metallic element, named after a Roman god, has a symbol derived from the Latin *hydrargyrum*, meaning 'water silver'.		
The symbol for this metal comes from the Latin *aurum*, which means 'shining dawn'.		

UNDERSTAND THESE TERMS

- element
- atom
- proton
- neutron
- electron
- energy levels

2 Calculate the number of atoms of each element in the following parts, giving your answers in standard form correct to three significant figures:

a Iron atoms in a 2.55 g nail (one atom of iron weighs 9.27×10^{-26} kg). [1]

b Atoms of gold in a bar weighing 1 kg (one atom of gold weighs 3.27×10^{-25} kg). [1]

c The number of carbon atoms in a piece of coal weighing 110 g, which is 75% carbon by mass (one carbon atom weighs 1.99×10^{-26} kg). [1]

d Oxygen atoms in a bottle of water of 500 cm³ (one oxygen atom weighs 2.66×10^{-26} kg). Show your working. [2]

e Lithium atoms in a lithium-ion battery, which contains 856 g of lithium carbonate, Li_2CO_3 (one lithium atom weighs 1.15×10^{-26} kg). Show your working. [3]

[Total: 8]

1.2 Inside the atom

1 a Look at the lithium atom in Figure 1.1. Name the parts labelled **A** to **E**.
   Use the words in the box.

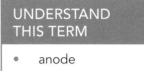

UNDERSTAND
THIS TERM

- anode

| proton | neutron | nucleus | energy level | electron |

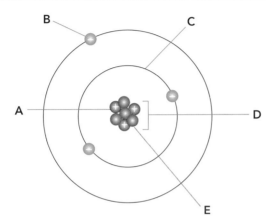

Figure 1.1: A lithium atom

b Give one reason why Figure 1.1 is not an accurate model of an atom.

c Copy and complete the table to show the names, masses and charges
  of subatomic particles.

Subatomic particle	Symbol	Relative mass	Relative charge
electron	e		
neutron	n		
proton	p		

2 a Explain what is meant by the term anode. [1]

  b Explain why electrons are attracted to the anode. [2]

  c In Rutherford's famous 'gold-foil experiment', alpha particles,
    which are the nuclei of helium atoms, were fired at thin gold foil.
    Some of the alpha particles were deflected by more than 90°.

    i Write the isotopic symbol for an alpha particle. [1]

    ii Describe what was deduced about the structure of the atom from
       Rutherford's experiment. [3]

    [Total: 7]

> **REFLECTION**
>
> Students commonly lose marks because they do not understand the command word and therefore answer the question in the wrong way, or they fail to follow a specific instruction within the question. What can you do in the exam to ensure you take note of command words and other instructional text?

1.3 Numbers of nucleons

1 **a** Give the number of neutrons and electrons in atoms of the following elements:

    i   fluorine-19

    ii calcium-44

    iii silver-109

  b Write isotopic symbols for the following ions:

    i   The +1 cation of potassium-39

    ii The +2 cation of beryllium-10

    iii The +6 cation of sulfur-34

    iv The –1 anion of iodine-135

    v The +7 cation of manganese-55

> **UNDERSTAND THESE TERMS**
>
> - atomic number
> - isotope
> - mass number

2 **a** Explain, in terms of subatomic particles, why atoms are neutral.   [3]

  b Radioactive decay of uranium-238 produces numerous isotopes, including thorium-230, radon-222 and bismuth-210. Complete the table to show the number of subatomic particles in each of these isotopes.   [3]

Isotope	Number of		
	Protons	Neutrons	Electrons
^{230}Th			
^{222}Rn			
^{210}Bi			

[Total: 6]

> **« RECALL AND CONNECT 1 «**
>
> As well as learning new definitions, you should be able to recall some key definitions from your earlier studies. Give definitions for the following:
>
> - compound
> - mixture
> - molecule

REFLECTION

You may have heard that the gap between IGCSE and AS & A Level chemistry is quite large. What do you think are some of the specific challenges of studying AS & A Level Chemistry, and what steps do you think you could take to help overcome them?

SELF-ASSESSMENT CHECKLIST

Let's revisit the Knowledge focus and Exam skills focus for this chapter.

Decide how confident you are with each statement.

Now I can:	Show it	Needs more work	Almost there	Confident to move on
describe the structure of the atom as mostly empty space surrounding a very small nucleus that consists of protons and neutrons, and state that electrons are found in shells in the space around the nucleus	Draw and label a diagram of an atom.			
describe the position of the electrons in shells in the space around the nucleus	Draw an atom and show the position of electron shells around the nucleus, including electrons per shell.			
identify and describe protons, neutrons and electrons in terms of their relative charges and relative masses	Create a table showing the subatomic particles and their properties.			
use and understand the terms atomic (proton) number and mass (nucleon) number	Write accurate definitions of these terms in your own words.			
describe the distribution of mass and charges within an atom	Create a table to show the masses and charges of subatomic particles.			
deduce the behaviour of beams of protons, neutrons and electrons moving at the same velocity in an electric field	Draw a diagram to show how beams of protons, neutrons and electrons are affected by electric fields.			

CONTINUED

Now I can:	Show it	Needs more work	Almost there	Confident to move on
understand that ions are formed from atoms or molecules by the gain or loss of electrons	Write equations to show the formation of positive and negative ions from elements.			
deduce the numbers of protons, neutrons and electrons present in both atoms and ions given the atomic (proton) number, mass (nucleon) number and charge	Write the number of subatomic particles for neutral elements, ions and their isotopes from the information provided.			
define the term *isotope* in terms of numbers of protons and neutrons	Write an accurate definition for *isotope* in your own words.			
use the notation ^x_yA for isotopes, where x is the mass (nucleon) number and y is the atomic (proton) number	Write isotopic symbols for isotopes of neutral atoms and ions.			
explain why isotopes of the same element have the same chemical properties	Draw the atoms ^{35}Cl and ^{37}Cl, and write a description of how their electronic structure is related to their chemical behaviour.			
explain why isotopes of the same element have different physical properties (limited to mass and density)	Draw the atoms ^1H and ^2D, and write a description of why H_2O and D_2O have different densities.			
understand the 'explain' command word and answer 'explain' questions	Give clear answers to 'explain' questions, using relevant information.			
distinguish between command words and other instructional text in questions	Identify any instructions in the questions and underline them to ensure you follow them.			

2 Electrons in atoms

An important part in answering questions correctly is to understand the command words in a question and what they are asking you to do. Command words help you provide the correct answers to the exam questions.

In this chapter pay attention to the 'identify' command word and make sure you are including what it is asking you to do in your answer. The definition for 'identify' is shown below.

| Identify | name/select/recognise |

2.1 Simple electronic structure

1   What alternative names are there for electron shells?

2   Figure 2.1 shows some simple electron configurations for some elements. Identify the three elements shown.

  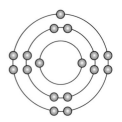

Figure 2.1

[Total: 3]

> **UNDERSTAND THESE TERMS**
> - energy levels
> - electronic configuration

≪ RECALL AND CONNECT 1 ≪

How can the number of electrons in an atom be determined from the symbol of the element in the Periodic Table?

2.2 Evidence for electronic structure

1   Give equations for the first and second ionisation energies of magnesium.

2   The table shows successive ionisation energies for an element.

Ionisation	1st	2nd	3rd	4th	5th
Ionisation energy / kJ mol⁻¹	799	2420	3660	25 000	32 800

Deduce which group of the Periodic Table the element belongs to. Explain your answer. **[Total: 6]**

> **UNDERSTAND THESE TERMS**
> - first ionisation energy, IE_1
> - successive ionisation energies
> - shielding

2.3 Sub-shells and atomic orbitals

1   Give the letters used to classify the atomic orbitals and what they stand for.

2   Give the letters used to classify the atomic orbitals that are relevant for elements up to atomic number $Z = 30$ and the number of electrons allowed in each.

3   Sketch the shape of a $3d_{z^2}$ orbital. **[Total: 1]**

> **UNDERSTAND THESE TERMS**
> - sub-shells (subsidiary quantum shells)
> - atomic orbitals

2.4 Electronic configurations

1   An element has the electronic configuration $1s^2 2s^2 2p^6 3s^2 3p^6 3d^{10} 4s^2 4p^6 4d^{10} 5s^2 5p^4$. Which block and group in the Periodic Table does this element belong to? Identify this element.

2   Give the electronic configurations of the following pairs of atoms and ions:

   a   K atom and K^+ ion.   [1]
   b   Ti atom and Ti^{2+} ion.   [1]

                                                                                    [Total: 2]

3   Give the electronic configuration of nitrogen using the 'electrons in boxes' notation. Explain your answer.   **[Total: 4]**

2.5 Periodic patterns of atomic and ionic radii

1   How is the atomic radius defined?

2   Deduce which of Na^+ and Mg^{2+} is the smaller ion. Explain your answer.   **[Total: 3]**

2.6 Patterns in ionisation energies in the Periodic Table

1   Write an equation including state symbols for the first ionisation of lithium.

2   The ionisation energy generally increases across a period.

   a   Give an example of a group of elements that deviates from this trend.
   b   Explain why this deviation occurs.   **[Total: 3]**

REFLECTION

Are you confident seeing the connections between the concepts in this chapter? Can you sketch out how all the key terms and concepts are related to the organisation of the Periodic Table? Try and annotate a copy of the Periodic Table with the concepts in this chapter.

SELF-ASSESSMENT CHECKLIST

Let's revisit the Knowledge focus and Exam skills focus for this chapter.

Decide how confident you are with each statement.

Now I can:	Show it	Needs more work	Almost there	Confident to move on
understand that electrons in an atom can only exist in certain energy levels (shells) outside the nucleus	Write a few bullet points to explain the evidence that shows electrons can only exist in certain energy levels (shells) outside the nucleus.			
use and understand the terms *shells*, *sub-shells*, *orbitals*, *principal quantum number (n)* and *ground state electronic configuration*	Draw a diagram or series of diagrams summarising the model of the atom using the key terms here.			
describe the number of orbitals making up s, p and d sub-shells, and the number of electrons that can fill s, p and d sub-shells	Draw the shape of each orbital and annotate this with the number of electrons that can fill the sub-shells.			
describe the order of increasing energy of the sub-shells within the first three shells and the 4s and 4p sub-shells	Draw a diagram showing the relative energies of the sub-shells within the first three shells and the 4s and 4p sub-shells.			
describe the electronic configurations in each shell, sub-shell and orbital	Summarise the electronic configurations in each shell, sub-shell and orbital in a short paragraph.			
explain the electronic configuration in terms of energy of the electrons and inter-electron repulsion	Write bullet points to explain how the pairing of electrons changes their relative energy.			
determine the electronic configuration given the atomic (proton) number and charge using either the full electronic configuration or shorthand electronic configuration, e.g., for Fe: $1s^2 2s^2 2p^6 3s^2 3p^6 3d^6 4s^2$ (full) or $[Ar]3d^6 4s^2$ (shorthand)	Write the full and shorthand electron configurations of five elements in the Periodic Table (atomic number up to 40).			

CONTINUED

Now I can:	Show it	Needs more work	Almost there	Confident to move on
use and understand the 'electrons in boxes' notation	Sketch the 'electrons in boxes' notation for five elements in the Periodic Table (atomic number up to 40).			
describe and sketch the shapes of s and p orbitals	Sketch the shapes of s and p orbitals, and briefly describe their shape.			
describe a free radical as a species with one or more unpaired electrons	Write the electron configuration of some free radicals.			
define the term *first ionisation energy*	Write a flash card with the definition of *first ionisation energy*. Give example equations.			
construct equations to represent first, second and subsequent ionisation energies	Write equations for all the ionisation energies for sodium.			
identify and explain the trend in ionisation energies across a period and down a group of the Periodic Table	Sketch graphs of the trend in ionisation energies across a period and down a group of the Periodic Table. Annotate the graph with labels explaining the key points.			
identify and explain the variation in successive ionisation energies of an element	Research the successive ionisation energies for sodium. Write them down in a list and annotate the list to explain the general trend and any big differences.			
describe and understand that ionisation energies are due to the attraction between the nucleus and the outer electron	Annotate a diagram of the model of the atom with labels summarising the forces holding electrons in place.			

CONTINUED

Now I can:	Show it	Needs more work	Almost there	Confident to move on
explain the factors influencing the ionisation energies of the elements (in terms of nuclear charge, atomic/ionic radius, shielding by inner shells and sub-shells, and spin-pair repulsion)	Construct a spider diagram to summarise the factors influencing the magnitude of ionisation energies.			
deduce the electronic configurations of elements using successive ionisation energy data	The first eight ionisation energies of an element are 1314, 3389, 5300, 7469, 10 990, 13 326, 71 334 and 84 078 kJ mol^{-1}. What is its electron configuration?			
deduce the position of an element in the Periodic Table using successive ionisation energy data	Add notes to a copy of the Periodic Table to show how successive ionisation energies relate to the position of an element.			
qualitatively explain the variations in atomic radius and ionic radius across a period and down a group	Make a flash card of bullet points explaining how atomic radius and ionic radius change across a period and down a group.			
understand the 'identify' command word and answer 'identify' questions	Write an 'identify' question involving patterns in the Periodic Table, complete with mark scheme.			

3 Atoms, molecules and stoichiometry

KNOWLEDGE FOCUS

In this chapter you will answer questions on:

- masses of atoms and molecules
- hydrated and anhydrous compounds
- accurate relative atomic masses
- amount of substance
- mole calculations
- chemical formulae and chemical equations
- solutions and concentration
- calculations involving gas volumes.

EXAM SKILLS FOCUS

In this chapter you will:

- practise showing your working
- understand how to recognise high-quality responses.

Even if the final answer in a multistep calculation is incorrect, you may still get credit for the method of calculation. Some calculations may have answers that are guessable. For example, you could be asked to carry out calculations to determine the identity of a Group 2 metal, or the value of n in a formula such as $(CH_2)_n(COOH)_2$. As these answers could be guessed, showing your working is essential to justify your choice.

Another important exam skill is knowing what a good answer looks like. For calculations, this means:

- showing a logical sequence of steps leading to the answer
- using appropriate units
- using an appropriate number of significant figures
- checking whether your answer is sensible.

As you work through the questions in this chapter, make sure you write down each step in a calculation and use the correct units taken from the information in the question. This is good practice to make sure you use these skills.

3.1 Masses of atoms and molecules

1 a It is incorrect to use relative molecular mass when referring to substances like silicon dioxide, diamond and sodium chloride. Why is this?

b Work out the relative molecular masses of the following compounds:
  i Butane, C_4H_{10}
  ii Sulfuric acid, H_2SO_4
  iii Ethanoic acid, CH_3COOH
  iv Paracetamol, $C_8H_9NO_2$
  v Morphine, $C_{17}H_{19}NO_3$

c Work out the relative formula masses of the following compounds:
  i Magnesium chloride, $MgCl_2$
  ii Sodium nitrate, $NaNO_3$
  iii Lithium aluminium hydride, $LiAlH_4$
  iv Ammonium iron(II) sulfate, $(NH_4)_2Fe(SO_4)_2$
  v Aluminium chloride hexahydrate, $AlCl_3.6H_2O$

UNDERSTAND THESE TERMS
• unified atomic mass unit
• formula unit
• relative isotopic mass
• relative molecular mass, M_r
• relative formula mass, M_r

2 5.21 g of a Group 2 metal carbonate were strongly heated, causing thermal decomposition.

a Write a balanced chemical equation to show decomposition of the Group 2 carbonate. State symbols should be included. Use M to represent the metal.   [2]

b The volume of gas collected, measured at r.t.p., was 1813 cm³. Using this information:
  i Determine the number of moles of CO_2 produced.   [1]
  ii Deduce the number of moles of the Group 2 carbonate that decomposed.   [1]
  iii Determine the relative formula mass of the Group 2 carbonate.   [1]
  iv Deduce the identity of the Group 2 metal.   [1]

[Total: 6]

3.2 Hydrated and anhydrous compounds

1   A common substance that contains waters of crystallisation is hydrated copper(II) sulfate, which has the formula $CuSO_4.5H_2O$.

   a   Why are waters of crystallisation present in some compounds?

   b   Why do you think the formula is not written as a molecular formula, $CuSO_9H_{10}$?

   c   Rewrite the formulae of the following hydrated compounds to show the component ions and waters of crystallisation:

      i $Na_3PO_{16}H_{24}$

      ii $H_{12}N_2O_{12}Zn$

      iii $H_{20}N_2O_{10}S$

   d   One form of the salt potassium tartrate has the formula $K_2C_4H_4O_6.0.5H_2O$. Does this mean there is half a molecule of water per formula unit of the salt?

2   A sample of hydrated copper nitrate, $Cu(NO_3)_2.xH_2O$, is found to contain 22.4% water. Determine the value of x.   **[Total: 4]**

> **UNDERSTAND THESE TERMS**
> - water of crystallisation
> - hydrated compound
> - anhydrous
> - molecular formula

3.3 Accurate relative atomic masses

1   Using the table below, show, by calculation, how the following pairs of compounds may be distinguished using high-resolution mass spectrometry:

   a CH_3CHO and CO_2

   b $C_9H_8O_4$ and $C_6H_{12}O_6$

   c $C_{12}H_{10}N_2O_5$ and $C_{18}H_{15}P$

> **UNDERSTAND THESE TERMS**
> - relative isotopic abundance
> - fragmentation

Isotope	Relative isotopic mass
^1H	1.0078246
^{12}C	12.0000000
^{14}N	14.0030738
^{16}O	15.9949141
^{31}P	30.973761998

2   The mass spectrum of a hydrocarbon is shown in Figure 3.1. The molecular ion peak has a mass-to-charge ratio of 86 and a relative abundance of 65.1%, while the relative abundance of the $[M + 1]^+$ peak is 4.3%.

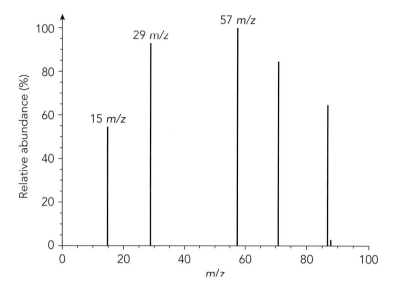

Figure 3.1

a   State what is meant by the term *molecular ion*.   [1]

b   Determine the number of carbon atoms in the hydrocarbon.   [1]

c   Give the formulae of the ions responsible for the peaks in the mass spectrum labelled 15 *m/z* and 29 *m/z*.   [2]

d   Explain the appearance of the peak labelled 57 *m/z* in the mass spectrum and give the formula of the ion responsible for this peak.   [2]

e   Deduce the molecular formula for the hydrocarbon.   [1]

[Total: 7]

UNDERSTAND
THIS TERM

• molecular ion

《 RECALL AND CONNECT 1 《

a   Give the full electronic configurations for the following elements:

  i   fluorine

  ii   aluminium

  iii   copper

b   Why is the first ionisation energy of sulfur lower than that of phosphorus?

3.4 Amount of substance

1 The structure of the common painkiller ibuprofen is shown in Figure 3.2. Worldwide production of ibuprofen in 2019 was 15,000 tonnes.

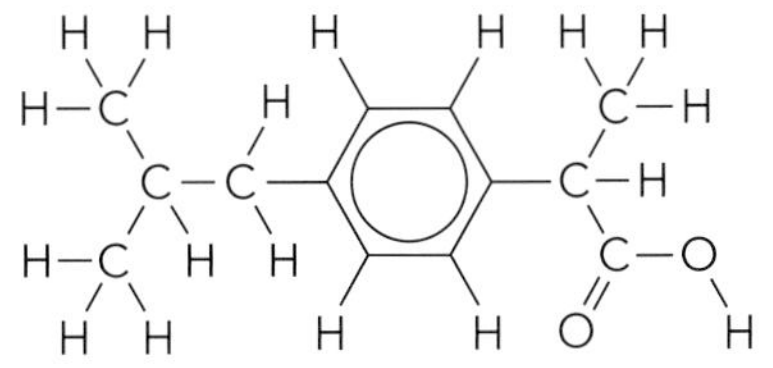

Figure 3.2

UNDERSTAND
THESE TERMS

• mole
• Avogadro constant, L
• molar mass

a Deduce the molecular formula of ibuprofen. [1]
b Calculate the relative molecular mass of ibuprofen. [1]
c Calculate the number of moles of ibuprofen produced in 2019, giving your answer in standard form. 1 tonne = 10^6 g. [1]
d Calculate the total number of carbon atoms in this amount of ibuprofen, giving your answer in standard form. [1]

[Total: 4]

3.5 Mole calculations

1 a 20 kg of iron(III) oxide are reduced with carbon monoxide to give 11 kg of iron metal.

$$Fe_2O_3 + 3CO \rightarrow 2Fe + 3CO_2$$

What is the percentage yield?

b A student wants to prepare 10 g of ethanal, CH_3CHO, by oxidation of ethanol, CH_3CH_2OH. Given that the reaction yield is 80%, work out the mass of ethanol that the student should use.

$$CH_3CH_2OH + [O] \rightarrow CH_3CHO + H_2O$$

c Suggest three reasons why the yields of chemical reactions are seldom 100%.
d Fe_2O_3 has an empirical formula but not a molecular formula. Why is this?
e A different type of iron oxide contains 72.3% Fe and 27.7% O by mass. What is its empirical formula?

UNDERSTAND
THESE TERMS

• stoichiometry
• empirical formula

2   Thionyl chloride ($SOCl_2$) is a powerful drying agent. It reacts with the waters of crystallisation present in hydrated salts such as nickel(II) chloride hexahydrate, producing anhydrous nickel(II) chloride, sulfur dioxide and hydrogen chloride:

$$NiCl_2.6H_2O(s) + 6SOCl_2(l) \rightarrow NiCl_2(s) + 6SO_2(g) + 12HCl(g)$$

In one reaction, 237.7 g of nickel(II) chloride hexahydrate are reacted with 1232 g of thionyl chloride, an excess.

   a   State the meaning of the term *mole*.   [1]
   b   Suggest reasons why a reaction might be carried out using an
       excess reactant.   [2]
   c   Calculate the number of moles of hydrated nickel(II) chloride used.   [1]
   d   Show that the thionyl chloride is in excess.   [2]
   e   Calculate the mass of nickel(II) chloride formed.   [1]
   f   Deduce the theoretical mass of thionyl chloride remaining,
       assuming 100% yield.   [2]

                                                                      [Total: 9]

3   6.66 g of a gaseous hydrocarbon **D** with a molar mass of 54 g mol^{-1} are passed over a large excess of heated copper(II) oxide, causing complete oxidation of **D**. The product mixture contains 21.7 g of CO_2 and 6.66 g of H_2O as well as copper metal.

   a   Calculate the number of moles of carbon present in 21.7 g of CO_2.   [1]
   b   Calculate the number of moles of hydrogen present in 6.66 g of H_2O.   [1]
   c   Calculate the number of moles of **D**.   [1]
   d   Using your answers to parts **a**, **b** and **c**, deduce the molecular
       formula of **D**.   [2]
   e   A student suggests that the general formula of the homologous series
       that **D** belongs to is C_nH_{n+2}. Explain why the student is incorrect. [1]
   f   Determine the correct general formula of the homologous series
       to which hydrocarbon **D** belongs.   [1]

                                                                      [Total: 7]

REFLECTION

This chapter contains several important equations relating to the mole, which must be memorised – no equations are given in the exam. You also must be confident rearranging these equations. What strategies do you find are most effective for helping you remember equations?

3.6 Chemical formulae and chemical equations

1 a What do you understand by the term *compound ion*?

b Using your knowledge of the formulae of compound ions and the charges on simple ions, work out the formulae of the following compounds from their names. Note that some of these are extension examples!

    i Potassium nitrate

    ii Calcium hydrogen carbonate

    iii Magnesium phosphate

    iv Silver(I) hydroxide

    v Aluminium ammonium sulfate

    vi Zinc(II) bromide

    vii Iron(II) oxide

    viii Chromium(III) sulfide

> **UNDERSTAND THESE TERMS**
>
> - oxidation number (oxidation state)
> - compound ion
> - state symbol
> - spectator ions
> - ionic equation

2 0.45 g of a hydrated metal (M) chloride, $MCl_2.4H_2O$, was heated to constant mass. The volume of $H_2O(g)$, measured under room conditions, was $221.5\,cm^3$.

$$MCl_2.4H_2O(s) \rightarrow MCl_2(s) + 4H_2O(g)$$

a State the type of reaction occurring when the hydrated metal chloride was heated. [1]

b Explain why the hydrated metal chloride was heated to constant mass. [1]

c Calculate the number of moles of water given off in the reaction. [1]

d Deduce the number of moles of the hydrated metal chloride that were heated. [1]

e Determine the identity of the metal, M. [2]

f Suggest the name for the hydrated metal chloride. [1]

[Total: 7]

3 a What law is being followed when ensuring a chemical equation is balanced?

b Copy and balance the following chemical equations.

    i ......Al + ...$Fe_2O_3 \rightarrow$ ......Fe + ...Al_2O_3

    ii ......Fe + ...$H_2O \rightarrow$ ......Fe_3O_4 + ...H_2

    iii ......C_3H_6 + ...$O_2 \rightarrow$ ......CO + ...H_2O

    iv ......$Ca_3(PO_4)_2$ + ...$C \rightarrow$ ......Ca_3P_2 + ...CO

    v ......$C_3H_6O_2$ + ...$O_2 \rightarrow$ ......CO_2 + ...H_2O

    vi ......$Cu(CN)_2 \rightarrow$ ......$CuCN$ + ...C_2N_2

    vii ......PCl_3 + ...$H_2O \rightarrow$ ......$P(OH)_3$ + ...HCl

    viii ......KBr + ...$Al(ClO_4)_3 \rightarrow$ ......$AlBr_3$ + ...$KClO_4$

    ix ......C_2H_5OH + ...$O_2 \rightarrow$ ......CO + ...H_2O

    x ......HCl + ...$MnO_2 \rightarrow$ ......$MnCl_2$ + ...H_2O + ...Cl_2

3.7 Solutions and concentration

1 **a** What is meant by the following terms?

    i Solute

    ii Solvent

    iii Solution concentration

    iv Titre

   b What is the difference between a chemical and physical change?

   c The state symbol (aq) means a substance has dissolved in water to form an aqueous solution. Do you consider the following processes to be chemical or physical changes?

    i Dissolving glucose: $C_6H_{12}O_6(s) \rightarrow C_6H_{12}O_6(aq)$

    ii Dissolving hydrogen chloride to make hydrochloric acid: $HCl(g) \rightarrow HCl(aq)$

    iii Dissolving carbon dioxide to make carbonated water: $CO_2(g) \rightarrow CO_2(aq)$

UNDERSTAND THESE TERMS
• solute
• solvent
• titre
• solution concentration

2 Washing soda solution is an aqueous solution of hydrated sodium carbonate $Na_2CO_3.10H_2O$. A batch of washing soda solution was analysed by titration to determine its concentration. $25.0\,cm^3$ of the solution was pipetted into a conical flask and a few drops of indicator were added. A solution of $0.5\,mol\,dm^{-3}$ hydrochloric acid was added from a burette until the endpoint was reached.

$$Na_2CO_3(aq) + 2HCl(aq) \rightarrow 2NaCl(aq) + CO_2(g) + H_2O(l)$$

The titration was repeated until concordant results were obtained (those agreeing within $0.1\,cm^3$). The results are shown in the table below:

Titration	Rough	1	2	3	4
Titre / cm³	17.15	16.80	16.95	16.75	16.70

   a Using the titration data, calculate the mean titre. [1]

   b Calculate the number of moles of hydrochloric acid reacting in the titration. [1]

   c Deduce the number of moles of sodium carbonate reacting in the titration. [1]

   d Hence, calculate the concentration of the washing soda solution in:

    i $mol\,dm^{-3}$ [1]

    ii $g\,dm^{-3}$ [1]

   e State an assumption made when calculating the concentration of washing soda solution. [1]

   f Give **two** reasons why titrations are repeated. [2]

[Total: 8]

3.8 Calculations involving gas volumes

1   0.25 g of ethane undergoes complete combustion in 900 cm³ of oxygen, which is an excess. Under the reaction conditions, the water produced is in the gaseous state.

   a   Write the equation for the complete combustion of ethane, including state symbols.

   b   Work out the volume of ethane reacting with oxygen.

   c   Work out the volumes of carbon dioxide and water formed.

   d   Hence, calculate the total volume of gases remaining at the end of the reaction.

UNDERSTAND THIS TERM
• molar gas volume

2   2.6 kg of butan-1-ol, $CH_3CH_2CH_2CH_2OH$, are completely burned in oxygen under room conditions.

   a   Define the term *molar gas volume*.   [1]

   b   Write a balanced equation for the reaction between butan-1-ol and excess oxygen.   [1]

   c   Calculate the number of moles of butan-1-ol reacting.   [1]

   d   Calculate the volume of oxygen gas required to ensure complete combustion of the butan-1-ol.   [2]

   e   Oxygen makes up 21% of air.

      Determine the minimum room size, in m³, in which this mass of butan-1-ol could be safely burned.   [2]

[Total: 7]

3   The lanthanide metal dysprosium reacts with dilute sulfuric acid to form a yellow solution of dysprosium sulfate and hydrogen gas under room conditions. When 0.298 g of dysprosium are reacted with excess dilute sulfuric acid, 66 cm³ of hydrogen gas were obtained.

   a   Using the information provided, give the overall equation for the reaction between dysprosium and sulfuric acid.   [4]

   b   Write the ionic equation for this reaction.   [1]

[Total: 5]

❬❬ RECALL AND CONNECT 2 ❬❬

State and explain the trend in atomic radius down Group 1.

REFLECTION

There were a lot of calculation questions in this chapter. Did you remember to show your working? How will you remember the four points given in the introduction to ensure that you give high-quality responses to calculation questions?

SELF-ASSESSMENT CHECKLIST

Let's revisit the Knowledge focus and Exam skills focus for this chapter.

Decide how confident you are with each statement.

Now I can:	Show it	Needs more work	Almost there	Confident to move on
define *unified atomic mass unit* as one-twelfth of the mass of a carbon-12 atom	Write a definition for this term in your own words.			
define and use the terms *relative atomic mass*, *isotopic mass* and *formula mass* in terms of unified atomic mass unit	Write definitions for these terms in your own words.			
define and use the term *mole* in terms of the Avogadro constant	Recall the value of the Avogadro constant and use it to calculate numbers of particles.			
write formulae of ionic compounds from ionic charges and oxidation numbers, including the prediction of ionic charge from the position of an element in the Periodic Table	Pick five metals and five non-metals from different groups in the Periodic Table and write the formulae of their ionic compound.			
recall of the names and formulae for the ions NO_3^-, CO_3^{2-}, SO_4^{2-}, OH^-, NH_4^+, Zn^{2+}, Ag^+, HCO_3^- and PO_4^{3-}	Practise pairing these ions up with different metals and naming the resulting compounds.			
find the molecular mass of an organic molecule from the molecular ion peak in a mass spectrum	Work out the molecular masses from the mass spectra in this chapter and Chapter 3 of the coursebook.			
deduce the number of carbon atoms in a compound using the [M + 1] peak and the relevant formula	Write the formula for determining number of carbon atoms from relative abundances and apply it to question 3.3.2.			
write and construct balanced equations, including ionic equations (not including spectator ions)	Write the ionic equations for the acid–base reactions featured in question 3.7.2.			

CONTINUED

Now I can:	Show it	Needs more work	Almost there	Confident to move on
use the correct state symbols in equations	Write down what each state symbol stands for, then add them to the equations in question 3.6.3b.			
define and use the terms *empirical formula* and *molecular formula*	Add these definitions to a set of flash cards and test your ability to recall them.			
calculate empirical and molecular formulae using given data	Know the relationship between empirical and molecular formula and answer question 3.5.1e.			
understand and use the terms *anhydrous*, *hydrated* and *water of crystallisation*	Add these definitions to a set of flash cards and test your ability to recall them.			
perform calculations, including use of the mole concept involving reacting masses (from formulae and equations), including percentage yield calculations, volumes of gases (e.g., in the burning of hydrocarbons), volumes and concentrations of solutions, limiting reagents and excess reagent	Memorise all the equations involving the mole, then answer the questions in sections 3.4–3.8.			
deduce stoichiometric relationships from calculations involving reacting masses, volumes of gases, and volumes and concentrations of solutions	Do the calculations involving reacting masses, reacting volumes and titrations in this chapter and in the flip cards.			
show my workings	For questions that require calculations, make sure your working is clear and logically leads to the answer.			
recognise high-quality responses	Ensure you have used the appropriate number of significant figures and units for all calculation questions you attempt.			

4 Chemical bonding

In this chapter you will practise your understanding of the command word 'suggest'.

Suggest	apply knowledge and understanding to situations where there are a range of valid responses in order to make proposals/put forward considerations

The 'suggest' command word can be used where there is no definitive answer (for example, two compounds might fit all the data given to help determine the identity of an unknown), or it may require you to draw upon wider knowledge to deal with an unfamiliar context. The latter usually requires analysis, critical thinking and problem-solving.

You can prepare for 'suggest' questions by working through past exam questions to enable you to understand unfamiliar chemistry and contexts, and by reading more widely.

4.1 Types of chemical bonding

UNDERSTAND THESE TERMS

- anion
- cation
- lattice
- van der Waals' forces
- intermolecular forces

1 What types of bonding could be present in:

  a metallic elements

  b non-metal elements

  c compounds?

4.2 Ionic bonding

1 a Explain what is meant by the term *ionic bonding*.

  b Copy and complete the table by writing the formulae and names of the ionic compounds formed from metals and non-metals. The first one has been done for you.

Metal	Non-metal	Formula	Name
Group 1, Period 3	Group 17, Period 3	NaCl	sodium chloride
Group 1, Period 2	Group 16, Period 2		
Group 2, Period 5	Group 16, Period 3		
Group 13, Period 2	Group 17, Period 4		
Group 14, Period 3	Group 15, Period 2		
Group 12, Period 4	Group 17, Period 5		

UNDERSTAND THESE TERMS

- ionic bonding
- electrovalent bond
- dot-and-cross diagram

  c Ionic compounds can be represented using dot-and-cross diagrams. Explain what a dot-and-cross diagram is.

  d Draw the dot-and-cross diagrams for:

    i silver iodide, AgI

    ii the polyatomic carbonate ion, CO_3^{2-}.

2 This question is about oxides of metals.

  a Describe, in terms of electron transfer and the particles involved, the formation of the ionic bond in calcium oxide. [3]

  b Aluminium oxide has a melting point of 2072 °C. Discuss this value in terms of its structure and bonding. [3]

c   Superoxides are compounds containing the superoxide anion, O_2^-.
One example is potassium superoxide, KO_2, which is used as an oxygen
generator in spacecraft to maintain breathable oxygen levels of 21%.

$$4KO_2(s) + 2H_2O(l) \rightarrow 4KOH(aq) + 3O_2(g)$$

   i   A spacecraft module has a volume of $4.5\,m^3$. Determine the number
of moles of oxygen required to ensure a breathable atmosphere. [2]

   ii Determine the mass of potassium superoxide required to produce
this amount of oxygen on board the spacecraft. [1]

[Total: 9]

≪ RECALL AND CONNECT 1 ≪

Ionic compounds are formed by electron transfer.

a   How do metals and non-metals typically transfer electrons and what are
the names of the charged particles formed?

b   What is ionisation energy and how is it related to reactivity?

4.3 Covalent bonding

1 a   Define the term *covalent bond*.

   b   Draw dot-and-cross diagrams for the following:

   i   Ammonia, NH_3.

   ii   Ethene, C_2H_4.

   iii The nitrile ion, CN^-.

   c   Draw the dot-and-cross diagram for sulfur dioxide, SO_2, and explain why
the sulfur atom is described as having an *expanded octet*.

   d   Explain what is meant by the term co-ordinate bond.

   e   Draw displayed formulae for the following substances, showing the
co-ordinate bond with an arrow.

   i   Hydroxonium ion, H_3O^+.

   ii   Dinitrogen oxide, N_2O.

   iii Nitrate ion, NO_3^-.

   iv   The complex formed between tetrahydrofuran and borane, BH_3.
The structure of tetrahydrofuran is shown in Figure 4.1.

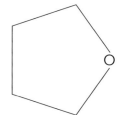

Figure 4.1: Structure of tetrahydrofuran

2 Many organic compounds undergo combustion reactions, generating carbon
dioxide or carbon monoxide.

   a   Write the equation for the incomplete combustion of pentane to give
carbon monoxide. [1]

   b   Carbon monoxide contains a co-ordinate bond.
Draw its dot-and-cross diagram. [1]

c Carbon monoxide is toxic because it binds irreversibly with iron(II) ions present in haemoglobin (Hb), preventing oxygen transport. Carbon dioxide binds reversibly with Hb. Compare these statements with reference to the bonding in carbon monoxide and carbon dioxide. [3]

d The table shows the covalent bond lengths and bond energies of different carbon–oxygen bonds.

Bond	Bond length / pm (1 × 10⁻¹² m)	Bond energy / kJ mol⁻¹
C—O	143	358
C=O	122	805
CO	113	1077

i Explain what is meant by the term *bond length*. [1]

ii State the relationship between the type of carbon–oxygen bond, bond lengths and bond strengths shown in the table. [2]

iii Explain this relationship. [2]

[Total: 10]

4.4 Shapes of molecules

1 a Define the term *lone pair*.

b Describe the principles behind VSEPR and how it is used to work out the shapes of molecules and ions.

c Draw 3D diagrams of the following molecules, giving the molecular geometry and bond angles. You should show any lone pairs present on the central atom.

i H_2O vi $BeCl_2$

ii CO_2 vii NH_2^-

iii NH_3 viii BH_4^-

iv PCl_5 ix BrO_3^-

v SF_6 x XeO_3F_2

d Which of the species in part c:

i is electron deficient?

ii has an expanded octet?

iii contains a co-ordinate bond?

2 Calcium carbide, CaC_2, used to be used in miners' *carbide lamps*. Water dripping on calcium carbide inside the lamp liberated ethyne gas (C_2H_2, commonly called acetylene), which was ignited to produce light. An alkaline by-product was also produced.

a Write the chemical equation, including state symbols, for the reaction between calcium carbide and water. [2]

b Draw a dot-and-cross diagram for ethyne. [1]

c Suggest why carbide lamps are no longer used in mines. [1]

Calcium carbide is also used in the manufacture of calcium cyanamide, $CaCN_2$, a fertiliser that is commercially known as 'nitrolime'.

d Draw the displayed formula of the cyanamide ion, CN_2^{2-}. [1]

e State and explain the shape of the CN_2^{2-} ion. [3]

Calcium cyanamide reacts with water to produce ammonia and calcium carbonate:

$$CaCN_2 + H_2O \rightarrow 2NH_3 + CaCO_3$$

f Calculate the mass of calcium cyanamide needed to produce 10.5 tonnes of ammonia if the process has a yield of 95%. [3]

[Total: 11]

4.5 Sigma (σ) and pi (π) bonds

1 **a** Describe the formation of the π bonds in ethene, illustrating your answer with a labelled diagram. Explain why a C=C bond is not twice as strong as a C—C bond.

b Describe how a sp^2 hybrid orbital is formed from atomic orbitals.

c Which type of hybrid orbital has 25% s character? Explain your answer.

d Why is ethene planar?

4.6 Metallic bonding

1 **a** What is the meaning of the term *metallic bonding*?

b Draw a diagram to show the metallic bonding in magnesium.

c Rank the following forces of attraction in order of increasing strength: hydrogen bonding, metallic bonding, permanent dipole–permanent dipole, ionic bonding, covalent bonding, instantaneous dipole–induced dipole.

> UNDERSTAND THESE TERMS
> - delocalised electrons
> - metallic bonding

2 The melting points of three metals are shown in the table.

Metal	Melting point / °C
sodium	98
caesium	29
strontium	769

Explain the trend shown in the melting points of these metals. **[Total: 4]**

4.7 Intermolecular forces

1 a Describe how instantaneous dipole–induced dipole forces arise.

b Explain what is meant by the term *electronegativity*.

c Explain how electronegativity is related to bond polarity.

d Draw the following molecules, showing the location of significant dipoles:

  i HBr

  ii $CHCl_3$

  iii $SOCl_2$

  iv NH_3

e Copy and complete the table to show whether the compounds would be ionic, covalent, or would have both ionic and covalent character (Pauling electronegativity values: aluminium 1.6; beryllium 1.6; bromine 3.0; caesium 0.8; carbon 2.6; chlorine 3.2; fluorine 4.0; hydrogen 2.2; phosphorus 2.2; potassium 0.8).

Compound	Ionic, covalent or both?
KCl	
$BeBr_2$	
PH_3	
CsF	
$AlCl_3$	
C_3H_8	

> **UNDERSTAND THESE TERMS**
>
> - electronegativity
> - polar bonds
> - bond polarity
> - instantaneous dipole–induced dipole forces (id–id forces)
> - permanent dipole–permanent dipole forces (pd–pd forces)

2 a State and explain the trend in electronegativity values across a period. [4]

b Nitrosyl chloride, ClNO, is used as an oxidising agent in organic synthesis.

  i Define *oxidising agent*. [1]

  ii Draw a dot-and-cross diagram of nitrosyl chloride. [1]

  iii Suggest the shape of nitrosyl chloride, explaining your answer. [3]

  iv Explain why the nitrosyl chloride molecule is polar. [2]

[Total: 11]

> **REFLECTION**
>
> There are some key words you must recall for AS & A Level Chemistry as you could be asked to define any of them in the exam. Research shows that active recall (learning by retrieving) helps memorise information more effectively than repeatedly reading it or writing it out. An example of active recall is trying to remember the definition on a flip card before you turn it over. Which methods do you find most effective?

4.8 Hydrogen bonding

1 **a** Hydrogen bonding is a special type of permanent dipole–permanent dipole. Explain how this type of intermolecular force arises.

b Draw diagrams to show the hydrogen bonding between:
  i Water molecules.
  ii Ammonia and methanol, CH_3OH.
  iii Water and methanal, H_2CHO.

c Explain why strong hydrogen bonds are only present in substances where hydrogen is bonded to fluorine, oxygen or nitrogen.

d Describe how hydrogen bonding gives water its anomalous properties.

UNDERSTAND THIS TERM
• hydrogen bond

2 The boiling points of three Group 16 hydrides are shown in the table.

Group 16 hydride	Boiling point / °C
H_2O	100
H_2S	−61
H_2Se	−41

Explain these values by considering the intermolecular forces involved. **[Total: 3]**

4.9 Bonding and physical properties

1 **a** What is the state of the following substances at room temperature? Explain your answers.
  i Mercury.
  ii Butane, C_4H_{10}.
  iii Tungsten carbide, W_2C.

b Explain the states of Group 17 (halogens) at room temperature.

UNDERSTAND THIS TERM
• hydrolysis

2 **a** Silicon dioxide is insoluble in water, whereas silicon tetrachloride, $SiCl_4$, dissolves in water to give an acidic solution. Explain these observations. Include equations and state symbols as necessary. [3]

b Tetrasilane, SiH_4, does not react with water. Suggest an explanation for this. [2]

c SiO_2 dissolves in hot, concentrated sodium hydroxide to form a compound with the following composition by mass: Na 37.7%, Si 23.0%, O 39.3%.
  i Determine the empirical formula of this compound. [3]
  ii Write a chemical equation for the reaction between SiO_2 and sodium hydroxide. [1]

[Total: 9]

≪ RECALL AND CONNECT 2 ≪

What is meant by an empirical formula and how is it related to the molecular formula?

REFLECTION

How did you find the 'suggest' questions in this chapter? Did you spot the two different types? Did you find one type easier than the other? What can you do to help you recognise which type of 'suggest' question is being asked in an exam?

SELF-ASSESSMENT CHECKLIST

Let's revisit the Knowledge focus and Exam skills focus for this chapter.

Decide how confident you are with each statement.

Now I can:	Show it	Needs more work	Almost there	Confident to move on
define *electronegativity* and explain the factors influencing the electronegativity values of the elements	Write an accurate definition of *electronegativity* that explains the interaction between nuclear charge, atomic radius and shielding.			
explain the trends in electronegativity across a period and down a group in the Periodic Table	Rank several elements in order of increasing or decreasing electronegativity, explaining your choice.			
use differences in the Pauling electronegativity values to predict if a compound has ionic or covalent bonds	Determine whether a compound is ionic or covalent based on the location of its elements in the Periodic Table.			
define *ionic bonding* and describe ionic bonding in compounds such as sodium chloride, magnesium oxide and calcium fluoride	Draw dot-and-cross diagrams of these compounds and write a description of how each is formed, including the number of electrons transferred.			

CONTINUED

Now I can:	Show it	Needs more work	Almost there	Confident to move on
define *covalent bonding* and describe covalent bonding in molecules such as hydrogen, oxygen, nitrogen, chlorine, hydrogen chloride, carbon dioxide, ammonia, methane, ethane and ethene	Draw dot-and-cross diagrams of these compounds and write a description of how each is formed in terms of electron sharing.			
describe how some atoms in Period 3 can expand their octet of electrons to form compounds such as sulfur dioxide, phosphorus pentachloride and sulfur hexafluoride	Draw dot-and-cross diagrams for these compounds, showing how sulfur and phosphorus have expanded their octets.			
describe co-ordinate bonding (dative covalent bonding) in ions such as NH_4^+ and in molecules such as Al_2Cl_6	Draw displayed formula and dot-and-cross diagrams of compounds containing co-ordinate bonds.			
use dot-and-cross diagrams to show the arrangement of electrons in compounds with ionic, covalent and co-ordinate bonding	Draw dot-and-cross diagrams for all the molecules and ions listed here, and be prepared to extend this to other examples.			
describe covalent bonding in terms of orbital overlap giving sigma (σ) and pi (π) bonds	Draw labelled diagrams to show formation of sigma (σ) and pi (π) bonds, specifying the type of orbital overlap.			
describe how sigma (σ) and (π) pi bonds form in molecules such as H_2, C_2H_6, C_2H_4, HCN and N_2	Draw labelled diagrams of these compounds, showing the locations of sigma (σ) and pi (π) bonds.			
describe the hybridisation of atomic orbitals to form sp, sp^2 and sp^3 orbitals	Draw diagrams to show the hybrid orbitals formed from these combinations of atomic orbitals.			

CONTINUED

Now I can:	Show it	Needs more work	Almost there	Confident to move on
Define the terms *bond energy* and *bond length*, and use these to compare the reactions of covalent molecules	Look up the bond energies and bond lengths of some single, double and triple covalent bonds, and explain how the values influence reactivity.			
describe and explain the shapes and bond angles in simple molecules (such as BF_3, CO_2, CH_4, NH_3, H_2O, SF_6 and PF_5) using 'valence shell electron pair repulsion' (VSEPR) theory	Draw 3D diagrams of the listed compounds, clearly showing their shapes and labelling the bond angles.			
predict the shapes and bond angles in other molecules and ions similar to those above	Draw 3D diagrams of other molecules and ions that may be linear, trigonal planar, bent, trigonal pyramidal, tetrahedral, trigonal bipyramidal and octahedral.			
describe hydrogen bonding and explain, in terms of hydrogen bonding, why some physical properties of water are unusual for a molecular compound	Draw a diagram showing hydrogen bonding in water and use it to explain the high boiling point, high surface tension and high viscosity of water, and the low density of ice.			
use electronegativity values to explain bond polarity and dipole moments in molecules	Draw diagrams of molecules containing polar covalent bonds, showing the location of dipole moments and identifying them as polar or non-polar.			
describe and understand the different types of intermolecular forces (van der Waals' forces) as either instantaneous dipoles or permanent dipoles	Draw a labelled diagram showing how these forces arise in neighbouring molecules.			

CONTINUED

Now I can:	Show it	Needs more work	Almost there	Confident to move on
describe metallic bonding	Draw a labelled diagram showing the arrangement of metal cations and delocalised electrons in a metal.			
describe the relative bond strengths of ionic, covalent and metallic bonds compared with intermolecular forces	Create a table showing the average strengths of these bonds and intermolecular forces in kJ mol⁻¹.			
show that I understand the 'suggest' command word and answer 'suggest' questions	Answer different 'suggest' questions and note the way this command word is sometimes used to get you to think analytically.			
understand that the 'suggest' command word may be used in two different ways and recognise which questions relate to higher-order thinking skills and carry higher marks	Make a list of the knowledge from other topics needed to answer the 'suggest' questions in this chapter.			

Exam practice 1

This section contains past paper questions from previous Cambridge exams which draw together your knowledge on a range of topics that you have covered up to this point. These questions give you the opportunity to test your knowledge and understanding. Additional past paper practice questions can be found in the accompanying digital material.

The following question has an example student response and commentary provided. Work through the question first, then compare your answer to the sample response and commentary. Are your answers different to the sample responses?

1   Fig. 1.1 shows how **first** ionisation energies vary across Period 2.

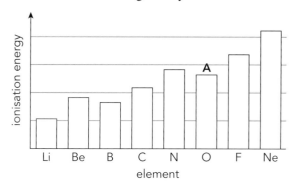

Fig. 1.1

a   Construct an equation to represent the **first** ionisation energy of oxygen. Include state symbols. [1]

b   i   State and explain the general trend in first ionisation energies across Period 2. [3]

    ii   Explain why ionisation energy **A** in Fig. 1.1 does **not** follow the general trend in first ionisation energies across Period 2. [2]

c   Element **E** is in Period 3 of the Periodic Table.
The first eight ionisation energy values of **E** are shown in the table.

ionisation	1st	2nd	3rd	4th	5th	6th	7th	8th
ionisation energy / kJ mol^{-1}	577	1820	2740	11600	14800	18400	23400	27500

Deduce the full electronic configuration of **E**.
Explain your answer. [3]

[Total: 9]

Cambridge International AS & A Level Chemistry (9701) Paper 22 Q1 March 2022

Example student response	Commentary
a $O_2 \rightarrow 2O^+ + 2e^-$	The student has confused oxygen in its normal state, where it is an O_2 molecule, with oxygen as an atom, which fits the definition of first ionisation energy. They have correctly formed a unipositive ion, but the equation does not have state symbols, which are essential to fit the definition of first ionisation energy. Correct state symbols are essential for ionisation energy equations even if the question does not state 'Include state symbols'. *This answer is awarded 0 out of 1 mark.*
b **i** First ionisation energies generally increase across the period. This is because going across the period there are more protons going into the nucleus, and increased nuclear charge. The electrons are going into the same principal energy level and so have similar shielding.	This is a good answer. However, the student has not explained that it is an attraction between the outer electron and the nucleus that must be overcome in ionisation. *This answer is awarded 2 out of 3 marks.*
ii The 1st ionisation energy goes down from N to O. N is $1s^2, 2s^2, 2p^3$ and O is $1s^2, 2s^2, 2p^4$. So in O there is a pair of electrons in one of the 2p orbitals. These negatively charged electrons repel each other so are easier to remove.	The student has set out the key knowledge needed to explain the dip in the first ionisation energies. It is always a good idea in these questions to write out the electron configurations of the elements involved to prompt correct thinking. The student has failed to mention that the repulsion of the electrons is significant enough to overcome the additional nuclear attraction. *This answer is awarded 1 out of 2 marks.*
c $1s^2\ 2s^2\ 2p^6\ 3s^2\ 3p^1$ There is a large jump in the magnitude of the ionisation energies between the removal of the 3rd and 4th electrons. This suggests that the 4th electron is in the next principle energy level nearer to the nucleus, so there must be 3 electrons in the outer shell.	This answer is correct and well explained. *This answer is awarded 3 out of 3 marks.*

The following question has an example student response and commentary provided. Work through the question first, then compare your answer to the sample response and commentary. Are your answers different to the sample responses?

2   An experiment was carried out to determine the percentage of iron in a sample of iron wire.

    A 3.35 g piece of the wire was reacted with dilute sulfuric acid, in the absence of air, so that all of the iron atoms were converted to iron(II) ions. The resulting solution was made up to 250 cm³.

    a   Write a balanced equation for the reaction between the iron in the wire and the sulfuric acid.   [1]

A 25.0 cm³ sample of this solution was acidified and titrated with 0.0250 mol dm⁻³ potassium dichromate(VI). 32.0 cm³ of the potassium dichromate(VI) solution was required for complete reaction with the iron(II) ions in the sample.

The relevant half-equations are shown.

$$Cr_2O_7^{2-} + 14H^+ + 6e^- \rightarrow 2Cr^{3+} + 7H_2O$$

$$Fe^{2+} \rightarrow Fe^{3+} + e^-$$

b Use the half-equations to write an equation for the reaction between the iron(II) ions and the acidified dichromate(VI) ions. [1]

c Calculate the amount, in moles, of dichromate(VI) ions used in the titration. [1]

d Calculate the amount, in moles, of iron(II) ions in the 25.0 cm³ sample of solution. [1]

e Calculate the amount, in moles, of iron in the 3.35 g piece of wire. [1]

f Calculate the mass of iron in the 3.35 g piece of wire. [1]

g Calculate the percentage of iron in the iron wire. [1]

[**Total: 7**]

Cambridge International AS & A Level Chemistry (9701) Paper 23 Q1a June 2016

Example student response	Commentary
a $Fe(s) + H_2SO_4(aq) \rightarrow FeSO_4(aq) + H_2(g)$	This is the correct response. Note that state symbols would be ignored as they were not requested. *This answer is awarded 1 out of 1 mark.*
b $Cr_2O_7^{2-} + 14H^+ + 6Fe^{2+} \rightarrow 2Cr^{3+} + 7H_2O + 6Fe^{3+}$	This is correct. *This answer is awarded 1 out of 1 mark.*
c 8×10^{-4} **d** 4.8×10^{-3}	Correct responses, but it is better to show all working so that credit can be given in case of errors in final values. *These answers are awarded 1 out of 1 mark each.*
e 4.8×10^{-3}	This is incorrect. The student has overlooked the fact that each titration only uses 25 cm³ of the 250 cm³ solution (i.e., a tenth) containing all the iron. The answer to part **d** should be multiplied by 10. *This answer is awarded 0 out of 1 mark.*
f $55.8 \times 4.8 \times 10^{-3} = 0.27$ g **g** $0.27/3.35 = 8\%$ pure	Underestimating the moles of iron due to the power of ten error above has caused the student to underestimate the mass, and therefore percentage purity, of iron in the wire. However, the error-carried-forward principle is applied. *These answers are awarded 1 out of 1 mark each.*

Now, based on your understanding of the commentary to the student response in question **2**, answer the following question.

3 The commonest form of iron(II) sulfate is the heptahydrate, $FeSO_4.7H_2O$. On heating at 90 °C this loses **some** of its water of crystallisation to form a different hydrated form of iron(II) sulfate, $FeSO_4.xH_2O$.

3.40 g of $FeSO_4.xH_2O$ was dissolved in water to form 250 cm³ of solution.

A 25.0 cm³ sample of this solution was acidified and titrated with 0.0200 mol dm⁻³ potassium manganate(VII).

In this titration, 20.0 cm³ of this potassium manganate(VII) solution was required to react fully with the Fe^{2+} ions present in the sample.

    a   The MnO_4^- ions in the potassium manganate(VII) *oxidise* the Fe^{2+} ions in the acidified solution.

        i   Explain, in terms of electron transfer, the meaning of the term *oxidise* in the sentence above. [1]

        ii   Complete and balance the ionic equation for the reaction between the manganate(VII) ions and the iron(II) ions.

            $MnO_4 (aq) + 5Fe^{2+}(aq) + ...H^+(aq) \rightarrow$

            $........(aq) + 5Fe^{3+}(aq) + ...H_2O(l)$ [3]

    b   **i**   Calculate the number of moles of manganate(VII) used in the titration. [1]

        ii   Use the equation in **a ii** and your answer to **b i** to calculate the number of moles of Fe^{2+} present in the 25.0 cm³ sample of solution used. [1]

        iii Calculate the number of moles of $FeSO_4.xH_2O$ in 3.40 g of the compound. [1]

        iv Calculate the relative formula mass of $FeSO_4.xH_2O$. [1]

        v   The relative formula mass of anhydrous iron(II) sulfate, $FeSO_4$, is 151.8.

            Calculate the value of x in $FeSO_4.xH_2O$. [1]

[Total: 9]

Cambridge International AS & A Level Chemistry (9701) Paper 21 Q2 June 2014

The following question has an example student response and commentary provided. Work through the question first, then compare your answer to the sample response and commentary. Are your answers different to the sample responses? How are they different?

4 Sulfides are compounds that contain sulfur but not oxygen.

Carbon disulfide, CS_2, is a volatile liquid at room temperature and pressure.

    a   State the meaning of *volatile*. [1]

    b   Draw a 'dot-and-cross' diagram of the CS_2 molecule. [2]

    c   Suggest the bond angle in a molecule of CS_2. [1]

d CS_2 is a liquid under room conditions, while CO_2 is a gas.

Explain what causes the difference in the physical properties between CS_2 and CO_2. [2]

[Total: 6]

*Cambridge International AS & A Level Chemistry (9701) Paper 21 Q1
November 2021*

Example student response	Commentary
a Volatile means a substance boils easily.	The definition of volatile could be improved. Volatile substances may boil more easily, but boiling and evaporation are not the same thing. *This answer is awarded 0 out of 1 mark.*
b	Unfortunately, the student has used the wrong central atom – this is often the element appearing the fewest times in the molecular formula, in this case carbon. Carbon also follows the octet rule in all its compounds but, here, it only has 6 electrons in its outer shell. *This answer is awarded 0 out of 2 marks.*
c 104.5°	Based on the student's diagram in (b) there is only one lone pair of electrons around the central S, so the bond angle proposed should be 109.5°. *This answer is awarded 0 out of 1 mark.*
d The bond between carbon and sulfur is more polar than the one between carbon and oxygen, therefore the pd-pd forces are stronger.	The wrong type of intermolecular force has been identified as both these molecules are non-polar. The student needed to consider the relative sizes of these molecules. *This answer is awarded 0 out of 2 marks.*

5 Now that you've gone through the commentary, try to write an improved answer to any part of question **4** where you did not score highly. This will help you check if you've understood why each mark has (or has not) been allocated. In your new answers, make sure you read the question and address the scope of the question.

5 States of matter

KNOWLEDGE FOCUS

In this chapter you will answer questions on:

- states of matter
- the gaseous state
- the liquid state
- the solid state
- fullerenes.

EXAM SKILLS FOCUS

In this chapter you will:

- recognise synoptic questions and understand how to answer them.

This chapter is all about the properties of particles in the solid, liquid and gaseous states of matter. These properties result from the type of bonding between the particles, which in turn influences the type of structure adopted. For this reason, there is significant overlap between the concepts in this chapter, and those covered as part of Chapter 4 Chemical bonding. It is common to encounter synoptic questions that will test your ability to see the connections between these related topics. This is a very common theme in chemistry, where the microscopic behaviour of particles and how they bond and interact with each can be used to explain macroscopic properties like pressure and melting points. To answer such questions, you will need to understand and describe the connection between the microscopic and macroscopic.

The Exam skills chapter at the end of this book has more support and suggestions for how to learn to recognise and use synoptic links between topics.

5.1 States of matter

1 a   Copy the boxes below and add particles to them to illustrate the arrangement of particles in solids, liquids and gases.

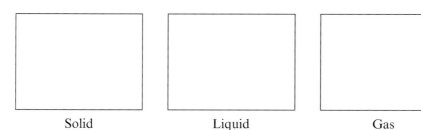

Solid	Liquid	Gas

   b   Copy and complete the table to describe the behaviour of particles in the three states of matter.

State	Solid	Liquid	Gas
density		medium	
particle arrangement			random
particle movement			rapid in all directions
particle energy	lowest		

   c   Which state would the following substances be in at the given temperatures?
   i   Chlorine (m.p. –101.5 °C, b.p. –34 °C) at –95 °C.
   ii   Mercury (m.p. –38 °C, b.p. 357 °C) at 220 °C.
   iii   Cyclohexane (m.p. 6.5 °C, b.p. 80.7 °C) at 110 °C.
   iv   Hydrogen sulfide (m.p. –85.5 °C, b.p. –59.5 °C) at –72 °C.

5.2 The gaseous state

1 a   Describe the origin of pressure in gases.

   b   Describe, as fully as you can, the changes occurring when liquid bromine is heated to its boiling point. Include references to the energy and behaviour of particles in your answer.

   c   Which forces of attraction are overcome when the following substances undergo evaporation?

   i   water   iii   sulfur
   ii   sodium   iv   magnesium oxide

   d   Which of the substances from part **c** would require the most energy for evaporation? Explain your answer.

UNDERSTAND
THESE TERMS

- kinetic theory
- real gas
- ideal gas

2 **a** What are the assumptions behind the ideal gas model?

   b What effect does temperature have on the extent to which a gas deviates from ideal behaviour?

   c Sketch graphs to show the following:

   i The relationship between pressure and volume for an ideal gas.

   ii The relationship between volume and temperature for an ideal gas.

   d Calculate the volume, in cm³, occupied by 2.75 moles of carbon dioxide at a temperature of 49 °C and pressure of 304 kPa. ($R = 8.31\,J\,K^{-1}\,mol^{-1}$)

   e A sample of bromine was left to evaporate at a temperature of 15 °C and a pressure of 99 kPa. The vapour occupied a volume of 2450 cm³. How many grams of bromine were in the sample?

3 **a** 0.17 g of a volatile hydrocarbon were injected into a gas syringe in an oven at 70 °C. The hydrocarbon evaporated and the volume recorded on the gas syringe was 67 cm³.

   Given that the pressure was 100 kPa, determine the relative molecular mass of the hydrocarbon. ($R = 8.31\,J\,K^{-1}\,mol^{-1}$) [3]

   b The hydrocarbon used in the experiment was saturated. Deduce its identity. [1]

   [Total: 4]

4 Two glass containers, **A** and **B**, are connected by a closed valve, as shown in Figure 5.1. Container **A** is filled with argon at a pressure of 95 kPa and temperature of 40 °C.

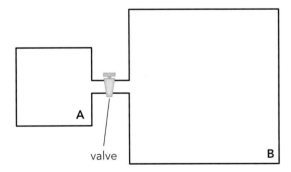

Figure 5.1

Container **B** is initially empty and has a volume four times bigger than that of container **A**. The valve is opened, and the temperature of the entire apparatus is heated to 150 °C.

Calculate the final pressure of the system in kilopascals. **[Total: 4]**

5.3 The liquid state

1 Describe, with reference to particles and energy, the changes occurring when

    a   gold is heated to its melting point

    b   steam is cooled to below the boiling point of water.

5.4 The solid state

> **UNDERSTAND THESE TERMS**
>
> • vaporisation
> • condensation
> • vapour pressure

≪ RECALL AND CONNECT 1 ≪

Knowing definitions for key terms is essential as you could be asked for any of them in the exam. Can you recall the definitions of the following key terms from bonding?

- ionic bonding
- covalent bonding
- co-ordinate bond
- metallic bonding
- electronegativity

1   a   Why are ionic lattices, metallic lattices and macromolecular structures referred to as 'giant'?

    b   Give three properties of ionic compounds and explain them in terms of structure and bonding.

    c   The metal iron is both ductile and malleable. Explain this in terms of its structure and bonding.

    d   '1095' High-carbon steel is an alloy of iron containing ~0.95% carbon. Its exceptional strength makes it ideal for use in the manufacture of precision cutting tools, but it requires careful handling due to its brittle nature. Explain why '1095' high-carbon steel has these properties.

    e   Copy and complete the table to help you revise the relationships between structure, bonding and forces between the particles involved.

Bonding	Structure	Particles	Forces between particles	Strength of forces	Melting and boiling points
ionic					
covalent					
metallic					

2 **a** Some physical properties of bromine and copper are shown in the table.

Element	Melting point / °C	Boiling point / °C	Electrical conductivity
bromine	−7.2	58.8	none
copper	1085	2562	high

    i Explain, in terms of structure and bonding, why these elements have different melting points. [5]

    ii Explain, in terms of structure and bonding, why these elements have different electrical conductivities. [2]

    iii Suggest why copper remains a liquid over a much greater temperature range compared to bromine. [1]

[Total: 8]

> **UNDERSTAND THESE TERMS**
>
> - alloy
> - giant molecular structure/giant covalent structure
> - allotrope

REFLECTION

Did you spot that question 5.4.2 was a synoptic question? Were you able to successfully link the microscopic behaviour of particles with the macroscopic properties given in the question? How can you ensure that you recognise synoptic questions in an exam?

5.5 Fullerenes

1 **a** What is an allotrope?

    b Discuss the electrical conductivities of diamond, graphite and buckminsterfullerene with reference to their bonding and structure.

    c Why is buckminsterfullerene more reactive than either diamond or graphite?

    d Diamond sublimes at around 4000 °C, whereas buckminsterfullerene sublimes at around 600 °C. What is the explanation for this?

    e What is the hybridisation of carbon in buckminsterfullerene?

UNDERSTAND THIS TERM

- buckminsterfullerene

« RECALL AND CONNECT 2 «

Incorrectly converting units is a frequent source of missed marks.
How do you convert between the following common units?

a   degrees Celsius and Kelvin

b   cubic centimetres and cubic decimetres

c   cubic centimetres and cubic metres

d   cubic decimetres and cubic metres

e   kilopascals and pascals

f   tonnes and grams

g   milligrams and grams

REFLECTION

You should now have an improved understanding of the properties and behaviour
of gases. Unlike solids and liquids, we cannot see gases, so their nature, as
described by the gas laws, is hidden from us. However, we can see evidence of
the gas laws in action in everyday life. You have learned, for example, that the
pressure of a gas is inversely proportional to its volume. A way to remember this
is to think of a balloon – if it is squeezed, its volume decreases but the pressure
increases to the point where the balloon may burst. Can you think of an everyday
example that shows the relationship between gas volume and temperature?

SELF-ASSESSMENT CHECKLIST

Let's revisit the Knowledge focus and Exam skills focus for this chapter.

Decide how confident you are with each statement.

Now I can:	Show it	Needs more work	Almost there	Confident to move on
explain the origin of pressure in a gas in terms of collisions between gas molecules and the walls of the container	Describe how the behaviour of particles in the gaseous state gives rise to pressure.			
explain that ideal gases have zero particle volume and no intermolecular forces of attraction	Compare the ideal gas model with the behaviour of real gases.			

CONTINUED

Now I can:	Show it	Needs more work	Almost there	Confident to move on
use the ideal gas equation $pV = nRT$ in calculations, including the determination of relative molecular mass	Perform calculations involving $pV = nRT$, be able to rearrange the question, and be accurate with unit conversions.			
describe the lattice structure of a crystalline solid: giant ionic structures, including sodium chloride and magnesium oxide; simple molecular structures, including iodine, buckminsterfullerene and ice; giant molecular structures, including silicon(IV) oxide, graphite and diamond; giant metallic structures, including copper	Draw simple diagrams showing the arrangement of particles in ionic compounds, simple molecular substances, giant molecular substances and metals.			
describe, interpret and predict the effect of different types of structure and bonding on the physical properties of substances, e.g., effect on melting point, boiling point, electrical conductivity and solubility	Answer the questions in this chapter that test understanding of how the arrangement of particles and types of bonds influence physical properties.			
deduce the type of structure and bonding present in a substance from given information	Match typical melting and boiling points, electrical conductivities and solubilities to different structure types.			
recognise synoptic questions and understand how to answer them	Create a mind map (spider diagram) to show the links between structure and bonding and physical properties.			

6 Enthalpy

KNOWLEDGE FOCUS

In this chapter you will answer questions on:

- what enthalpy changes are
- standard enthalpy changes
- measuring enthalpy changes
- Hess's law
- bond energies and enthalpy changes
- calculating enthalpy changes using bond energies.

EXAM SKILLS FOCUS

In this chapter you will:

- understand how mark schemes are applied to calculation questions.

Mark schemes are written for expert markers, and it can be easy for students to apply them incorrectly. In this chapter you will gain an awareness of how mark schemes can be applied to calculation questions, including when you may earn 'error carried forward' marks. These are marks earned from a correct method when an earlier step in the calculation has been done incorrectly and the incorrect value is then used in later steps. Remember to use the skills you have learned in Chapter 3 to show your working for each calculation. This will make sure you are showing that you are using the correct method even if an earlier step in the calculation was incorrect.

The Exam skills chapter at the end of this book has more support and suggestions for how to use the number of marks available to manage your time in answering different types of questions.

6.1 What are enthalpy changes?

1 Name four things that could be classed as the surroundings in a chemical system.

2 The combustion of methane is an exothermic process with a value of $-890.3\,kJ\,mol^{-1}$. Draw a fully labelled enthalpy profile diagram for the reaction. **[Total: 5]**

6.2 Standard enthalpy changes

1 What are the standard conditions for enthalpy changes?

2 a Define the term *standard enthalpy of formation*. [2]

b Write an equation to describe the standard enthalpy of formation of lithium oxide. [2]

[Total: 4]

≪ RECALL AND CONNECT 1 ≪

What is the standard state of ionic substances like sodium chloride?

6.3 Measuring enthalpy changes

1 What is the equation for the energy transferred as heat (q) in a calorimetry experiment?

2 $50.0\,cm^3$ of $0.50\,mol\,dm^{-3}$ aqueous hydrochloric acid are reacted with $50.0\,cm^3$ of $0.50\,mol\,dm^{-3}$ aqueous sodium hydroxide, leading to neutralisation.

$$NaOH(aq) + HCl(aq) \rightarrow NaCl(aq) + H_2O(l)$$

$$\Delta H = -57.1\,kJ\,mol^{-1}$$

The initial temperature of each solution is 12 °C.

Calculate the maximum final temperature of the reaction mixture.

(Assume that the specific heat capacity of the reaction mixture, $c = 4.18\,J\,K^{-1}\,g^{-1}$ and that the density of the reaction mixture = $1.00\,g\,cm^{-3}$.) **[Total: 4]**

UNDERSTAND THESE TERMS

- activation energy, E_a
- standard enthalpy change of reaction, $\Delta H_r^{\ominus}$
- standard enthalpy change of formation, $\Delta H_f^{\ominus}$
- standard enthalpy change of combustion, $\Delta H_c^{\ominus}$
- standard enthalpy change of neutralisation, $\Delta H_{neut}^{\ominus}$
- specific heat capacity, c

6.4 Hess's law

1 Which law of thermodynamics leads to Hess's law?

2 Calculate the enthalpy of formation of buta-1,3-diene, $C_4H_6(g)$, using the enthalpy of combustion data, ΔH_c, in the table.

	Substance	ΔH_c / kJ mol^{-1}
ΔH_1	$C_4H_6(g)$	−2546
ΔH_2	$C(s)$	−394
ΔH_3	$H_2(g)$	−286

[Total: 3]

3 It is impossible to find the standard enthalpy of formation of ethyne, C_2H_2, by experimental methods. Use the enthalpy of combustion data, ΔH_c, given in the table to calculate a value for this reaction.

	Substance	ΔH_c / kJ mol^{-1}
ΔH_1	$C(s)$	−394
ΔH_2	$H_2(g)$	−286
ΔH_3	$C_2H_2(g)$	−1300

[Total: 3]

4 Calculate the enthalpy change for the hydration of ethene using the enthalpy of formation data, ΔH_f, given in the table. The equation for the hydration of ethene is:

$$C_2H_4(g) + H_2O(l) \rightarrow C_2H_5OH(l)$$

	Substance	ΔH_f / kJ mol^{-1}
ΔH_1	$C_2H_4(g)$	+52
ΔH_2	$H_2O(l)$	−286
ΔH_3	$C_2H_5OH(l)$	−278

[Total: 3]

6.5 Bond energies and enthalpy changes

1 Explain, using ideas about bond energies, why a reaction might be endothermic.

2 a Define the terms *exact bond energy* and *average bond energy*.

   b Explain why average bond energies are provided in data books for use in calculations. [Total: 5]

3 Draw an energy diagram to show bond breaking and bond forming for the combustion of methanal $H_2C{=}O$. Bond energy values are not needed. [Total: 4]

6.6 Calculating enthalpy changes using bond energies

1 When is it necessary to use bond energies to carry out calculations of enthalpy changes?

2 Hydrogen fluoride reacts with ethyne (C_2H_2) in a gas phase reaction to make 1,1-difluoroethane. An equation using displayed formulae is shown in Figure 6.1. All compounds are in the gaseous state.

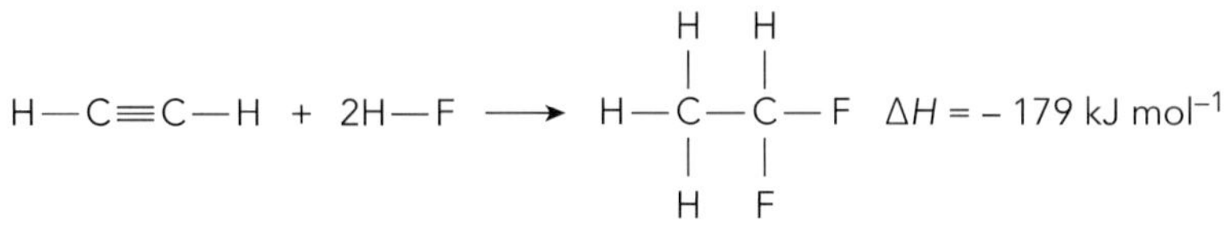

$$H-C\equiv C-H \ + \ 2H-F \ \longrightarrow \ \begin{matrix} H & H \\ | & | \\ H-C-C-F \\ | & | \\ H & F \end{matrix} \quad \Delta H = -179 \text{ kJ mol}^{-1}$$

Figure 6.1: Structure of 1,1-difluoroethane

The table shows some relevant average bond energies.

Bond	C—H	C≡C	H—F	C—C
Average bond energy / kJ mol^{-1}	412	837	562	348

Calculate a value for the bond enthalpy of a C—F bond in 1,1-difluoroethane.

[Total: 3]

REFLECTION

How well do you understand how mark schemes are applied to calculation questions? Are you able to give yourself marks even if your final answer is incorrect? Try some other questions from Exam practice 2 and see if you can apply mark schemes in the same way.

SELF-ASSESSMENT CHECKLIST

Let's revisit the Knowledge focus and Exam skills focus for this chapter.

Decide how confident you are with each statement.

Now I can:	Show it	Needs more work	Almost there	Confident to move on
explain and use the term *enthalpy change (ΔH)* and apply it to exothermic (ΔH is negative) and endothermic (ΔH is positive) chemical reactions	Write a definition of the term *enthalpy change* and give examples of exothermic and endothermic chemical changes.			

CONTINUED

Now I can:	Show it	Needs more work	Almost there	Confident to move on
construct and interpret reaction pathway diagrams in terms of enthalpy changes and activation energy	Draw reaction pathway diagrams for endothermic and exothermic chemical reactions, and fully label them with the key terms.			
define and use the term *standard conditions*	State the standard conditions.			
define and use the term *enthalpy change* with reference to enthalpy changes of reaction, formation, combustion and neutralisation	Write equations to represent the following: $\Delta H_{formation}$ of water, $\Delta H_{combustion}$ of magnesium, $\Delta H_{neutralisation}$.			
explain energy transfers during chemical reactions in terms of breaking and making chemical bonds	Look up a chemical reaction for an organic molecule. Draw it out using displayed formulae and annotate it with information about bond breaking and bond making.			
use bond energies to calculate enthalpy change of reaction	Find a list of bond energies using the internet and calculate the enthalpy change for the reaction you chose above.			
understand that some bond energies are exact and some bond energies are averages	Explain the difference between exact bond energies and average bond energies, and explain why average bond energies are generally used in calculations.			
calculate enthalpy changes from experimental results, including use of the relationships: $q = mc\Delta T$ and $\Delta H = -mc\Delta T$	Choose a past exam paper and use data from the paper that fits these relationships to perform some calculations.			
use Hess's law to construct simple energy cycles	Draw a visual representation of how Hess's cycles work.			

CONTINUED

Now I can:	Show it	Needs more work	Almost there	Confident to move on
carry out calculations using energy cycles to determine enthalpy changes that cannot be found by direct experiment	Find a question on Hess's law and carry out the calculations.			
understand how mark schemes are applied to calculation questions	Write a calculation question on this topic and then write its accompanying mark scheme.			

7 Redox reactions

It is essential to manage your time in the exam. If you do not, you can easily spend too long on a question, which puts you under time pressure for the rest of the paper. Paper 1 has 40 multiple choice questions to be completed in 75 minutes.

Another important exam skill is recognising multiple choice question distractors. Distractors are the incorrect answer choices. Sometimes, distractors are based on common student mistakes and misconceptions, so they stand out as plausible answers and trap unwary students. Good understanding, and plenty of practice of multiple choice questions, are key to mastering multiple choice questions and avoiding distractors. The Exam skills chapter provides more strategies for learning how to answer multiple choice questions.

7.1 What is a redox reaction?

1 **a** Why must oxidation and reduction always occur simultaneously in a reaction?

b Why is the number of electrons lost in the oxidation always the same as the number gained in the reduction?

c What are the limitations of defining oxidation and reduction in terms of addition or removal of hydrogen and oxygen?

d Identify the species that have been oxidised and reduced in the following equations, giving your reasons:

  i $H_2(g) + 0.5O_2(g) \rightarrow H_2O(l)$

  ii $Fe_2O_3(s) + 2Al(s) \rightarrow Al_2O_3(s) + 2Fe(l)$

  iii $CH_3CN(l) + 2H_2(g) \rightarrow CH_3CH_2NH_2(g)$

e Write the ionic half-equations from the following equations and identify the species that have been oxidised and reduced:

  i $Mg(s) + Cu(NO_3)_2(aq) \rightarrow Mg(NO_3)_2(aq) + Cu(s)$

  ii $ZnI_2(l) \rightarrow Zn(l) + I_2(g)$

  iii $3H_2SO_4(aq) + 2Al(s) \rightarrow Al_2(SO_4)_3(aq) + 3H_2(g)$

f Write balanced chemical equations from the following half-equations by considering the number of electrons transferred:

  i $Pb^{2+} \rightarrow Pb^{4+} + 2e^-$

   $0.5F_2 + e^- \rightarrow F^-$

  ii $2S_2O_3^{2-} \rightarrow S_4O_6^{2-} + 2e^-$

   $0.5I_2 + e^- \rightarrow I^-$

  iii $BrO_3^- + 6H^+ + 5e^- \rightarrow 0.5Br_2 + 3H_2O$

   $Br^- \rightarrow 0.5Br_2 + e^-$

  iv $Cr_2O_7^{2-} + 6e^- + 14H^+ \rightarrow 2Cr^{3+} + 7H_2O$

   $Zn \rightarrow Zn^{2+} + 2e^-$

  v $MnO_4^- + 5e^- + 8H^+ \rightarrow Mn^{2+} + 4H_2O$

   $C_2O_4^{2-} \rightarrow 2CO_2 + 2e^-$

2 When chlorine gas is passed through a solution of potassium bromide, the solution turns orange.

a Explain this observation. [2]

b Write an ionic equation for the reaction taking place. [1]

c By writing half-equations, explain, in terms of electron transfer, why this is a redox reaction. [2]

[Total: 5]

UNDERSTAND THESE TERMS

- oxidation
- reduction
- redox reaction

≪ RECALL AND CONNECT 1 ≪

Redox equations are often written as ionic equations. To write ionic equations, you need to know which substances can ionise (or dissociate) in aqueous solution. A useful indicator of this is if a substance has the state symbol 'aq'. The 'solubility rules' you learned for IGCSE are also helpful – can you recall these?

7.2 Oxidation numbers

1 **a** Copy and complete the table to summarise the important oxidation number rules.

Group or element	Oxidation number
uncombined elements	
Group 1 metals	
Group 2 metals	
fluorine	
oxygen	
hydrogen	

b Why is the oxidation number of an uncombined element zero?

c The formal definition of oxidation number (not required learning!) is *'the charge of an atom after ionic approximation of its heteronuclear bonds.'*

  i 'Ionic approximation of heteronuclear bonds' means all bonds between different atoms are treated as ionic, even covalent bonds. How is this done? (See the rules on page 158 of the coursebook for a hint.)

  ii Why do you think all bonds are treated as ionic in this way?

2 Which of the following is a redox reaction?

  A $H_3PO_4(aq) + 3KHCO_3(aq) \rightarrow K_3PO_4(aq) + 3CO_2(g) + 3H_2O(l)$

  B $SiO_2(s) + 2NaOH(aq) \rightarrow Na_2SiO_3(aq) + H_2O(l)$

  C $Cr_2O_7^{2-}(aq) + H_2O(l) \rightarrow 2CrO_4^{2-}(aq) + 2H^+(aq)$

  D $H_2O_2(aq) \rightarrow H_2O(l) + 0.5O_2(g)$ [Total: 1]

7.3 Applying the oxidation number rules

1 **a** Work out the oxidation number of the stated element in the following compounds:

  i N in NH_3
  ii O in H_2O_2
  iii P in H_3PO_4
  iv Br in HBrO
  v B in $NaBH_4$
  vi C in $Na_2C_2O_4$
  vii N in $LiNO_3$
  viii S in $(NH_4)_2SO_4$
  ix O in LiO_2
  x Fe in Fe_3O_4

b Work out the oxidation number of the stated element in the following compound ions:

   i S in SO_3^{2-}

   ii Cr in $Cr_2O_7^{2-}$

   iii Mn in MnO_4^-

   iv V in VO_2^+

   v N in NO_2^-

   vi Cl in ClO_4^-

   vii Xe in XeF_5^+

   viii S in $S_4O_6^{2-}$

2 a Manganese violet is a pigment used in cosmetics such as eye liner. It has the formula $NH_4MnP_2O_7$ and contains the pyrophosphate ion, $P_2O_7^{2-}$. Deduce the oxidation state of manganese in this compound. [1]

   b X is a compound of manganese that contains manganese, nitrogen, hydrogen and chlorine. X was prepared by adding ammonia solution to $25.0\,cm^3$ of $0.05\,mol\,dm^{-3}$ manganese(II) chloride solution, adding an excess of an oxidising agent and then adding hydrochloric acid. An excess of silver nitrate solution was added to X, which produced $0.884\,g$ of a white precipitate.

   i Calculate the number of moles of manganese(II) chloride used. [1]

   ii Identify the white precipitate. [1]

   iii Calculate the number of moles of the white precipitate. [1]

   iv Calculate the mole ratio of manganese ions to chloride ions in X. [1]

   v Hence, determine the oxidation number of manganese in X. [1]

   vi Suggest a practical reason why a whole number mole ratio was not obtained in the experiment. Explain your choice. [2]

   [Total: 8]

7.4 Redox and oxidation number

1 Show, in terms of oxidation number changes, that the following reactions are redox reactions. You should state which elements are being oxidised and reduced. The first one has been done for you:

   a $2Al + 3H_2SO_4 \rightarrow Al_2(SO_4)_3 + 3H_2$
   Element oxidised: Al, from 0 to +3
   Element reduced: H, from +1 to 0

   b $6HI + SO_2 \rightarrow H_2S + 3I_2 + 2H_2O$

   c $4HCl + MnO_2 \rightarrow MnCl_2 + 2H_2O + Cl_2$

   d $Cr_2O_7^{2-} + 6Fe^{2+} + 14H^+ \rightarrow 2Cr^{3+} + 7H_2O + 6Fe^{3+}$

   e $3Cu + 8HNO_3 \rightarrow 3Cu(NO_3)_2 + 2NO + 4H_2O$

   f $2MnO_4^- + 3C_2O_4^{2-} + 4H_2O \rightarrow 2MnO_2 + 6CO_2 + 8OH^-$

   g $4FeO_4^{2-} + 10H_2O \rightarrow 3O_2 + 4Fe(OH)_3 + 8OH^-$

7.5 Oxidising agents and reducing agents

1 Identify the oxidising and reducing agents in the following reactions, explaining your answers in terms of oxidation number changes. The first one has been done for you.

    a $2KI + Br_2 \rightarrow 2KBr + I_2$

    Oxidising agent: Br_2 as it is reduced from 0 to -1

    Reducing agent: I^- as it is oxidised from -1 to 0

    b $HNO_3 + 2NO + H_2O \rightarrow 3HNO_2$

    c $PbO_2 + 4HCl \rightarrow PbCl_2 + 2H_2O + Cl_2$

    d $MnO_4^- + 8H^+ + 5Fe^{2+} \rightarrow Mn^{2+} + 5Fe^{3+} + 4H_2O$

    e $IO_3^- + 6H^+ + 5I^- \rightarrow 3I_2 + 3H_2O$

    f $2S_2O_3^{2-} + I_2 \rightarrow 2I^- + S_4O_6^{2-}$

2 Consider the following reaction:

$$2Ca_3(PO_4)_2 + 6SiO_2 + 10C \rightarrow 6CaSiO_3 + P_4 + 10CO$$

Which statement is correct?

    A $Ca_3(PO_4)_2$ is the oxidising agent as it loses electrons.

    B C is the reducing agent as it loses electrons.

    C C is the oxidising agent as it loses electrons.

    D $Ca_3(PO_4)_2$ is the reducing agent as it gains electrons.   **[Total: 1]**

7.6 Naming compounds

1 Give the systematic names for the following compounds and ions:

    a Fe_2O_3 **f** $HBrO_3$

    b $NaClO_2$ **g** KNO_2

    c $(NH_4)_2SO_3$ **h** $(NH_4)_2CrO_4$

    d $CaSO_4$ **i** $NiCl_2.H_2O$

    e $Ba_3(PO_3)_2$ **j** $(NH_4)_2Fe(SO_4)_2.6H_2O$

2 For which compound in the table is all the information correct?

	Compound	Oxidation number of bolded element	Systematic name
A	$(NH_4)_2\mathbf{Mo}O_4$	+6	diammonium molybdate(IV)
B	$H\mathbf{I}O_3$	+5	iodic(V) acid
C	$K_2\mathbf{Mn}O_4$	+7	potassium manganate(V)
D	$Na\mathbf{Cl}O_4$	+5	sodium chlorate(VII)

[Total: 1]

7.7 From name to formula

1 Write the formula of the following compounds from their systematic names:

a copper(I) oxide

b iron(III) sulfide

c sodium sulfate

d magnesium nitrate(III)

e ammonium sulfate(IV)

f potassium vanadate(V)

g titanium(III) nitride

h chloric(V) acid

i strontium dichromate(VI)

j palladium(II) phosphide

k cobalt(II) sulfate monohydrate

7.8 Balancing chemical equations using oxidation numbers

1 Balance the following chemical reactions by considering oxidation number changes:

a $\_HBr(aq) + \_H_2SO_4(aq) \rightarrow \_Br_2(aq) + \_SO_2(g) + \_H_2O(l)$

b $\_PbO_2(s) + \_H^+(aq) + \_SO_3^{2-}(aq) \rightarrow \_Pb^{2+}(aq) + \_H_2O(l) + \_SO_4^{2-}(aq)$

c $\_MnO_4^-(aq) + \_H^+(aq) + \_Fe^{2+}(aq) \rightarrow \_Mn^{2+}(aq) + \_Fe^{3+}(aq) + \_H_2O(l)$

d $\_V^{2+}(aq) + \_MnO_4^-(aq) + \_H_2O(l) \rightarrow \_VO_3^-(aq) + \_Mn^{2+}(aq) + \_H^+(aq)$

e $\_KMnO_4(aq) + \_HCl(aq) \rightarrow \_MnCl_2(aq) + \_KCl(aq) + \_Cl_2(aq) + \_H_2O(l)$

f $\_CuS(aq) + \_HNO_3(aq) \rightarrow \_CuSO_4(aq) + \_NO(aq) + \_H_2O(l)$

g $\_KI(aq) + \_H_2SO_4(aq) \rightarrow \_KHSO_4(aq) + \_I_2(aq) + \_S(s) + \_H_2O(l)$

h $\_MnO_4^-(aq) + \_H_2O(l) + \_I^-(aq) \rightarrow \_MnO_2(aq) + \_OH^-(aq) + \_I_2(aq)$

2 Sodium iodide reacts with concentrated sulfuric, as shown by the reaction:

$$\mathbf{a}NaI + \mathbf{b}H_2SO_4 \rightarrow \mathbf{c}NaHSO_4 + \mathbf{d}I_2 + \mathbf{e}H_2S + \mathbf{f}H_2O$$

Which coefficients correctly balance the equation?

	a	b	c	d	e	f
A	8	9	8	4	1	4
B	8	1	8	4	1	4
C	1	8	1	4	1	4
D	9	8	9	1	4	1

[Total: 1]

7.9 Disproportionation

1 Balance the following disproportionation reaction equations by considering oxidation number changes:

a ....Cl_2 + ...$NaOH \rightarrow$ ....$NaCl$ + ...$NaClO$ + ...H_2O

b ....Cl_2 + ...$NaOH \rightarrow$ ....$NaCl$ + ...$NaClO_3$ + ...H_2O

c ....$ClO^- \rightarrow$ ....Cl^- + ...ClO_3^-

d ....$Cu^+ \rightarrow$ ....Cu + ...Cu^{2+}

e ....NH_3 + ...$NO \rightarrow$ ....N_2 + ...H_2O

f ....KOH + ...$Br_2 \rightarrow$ ....$KBrO_4$ + ...H_2O + ...KBr

2 Bromine fluoride decomposes to form bromine trifluoride and bromine:

$$3BrF \rightarrow BrF_3 + Br_2$$

Show how this reaction is a disproportionation. **[Total: 2]**

3 Sodium dithionite reacts with sodium hydroxide:

$$\mathbf{v}Na_2S_2O_4 + \mathbf{w}NaOH \rightarrow \mathbf{x}Na_2SO_3 + \mathbf{y}Na_2S + \mathbf{z}H_2O$$

1 Sulfur changes oxidation number from +3 to +4 and from +3 to +2.

2 **v** and **w** are different numbers.

3 NaOH is the reducing agent.

Which statements are correct?

A **1**, **2** and **3** are correct.

B **1** and **2** only are correct.

C **2** and **3** only are correct.

D **1** only is correct. **[Total: 1]**

≪ RECALL AND CONNECT 2 ≪

Write full and ionic equations, including state symbols, for the following reactions:

a Solid magnesium carbonate reacting with sulfuric acid.

b Iron reacting with hydrochloric acid to make iron(III) chloride.

c Solid copper oxide reacting with sulfuric acid.

d Calcium hydroxide solution reacting with hydrochloric acid.

REFLECTION

One reason redox is a challenging topic is because it contains lots of skills that require lots of practice to master. Many of these skills involve writing chemical equations and half-equations. What common mistakes do you think students make when writing chemical equations? How do you think you could avoid making common mistakes?

SELF-ASSESSMENT CHECKLIST

Let's revisit the Knowledge focus and Exam skills focus for this chapter.

Decide how confident you are with each statement.

Now I can:	Show it	Needs more work	Almost there	Confident to move on
calculate oxidation numbers of elements in compounds and ions	Construct a table of the important oxidation number rules and use these to work out oxidation numbers for the substances in this chapter.			
explain and use the terms *redox, oxidation, reduction* and *disproportionation* in terms of electron transfer and changes in oxidation number	Using these terms, annotate the equations covered in Chapter 14 of the coursebook to show which are redox reactions.			
explain and use the terms *oxidising agent* and *reducing agent*	Make a list of the reactions from Chapters 11 and 12 in the coursebook and label the oxidising and reducing agents.			
use changes in oxidation numbers to help balance chemical equations	Write half-equations for the required halogen disproportionation reactions and use these to derive the coefficients.			
use Roman numerals to indicate the degree of oxidation or reduction of an element in a compound	Write the formulae of the possible nitrates, sulfates, and chlorates, and state which contain the most oxidised elements.			
effectively manage time spent on multiple choice questions	Attempt the multiple choice questions in the accompanying digital material.			
practise recognising distractor answer choices in multiple choice questions	When answering multiple choice questions, note how the distractors have been selected.			

8 Equilibria

Some chemistry questions require a longer answer (around 6–8 marks). These questions may combine different command words, such as *identify* and *explain* or *state* and *explain*. It is important to cover all parts of the question as you write your answer. In this chapter you will practise some of these longer answers – comparing your answers with the examples given in the Answers section will help you to reduce the risk that you might miss something out.

8.1 Reversible reactions and equilibrium

1 How is a reversible reaction indicated in an equation?

2 State two features of a reaction in dynamic equilibrium. **[Total: 2]**

3 Figure 8.1 shows how the partial pressure of substances in a reaction changes over time. State the equation for the reaction and explain how the graph provides evidence for the equation. Put an X on the graph to show the point when equilibrium is reached. **[Total: 5]**

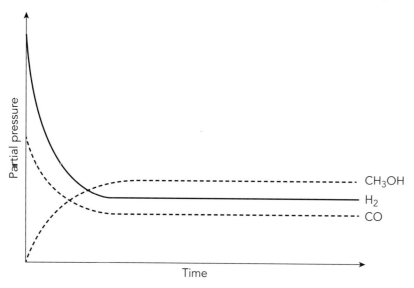

Figure 8.1

8.2 Changing the position of equilibrium

1 Equation 1: $CaCO_3(s) \rightarrow CaO(s) + CO_2(g)$

Equation 2: $CH_3COOH(l) + CH_3CH_2OH(l) \rightleftharpoons CH_3COOCH_2CH_3(l) + H_2O(l)$

If both reactions are carried out in beakers, why can the reaction in equation 2 reach equilibrium but the reaction in equation 1 cannot?

2 State Le Chatelier's principle.

3   The reaction between solutions of iron(III) ions (Fe^{3+}) and thiocyanate ions
    (SCN^-) is reversible. The reaction can be described by the ionic equation
    in the table.

	$Fe^{3+}(aq)$	+	$SCN^-(aq)$	$\rightleftharpoons$	$FeSCN^{2+}(aq)$
Colour of solution	yellow		colourless		red

When the reaction reaches equilibrium at room temperature the solution is orange.
When the temperature is increased the colour of the reaction mixture becomes
more yellow.

State whether the forward reaction is endothermic or exothermic.
Explain your answer.   **[Total: 3]**

≪ RECALL AND CONNECT 1 ≪

What is gas pressure?

8.3 Equilibrium expressions and the equilibrium constant, K_c

1   What is the K_c expression for the reversible reaction $2X(g) + Y(g) \rightleftharpoons 2Z(g)$

2   State what happens to the equilibrium constant K_c when the temperature
    is increased for an exothermic reaction.   **[Total: 3]**

8.4 Equilibria in gas reactions: the equilibrium constant, K_p

1   How are the pressure units atmosphere and Pascals related?
    Why are pressure values often quoted in atmosphere?

2   At equilibrium, a vessel contains 0.05 mol of $SO_2(g)$, 0.08 mol of $O_2(g)$
    and 0.07 mol of $SO_3(g)$. What is the mole fraction of SO_3?

3   Sulfur dioxide and oxygen were mixed in a 2:1 mol ratio and sealed in a flask
    with a catalyst according to the equation:

$$2SO_2(g) + O_2(g) \rightleftharpoons 2SO_3(g)$$

The partial pressure of sulfur dioxide in the equilibrium mixture was 24 kPa,
and the total pressure in the flask was 104 kPa.

Deduce the partial pressure of oxygen and sulfur trioxide and calculate
a value for the equilibrium constant K_p. Include the units of K_p.   **[Total: 5]**

UNDERSTAND THESE TERMS

- equilibrium reaction
- dynamic equilibrium
- closed system
- reversible reaction

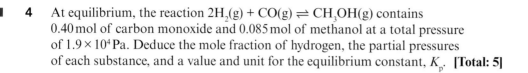

4   At equilibrium, the reaction $2H_2(g) + CO(g) \rightleftharpoons CH_3OH(g)$ contains 0.40 mol of carbon monoxide and 0.085 mol of methanol at a total pressure of 1.9×10^4 Pa. Deduce the mole fraction of hydrogen, the partial pressures of each substance, and a value and unit for the equilibrium constant, K_p. **[Total: 5]**

8.5 Equilibria and the chemical industry

1   Why is equilibrium position an important consideration in the chemical industry?

2   The Haber process for the industrial production of ammonia is summarised as follows:

$$N_2(g) + 3H_2(g) \rightleftharpoons 2NH_3(g)$$

$$\Delta H_r = -92 \, kJ \, mol^{-1}$$

The compromise conditions of the reaction are a temperature of $450\,°C$ and pressure of 1.50×10^7 Pa using an iron catalyst. Additionally, the ammonia formed is immediately condensed and removed.

For each of the conditions, explain their use with reference to the position of equilibrium and the yield of ammonia.   **[Total: 6]**

> **UNDERSTAND THESE TERMS**
>
> *   equilibrium constant, K_c or K_p
> *   equilibrium expression
> *   partial pressure
> *   mole fraction

8.6 Acid–base equilibria

« RECALL AND CONNECT 2 «

What is the pH of a solution containing 1×10^{-5} mol dm^{-3} H$^+$ ions?

1   What are the ions formed by ethanoic acid, CH_3COOH, when it is dissolved in water?

2   The ionisation of water is a reversible reaction, as shown by the equation $2H_2O \rightleftharpoons H_3O^+ + OH^-$. Describe this reaction in terms of the Brønsted–Lowry theory of acids and bases.   **[Total: 3]**

3   Carbonic acid is an equilibrium mixture of carbon dioxide dissolved in water. The following equilibrium is set up: $CO_2(g) + H_2O(l) \rightleftharpoons HCO_3^-(aq) + H^+(aq)$

Explain, in terms of the equilibrium, why carbonic acid is classed as a weak acid.   **[Total: 2]**

8.7 Indicators and acid–base titrations

1   What is an acid–base indicator?

2   Figure 8.2 shows the pH change for an acid–base titration.

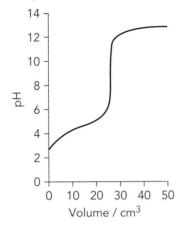

Figure 8.2

The table shows some information about two commonly used indicators, methyl orange and phenolphthalein.

Identify what class of acid and base (weak/strong) are used and identify a suitable indicator for the endpoint of the titration. Explain your answer.   **[Total: 6]**

Indicator	Colour change range	Colour at lower pH	Colour at higher pH
methyl orange	pH 3.2–4.4	red	yellow
phenolphthalein	pH 8.2–10	colourless	pink

REFLECTION

How well are you organising your answers to longer questions? The answer section to this chapter shows a number of different ways to set out your answer – you don't just have to write a paragraph. It is worthwhile experimenting with different ways to set out your answer so that you are reminded to cover all parts of the question. Suggested ways to set out your answer include bullet points, lists, tables, diagrams and flowcharts. Look back at some of your answers and try a different way of setting out the ideas.

SELF-ASSESSMENT CHECKLIST

Let's revisit the Knowledge focus and Exam skills focus for this chapter.

Decide how confident you are with each statement.

Now I can:	Show it	Needs more work	Almost there	Confident to move on
explain what is meant by a reversible reaction	Make a flash card of the key term *reversible reaction*.			
explain what is meant by dynamic equilibrium in terms of the rate of forward and backward reactions being equal and the concentration of reactants and products remaining constant	Make a flash card of the key term *dynamic equilibrium*.			
explain why a closed system is needed for equilibrium to be established	Draw a series of diagrams to show why a closed system is needed for equilibrium to be established.			
define Le Chatelier's principle as: 'If a change is made to a system at dynamic equilibrium the position of equilibrium moves to minimise this change'	Write down the definition of Le Chatelier's principle, cover it, then try to rewrite it from memory.			
use Le Chatelier's principle to qualitatively deduce the effects of changes in temperature, concentration, pressure or presence of a catalyst on a reaction at equilibrium	Construct a table showing the effect of changes in temperature, concentration, pressure or presence of a catalyst on endothermic and exothermic reactions, and on reactions with different numbers of moles of reactant and product gases.			
deduce expressions for equilibrium constants in terms of concentrations, K_c	Find or construct five equations for aqueous reactions. Write K_c expressions for them and deduce the units.			

CONTINUED

Now I can:	Show it	Needs more work	Almost there	Confident to move on
use the terms *mole fraction* and *partial pressure*	Write a definition for the terms *mole fraction* and *partial pressure*.			
deduce expressions for equilibrium constants in terms of partial pressures, K_p	Find or construct five equations for gaseous reactions. Write K_p expressions for them and deduce the units.			
use K_c and K_p expressions to carry out equilibrium calculations	Draw a flowchart of the steps needed when carrying out K_c and K_p calculations from given amounts of substances (in moles).			
calculate the quantities present at equilibrium from given data	Choose an equation for a chemical system at equilibrium. Annotate the equation with bullet points to show how to calculate the equilibrium quantities using the ICE (initial, change, equilibrium) method.			
understand which factors affect the value of the equilibrium constant	Make a list of factors that do and do not affect the equilibrium constant.			
describe and explain the conditions used in the Haber process and the Contact process	Make flash cards summarising the conditions for the Haber process and the Contact process, and the reasons why these conditions are optimum.			
write the formula and give the names of common acids and alkalis (HCl, H_2SO_4, HNO_3, CH_3COOH, $NaOH$, KOH, NH_3)	Write the names of each of the acids and alkalis given.			

CONTINUED

Now I can:	Show it	Needs more work	Almost there	Confident to move on
describe the Brønsted–Lowry theory of acids and bases	Draw Lewis dot-and-cross diagrams illustrating the reaction of ammonia and hydrogen chloride, and annotate this with the Brønsted–Lowry theory of acids and bases.			
describe strong acids and strong bases, and weak acids and weak bases in terms of being fully dissociated or partially dissociated	Using HNO_3 as an example of a strong acid and HCOOH as an example of a weak acid, show the dissociation equations and illustrate the extent of dissociation.			
describe acid, alkaline and neutral solutions in terms of pH	Give the pH values for acid, alkaline and neutral solutions.			
qualitatively explain the differences in behaviour of strong and weak acids in terms of electrical conductivity, universal indicator, pH and reactivity with reactive metals	Explain the differences in behaviour of strong and weak acids in terms of electrical conductivity, universal indicator, pH and reactivity with reactive metals.			
describe neutralisation reactions in terms of $H^+(aq) + OH^-(aq) \rightarrow H_2O(l)$	Write equations for some neutralisation reactions, and colour-code the atoms that lead to the formation of water.			
sketch pH titration curves using combinations of strong and weak acids with strong and weak alkalis	Draw sketches of pH titration curves using combinations of strong and weak acids with strong and weak alkalis.			
select suitable indicators for acid–alkali titrations using data provided	On the sketches above, show the colour changes of common indicators.			
practise and improve longer answers	Look back at some of your longer answers and consider how they could be better organised.			

9 Rates of reaction

The 'sketch' command word is often used for topics where information is shown graphically, or where simple diagrams can efficiently communicate important ideas. Various types of graphs, periodic trends, Boltzmann distribution curves, reaction pathway diagrams and types of structure are examples of things you could be asked to sketch. Remember, the exam is timed, so your sketch drawings need to be simple and show only the features required by the question.

Sketch	make a simple drawing showing the key features

9.1 Rate of reaction

1 **a** To study the rates of the following reactions, which is the best variable to measure over time, and which instrument or experimental technique would you use?

   i $H_2O_2(aq) \rightarrow H_2O(aq) + 0.5O_2(g)$

   ii $CH_3COCH_3(aq) + I_2(aq) \rightarrow ICH_2COCH_3(aq) + HI(aq)$

   iii $MnO_4^- + 8H^+ + 5Fe^{2+} \rightarrow Mn^{2+} + 5Fe^{3+} + 4H_2O$

   iv $CH_3CH_2CHBrCH_3(l) + NaOH(aq) \rightarrow CH_3CH_2CH(OH)CH_3(aq) +$ NaBr(aq)

b 'Reactivity' is a very common word used in chemistry.

   i What does 'reactivity' mean, and how is it connected to reaction kinetics?

   ii Hydrochloric acid is a strong acid, whereas ethanoic acid is a weak acid. How could you compare the reactivities of these two different acids using reaction kinetics?

UNDERSTAND THESE TERMS
• rate of reaction
• reaction kinetics
• collision theory
• ineffective collisions
• effective collisions
• catalyst

2 **a** State the main features of collision theory. [4]

b To improve their combustion efficiency, linear alkanes undergo a process called catalytic reforming, which produces cyclic molecules. Reformation of hexane into methylcyclopentane is an exothermic reaction that produces one other product.

   i Write a chemical equation for the reformation of hexane into methylcyclopentane. [1]

   ii Catalytic reforming uses heterogeneous catalysts such as platinum on silica. Explain what is meant by the term heterogeneous catalyst. [1]

   iii Sketch a reaction pathway diagram to show the conversion of hexane into methylcyclopentane. Label the diagram to show the enthalpy change, ΔH, and the activation energies for the catalysed and uncatalysed reactions. [3]

   [Total: 9]

≪ RECALL AND CONNECT 1 ≪

a Can you recall the ideal gas equation?

b What are the correct units for each of the terms in the equation?

c What does it tell us about the relationship between i) volume and pressure and ii) volume and amount of gas?

9.2 The effect of concentration on rate of reaction

1   a   What is meant by *concentration* in chemistry and what are its standard units?

   b   How does concentration affect the rate of chemical reactions?

   c   Why might increasing the concentration not significantly increase the rate of reaction?

   d   Explain fully how doubling the volume of a gaseous reaction would alter its rate of reaction.

2   Nitrogen dioxide undergoes decomposition to form nitrogen monoxide and oxygen, as shown in the following equation:

$$2NO_2(g) \rightarrow 2NO(g) + O_2(g)$$

   a   Show, using oxidation numbers, that this is a redox reaction.   [2]

   b   With reference to Le Chatelier's principle and reaction kinetics, state and explain one advantage and one disadvantage of using a higher pressure.   [4]

   c   Reaction kinetics data for this reaction is shown in the table.

Time / s	$[NO_2] \times 10^{-3}$ / mol dm^{-3}
0	4.44
90	3.14
216	2.22
288	1.91
450	1.44
702	1.04
900	0.87
1350	0.61
1800	0.48

   i   Plot these data and draw a line of best fit.   [2]

   ii   Using collision theory, explain the change in overall rate over time.   [3]

[Total: 11]

9.3 The effect of temperature on rate of reaction

UNDERSTAND
THIS TERM

• Boltzmann
  distribution

1 Explain, in terms of collision theory, why increasing reaction temperature by 10 °C typically doubles the rate of reaction.

2 In the first stage of the Ostwald process used to manufacture nitric acid, ammonia is oxidised to nitrogen(II) oxide:

$$4NH_3(g) + 5O_2(g) \rightarrow 4NO(g) + 6H_2O(g)$$

The Boltzmann distribution for a mixture of ammonia and oxygen at 298 K is shown in Figure 9.1. E_a represents the activation energy for the reaction.

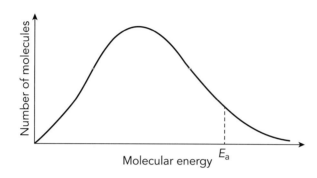

Figure 9.1

a Using the same axes, sketch a second curve to indicate the Boltzmann distribution at 450 K. [2]

b With reference to the Boltzmann distribution, state and explain the effect of increasing temperature on the rate of formation of nitrogen(II) oxide. [3]

[Total: 5]

9.4 Catalysis

1 Ethanol reacts with butanoic acid to give an ester with a fruity aroma similar to pineapple. The reaction is an acid-catalysed condensation reaction.

UNDERSTAND
THIS TERM

• catalysis

a What is meant by the term *acid catalysed*?

b What is meant by the term *condensation reaction*?

c Write a balanced chemical equation for this reaction.

d Name the ester formed.

e Why is monitoring pH change over time not an effective method to study the kinetics of this reaction?

2   Methanol is manufactured from carbon monoxide and hydrogen using a catalyst that contains chromium(III) oxide:

$$CO(g) + 2H_2(g) \rightarrow CH_3OH(g)$$

a   Give the formula for chromium(III) oxide.   [1]

b   The carbon monoxide and hydrogen needed for this reaction can be manufactured by reacting coke, a form of carbon, with steam. Write a chemical equation for this reaction, including state symbols.   [1]

c   The chromium(III) oxide catalyst increases the rate of methanol production. Use the Boltzmann distribution in Figure 9.2 to explain why a catalyst increases the rate of this reaction.   [4]

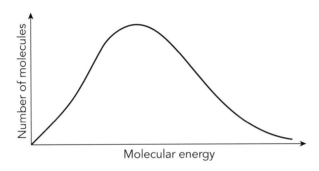

Figure 9.2

[Total: 6]

《 RECALL AND CONNECT 2 《

Write equations for the following standard enthalpy changes:

a   The standard enthalpy of combustion of propane, C_3H_8.

b   The standard enthalpy of formation of aluminium oxide.

c   The standard enthalpy of neutralisation for the reaction between potassium hydroxide and sulfuric acid.

REFLECTION

The first step towards greater confidence and reducing stress is identifying topics where you feel you need to improve your understanding. To do this, make a list of all the syllabus topics and highlight them using a 'traffic light' system: red for a topic you don't understand, yellow for a topic that needs improvement and green for a topic you feel confident with. The red topics are the priority ones to address.

SELF-ASSESSMENT CHECKLIST

Let's revisit the Knowledge focus and Exam skills focus for this chapter.

Decide how confident you are with each statement.

Now I can:	Show it	Needs more work	Almost there	Confident to move on
explain and use the terms rate of reaction, frequency of collisions, effective and non-effective collisions	Write alternative definitions for these key terms without using the words 'rate', 'frequency' or 'effective'/ 'non-effective'.			
explain, in terms of frequency of effective collisions, the effect of changes of concentration and pressure on the rate of reaction	Write a description of how concentration and pressure changes affect the rates of solution phase and gas phase reactions.			
use experimental data to calculate the rate of a reaction	Plot a graph from concentration vs. time data and find the rate by drawing tangents to the curve.			
define activation energy, E_a	Label the activation energy on a reaction pathway diagram and explain its significance in terms of collision theory.			
sketch and use the Boltzmann distribution curve to explain the importance of activation energy	Write a description of the relationship between the Boltzmann distribution and collision energy.			
explain the effect of temperature change on rate of reaction in terms of the Boltzmann distribution and the frequency of effective collisions	Sketch Boltzmann distribution curves for two different reaction temperatures and describe how it links with collision theory.			
explain and use the terms catalyst and catalysis	Describe why iron in the Haber process can be described as a heterogeneous catalyst.			

Now I can:	Show it	Needs more work	Almost there	Confident to move on
explain how a catalyst works in terms of difference in activation energy and difference in mechanism	Sketch a reaction pathway diagram for a catalysed and uncatalysed reaction.			
explain the effect of catalysts in terms of the Boltzmann distribution	Sketch a Boltzmann distribution curve for a reaction with and without a catalyst and describe how it explains how the rate is increased with a catalyst.			
construct and interpret a reaction pathway diagram in the presence and absence of a catalyst	Label a reaction pathway diagram to show the different pathways and activation energies for catalysed and uncatalysed reactions.			
show that I understand the 'sketch' command word and answer 'sketch' questions	Sketch Boltzmann distribution curves to show the effects of increasing reaction temperature and adding a catalyst on reaction rates.			

Exam practice 2

This section contains past paper questions from previous Cambridge exams which draw together your knowledge on a range of topics that you have covered up to this point. These questions give you the opportunity to test your knowledge and understanding. Additional past paper practice questions can be found in the accompanying digital material.

The following question has an example student response and commentary provided. Work through the question first, then compare your answer to the sample response and commentary. Are your answers different to the sample responses?

1   Until 1985, carbon was thought to exist in only two structural forms or *allotropes*. In 1985 another form, buckminsterfullerene, was discovered, in which the carbon exists as spherical molecules.

    a   The other two forms of carbon have very different structures.

        i   Name these two forms.   [1]

        ii   Give **three** differences in physical properties between these two forms.   [3]

    b   The diagram shows the structure of buckminsterfullerene.

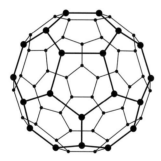

buckminsterfullerene

The molecule of buckminsterfullerene contains 60 carbon atoms. Suggest a reason why buckminsterfullerene reacts with hydrogen under suitable conditions and give a formula for the product.   [2]

c   In 2010, two scientists from the University of Manchester were awarded
    the Nobel Prize for Physics for their work on graphene, a new structural
    form of carbon. Graphene is one of the new 'nano-materials' being
    developed for commercial uses in the next 10 years.

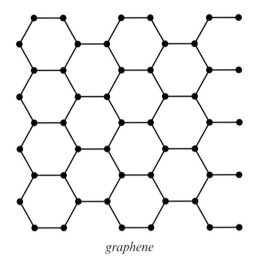

graphene

i   Graphene is in the form of sheets of carbon one atom thick. Calculate
    the number of carbon atoms present in a sheet of graphene with a mass
    of one thousandth of a gram (0.001 g).

The number of hexagons in a large sheet of graphene can be assumed to be one
half of the number of carbon atoms. Each hexagon has an area of 690 nm^2.

ii   Calculate the area of the sheet of graphene in **i** in nm^2.

iii Would you expect samples of graphene and buckminsterfullerene
     to be electrical conductors? Explain your answers.   [4]

                                                              [Total: 10]

Cambridge International AS & A Level Chemistry (9701) Paper 43 Q9
November 2013

Example student response	Commentary
a i Diamond and graphene.	Diamond is correct, but the question asks about the forms of carbon known **up to 1985**. Also, graphene is named as a form of carbon in this question. Your answers must offer new information not already provided as part of the question. *This answer is awarded ½ out of 1 mark.*
ii Graphene is less dense than diamond. Graphene conducts electricity, diamond does not. Diamond is shiny, graphene is dull grey.	Although graphene is the wrong allotrope, the student has correctly compared density and electrical conductivity. However, 'shiny' is not an accurate physical property of diamond (this is only true of cut and polished diamonds). *This answer is awarded 2 out of 3 marks.*

Example student response	Commentary
b Fullerenes are reactive due to their large surface area. $C_{60}H_{122}$	Both responses are incorrect. The student needed to recognise how the bonding and hybridisation of the carbon atoms in fullerenes allows them to undergo similar reactions to alkenes. *This answer is awarded 0 out of 2 marks.*
c i moles = 0.001/12 = 0.000083 atoms = 0.000083 × 6 × 10^{23} = 5 × 10^{19} hexagons = 5 × 10^{19}/2 = 2.5 × 10^{19}	The correct method has been used, but one mark is lost because the student should use precise values for physical constants. *This answer is awarded 0 out of 1 mark.*
ii area = 2.5 × 10^{19} × 690 = 1.725 × 10^{22}	The rest of the calculation is performed correctly, so the error-carried-forward rule (see Chapter 6) is applied. *This answer is awarded 1 out of 1 marks.*
iii Graphene conducts as it has free electrons, but buckminsterfullerene does not conduct because, although it has free electrons, they cannot move from one molecule to the next.	Both responses here are correct. *This answer is awarded 2 out of 2 marks.*

2   Now write an improved answer to the parts of question **1** where you did not gain full marks.

The following question has an example student response and commentary provided. Work through the question first, then compare your answer to the sample response and commentary. Are your answers different to the sample responses?

3   Thiophene, C_4H_4S(l), is an organic compound that is found as a contaminant in crude oil.

   a   Construct the equation for the complete combustion of thiophene, C_4H_4S(l).

   Include state symbols in your answer.   [2]

   b   A student carries out an experiment to determine the enthalpy change of combustion of C_4H_4S(l).

   Explain the meaning of the term *enthalpy change of combustion*.   [2]

c   The student uses the following apparatus in the experiment.

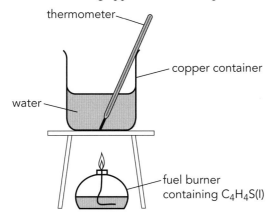

mass of water in copper container / g	200
initial temperature of water / °C	18.5
highest temperature of water / °C	37.5

Calculate the heat energy released, in J, by the reaction.

Assume that 4.18 J of heat energy changes the temperature of 1.0 cm^3 of water by 1.0 °C.

Assume no heat is lost to the surroundings.   [2]

d   The student used 0.63 g of $C_4H_4S(l)$ in the experiment.

Calculate the enthalpy change of combustion of thiophene, $\Delta H_c(C_4H_4S(l))$, in kJ mol^{-1}. Include a sign in your answer.   [2]

[Total: 8]

Cambridge International AS & A Level Chemistry (9701) Paper 23 Q3b
November 2019

Example student response	Commentary
a $C_4H_4S + 6O_2 \rightarrow 4CO_2 + 2H_2O + SO_2$	The equation contains the correct reactants and products but the student has forgotten to give the state symbols. *This answer is awarded 1 out of 2 marks.*
b Enthalpy change when one mole of a substance burns in air.	Mentioning one mole of the substance is burned gains one mark. However, the student has missed out the 'negative' sign and a crucial word so the response is not awarded the second available mark. *This answer is awarded 1 out of 2 marks.*
c $Q = mc\,\Delta T = 200 \times 4.18 \times (37.5 - 18.5)$ $Q = 15\ 488$	The working-out line is correct and gains one mark. In the final answer, the student has made a transcription error – they have incorrectly copied their calculator output – and so the response does not get the second mark. *This answer is awarded 1 out of 2 marks.*

Example student response	Commentary
d n(thiophene) = 0.63/84.1 = 7.49×10^{-3} 15 488/7.49×10^{-3} = 2 067 823 J = 2067 kJ mol^{-1}	The student has correctly calculated the M_r of thiophene and the number of moles of thiophene. For the second part of the calculation, they have used the incorrect value from part **c**. As the method is correct, the marker would apply the error-carried-forward rule and marks are given for the correct method using the incorrect earlier value. So, they receive the second mark even though the response does not match the value given in the mark scheme. *This answer is awarded 2 out of 2 marks.*

4   Now that you have read the sample response, rewrite your answer to any part of question **3** where you did not score highly. Use the commentary to help you.

The following question has an example student response and commentary provided. Work through the question first, then compare your answer to the sample response and commentary. Are your answers different to the sample responses? How are they different?

5   When a concentrated solution of bromic(V) acid, $HBrO_3$, is warmed, it decomposes to form bromine, oxygen and water only.

Write an equation for this reaction. The use of oxidation numbers may be helpful.   **[Total: 1]**

Cambridge International AS & A Level Chemistry (9701) Paper 42 Q2ciii March 2018

Example student response	Commentary
$2HBrO_3 \rightarrow Br_2 + 5/2O_2 + H_2O$	Although the question advises the use of oxidation numbers, this student appears to have balanced the equation by inspection. *This answer is awarded 1 out of 1 mark.*

Now, based on your understanding of the commentary to the student response in question **5**, write your answer to the following question.

6   Nitrobenzene, $C_6H_5NO_2$, can be reduced to phenylamine, $C_6H_5NH_2$, in acid solution in a two step process.

   a   Balance the half-equation for this reaction to work out how many moles of electrons are needed to reduce one mole of nitrobenzene.

$$C_6H_5NO_2 + \ldots\ldots e^- + \ldots\ldots H+ \rightarrow C_6H_5NH_2 + \ldots\ldots H_2O \qquad [1]$$

b The reducing agent normally used is granulated tin and concentrated hydrochloric acid. In the first step, the reduction of nitrobenzene to phenylammonium chloride can be represented by the equation shown.

Use oxidation numbers or electrons transferred to balance this equation. You might find your answer to **a** useful.

......$C_6H_5NO_2$ + ...HCl + ...Sn → ......$C_6H_5NH_3Cl$ + ...$SnCl_4$ + ...H_2O [2]

[Total: 3]

Cambridge International AS & A Level Chemistry (9701) Paper 41 Q6a June 2016

The following question has an example student response and commentary provided. Work through the question first, then compare your answer to the sample response and commentary. Are your answers different to the sample responses? How are they different?

7   a At room temperature N_2O_3 dissociates.

$$N_2O_3(g) \rightleftharpoons NO(g) + NO_2(g)$$

Write the expression for K_p for this equilibrium. Include the units in your answer.   [1]

A 1.00 dm^3 flask at 25 °C is filled with pure $N_2O_3(g)$ at an initial pressure of 0.60 atm. At equilibrium, the partial pressure of $NO_2(g)$ is 0.48 atm.

b Calculate the partial pressures of NO(g) and $N_2O_3(g)$ at equilibrium. Hence, calculate the value of K_p at 25 °C.   [2]

[Total: 3]

Cambridge International AS & A Level (9701) Paper 42 Q1c March 2019

Example student response	Commentary
a K_p = p(NO)p(NO_2)/p(N_2O_3) with a unit of mol dm^{-3}	The expression is correct but the student has an incorrect unit. Since both the expression and the unit are needed for 1 mark, no mark has been awarded. The reaction is in the gas phase, so the units should be those of pressure. *This answer is awarded 0 out of 1 mark.*
b p(NO) = p(NO_2) = 0.48 mol dm^{-3} p(N_2O_3) = 0.60 − 0.48 = 0.12 mol dm^{-3} K_p = 0. 482/0.12 = 1.92 mol dm^{-3}	The whole of the calculation here is correct and is well labelled making it easy to find the values needed. The unit is incorrect throughout, but this error is ignored in the mark scheme and the response is given 2 marks. *This answer is awarded 2 out of 2 marks.*

8   Now write an improved answer to question **7** using the commentary to guide you.

81

The following question has an example student response and commentary provided. Work through the question first, then compare your answer to the sample response and commentary. Are your answers different to the sample responses? How are they different?

9 The rate of chemical reactions is affected by changes in temperature and pressure.

    a i Draw a curve on the axes to show the Boltzmann distribution of energy of particles in a sample of gaseous krypton atoms at a given temperature.

        Label the curve **T1** and label the axes.

[2]

    ii On the diagram in **a i**, draw a second curve to show the distribution of energies of the krypton atoms at a higher temperature.

        Label the second curve **T2**. [1]

    b The Boltzmann distribution assumes that the particles behave as an ideal gas.

        i State **two** assumptions of the kinetic theory as applied to an ideal gas. [2]

        ii 2.00 g of krypton gas, $Kr(g)$, is placed in a sealed 5.00 dm³ container at 120 °C.

           Calculate the pressure, in Pa, of $Kr(g)$ in the container.

           Assume $Kr(g)$ behaves as an ideal gas.

           Show your working. [3]

        iii State and explain the conditions at which krypton behaves most like an ideal gas. [2]

[Total: 10]

Cambridge International AS & A Level Chemistry (9701) Paper 22 Q1a, b
March 2021

Example student response	Commentary
a **i**	This is missing the y-axis label and the curve is incorrectly drawn (wrong shape). *This answer is awarded 0 out of 2 marks.*
ii	The curve for T2 is not the right shape and should not cross the original T1 curve twice. *This answer is awarded 0 out of 1 mark.*
b **i** Gas molecules move at high speeds and constantly collide with the walls of the container.	Neither of these are valid assumptions of the ideal gas model. *This answer is awarded 0 out of 2 marks.*
ii P = (0.0239 × 8.31 × 120)/5 = 4.8 kPa	One mark is awarded for correctly calculating moles of krypton, but the unit conversions are incorrect. To convert dm³ to m³, divide by 1000. To convert degrees Celsius to Kelvin, add 273. *This answer is awarded 1 out of 3 marks.*
iii When the temperature is very high and the pressure is low.	No marks awarded here because two correct conditions have been stated but with no explanation. *This answer is awarded 0 out of 2 marks.*

10 Now that you have read the sample response, rewrite your answer to any part of question **9** where you did not score highly. Use the commentary to help you.

10 Periodicity

Chemistry is an interconnected subject and understanding of the Periodic Table is key to lots of concepts. To provide an appropriate response to questions, you will need to make sure you understand how the concepts connect to each other and the arrangement of the Periodic Table. The questions included in this chapter will help you to develop this skill.

Give	produce an answer from a given source or recall/memory

You usually don't need to give too much information for a 'give' question. This command word is similar to 'state' and is sometimes combined with another word, such as 'explain'. You need to recall the answer from your prior knowledge, or use source material – such as the Periodic Table – to find the answer.

10.1 Structure of the Periodic Table

1 What are the vertical columns in the Periodic Table called?

2 Explain why sodium is classified as an s-block element whereas phosphorus is classified as a p-block element. **[Total: 2]**

10.2 Periodicity of physical properties

1 What are the four physical properties that show periodic trends across Period 3?

2 State and explain the general trend in atomic radius across Period 3. **[Total: 4]**

3 The trend in first ionisation energy across Period 3 is shown in Figure 10.1.

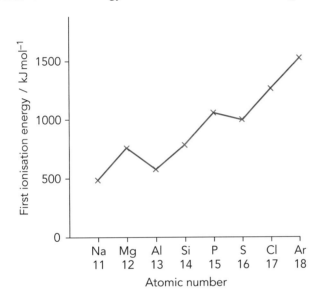

Figure 10.1

Explain the reasons for the dips between:

a Magnesium and aluminium. [4]

b Phosphorus and sulfur. [2]

[Total: 6]

UNDERSTAND THESE TERMS

- electronegativity
- amphoteric
- periodicity
- first ionisation energy, IE_1
- atomic radius

10.3 Periodicity of chemical properties

1 Give the formulae of the chlorides formed by the Period 3 elements.

2 Give the observations shown when a piece of sodium is added to cold water. Briefly explain each observation. **[Total: 4]**

> **≪ RECALL AND CONNECT 1 ≪**
>
> What are the three types of bonding structures found in compounds?

10.4 Oxides of Period 3 elements

1 Give the formulae of the oxides formed by the Period 3 elements.

2 a State the oxidation state of sulfur in the oxides SO_2 and SO_3.

   b Give the equation for the formation of SO_3.   **[Total: 2]**

10.5 Effect of water on oxides and hydroxides of Period 3 elements

1 Briefly summarise the acid–base behaviour of the oxides of Period 3 elements.

2 Silicon dioxide is insoluble. Explain this property of silicon dioxide using ideas about structure and bonding.

   Give an equation illustrating the acid–base behaviour of silicon dioxide. Include the necessary conditions.   **[Total: 4]**

10.6 Chlorides of Period 3 elements

1 In which chloride does the Period 3 element have the highest oxidation state?

2 Under certain conditions, aluminium chloride exists as the structure shown in Figure 10.2.

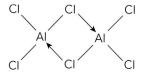

Figure 10.2

Name this type of structure and draw a dot-and-cross diagram to show the bonding.   **[Total: 2]**

10.7 Effect of water on chlorides of Period 3 elements

1 What is the trend in reactivity of the Period 3 chlorides with water going across the Period (increasing atomic number)?

2 The non-metal chlorides $SiCl_4$ and PCl_5 are hydrolysed in water. Write equations for the reactions and state the observations made.   **[Total: 5]**

10.8 Deducing the position of an element in the Periodic Table

1 List the different pieces of evidence that could be used to determine the position of an element in the Periodic Table.

2 The table shows some properties of an element, A. Each statement gives evidence that will suggest the position of the element in the Periodic Table. For each statement, suggest a conclusion that could be drawn.

Statement	Conclusion
forms a chloride, which reacts with water to form a solution of pH 1	
forms an oxide, which has a melting point of 1610 °C	
the oxide of A does not dissolve in or react with aqueous sodium hydroxide	

[Total: 3]

REFLECTION

How well are you able to make connections between the fundamental chemistry concepts and the observations of the physical and chemical properties of the elements of Period 3 and their compounds? Are you able to identify the key concepts that relate to questions you are asked?

SELF-ASSESSMENT CHECKLIST

Let's revisit the Knowledge focus and Exam skills focus for this chapter.

Decide how confident you are with each statement.

Now I can:	Show it	Needs more work	Almost there	Confident to move on
describe and explain the periodicity in the variation of atomic radius, ionic radius, melting point and electrical conductivity of the elements	Write the symbols of the elements in Period 3 across the middle of the page. Add short descriptions of the variation in atomic radius, ionic radius, melting point and electrical conductivity of the elements. Add explanations in a different colour.			

CONTINUED

Now I can:	Show it	Needs more work	Almost there	Confident to move on
describe and write equations for the reactions of Period 3 elements with oxygen to give Na_2O, MgO, Al_2O_3, P_4O_{10} and SO_2	Construct a table summarising the reactions of the Period 3 elements with oxygen, including observations and equations.			
describe and write equations for the reactions of Period 3 elements with chlorine to give NaCl, $MgCl_2$, $AlCl_3$, $SiCl_4$ and PCl_5	Construct a table summarising the reactions of the Period 3 elements with chlorine, including observations and equations.			
describe and write equations for the reactions of Na and Mg with water	Give equations, including state symbols, for the reactions of Na and Mg with water. Annotate your equations with observations and how they link to the species involved in the reactions.			
describe and explain the variation in the oxidation number of the oxides Na_2O, MgO, Al_2O_3, P_4O_{10}, SO_2 and SO_3, and the chlorides NaCl, $MgCl_2$, $AlCl_3$, $SiCl_4$ and PCl_5 in terms of their outer-shell electrons	Draw a visual summary of the oxidation numbers of the oxides and chlorides of Period 3, linking this to their outer-shell electrons.			
describe and write equations for the reactions, if any, of Na_2O, MgO, Al_2O_3, SiO_2, P_4O_{10}, SO_2 and SO_3 with water, including the likely pH of the solutions obtained	Draw a spider diagram of the reactions, if any, of Na_2O, MgO, Al_2O_3, SiO_2, P_4O_{10}, SO_2 and SO_3 with water. Include equations and the pH of the solutions formed.			

CONTINUED

Now I can:	Show it	Needs more work	Almost there	Confident to move on
describe, explain and write equations for the acid/base behaviour of Na_2O, MgO, Al_2O_3, P_4O_{10}, SO_2, SO_3, $NaOH$, $Mg(OH)_2$ and $Al(OH)_3$	Group the Period 3 oxides according to whether they react with acids, bases or both. Annotate your groups with equations of their reactions.			
describe the amphoteric behaviour of Al_2O_3 and $Al(OH)_3$	Draw a visual summary of the amphoteric behaviour of Al_2O_3 and $Al(OH)_3$.			
describe and write equations for the reactions, if any, of $NaCl$, $MgCl_2$, $AlCl_3$, $SiCl_4$ and PCl_5 with water, including the likely pH of the solutions obtained	Draw a spider diagram of the reactions, if any, of $NaCl$, $MgCl_2$, $AlCl_3$, $SiCl_4$ and PCl_5 with water. Include equations and the pH of the solutions formed.			
deduce the types of bonding present in oxides and chlorides of Period 3 from their chemical and physical properties	Write some bullet points of how chemical and physical properties can predict the bonding present in oxides and chlorides of Period 3.			
predict the characteristic properties of an element in a given group using knowledge of periodicity	Write some bullet points of how periodicity can be used to predict the characteristic properties of an element in a given group.			
deduce the nature, position in the Periodic Table and identity of unknown elements from given information	Write some bullet points of how different pieces of information can be used to deduce the nature, position in the Periodic Table, and identity of an unknown element.			
show that I understand the 'give' command word and answer 'give' questions	Answer questions using the command word 'give' on different topics.			

11 Group 2

Questions may ask you to provide a fact or short answer to a question. In this topic you may be asked to state the variation in solubility of sulfates in Group 2. The 'state' command word is often used for short answer questions. The definition for 'state' is shown below.

State	express in clear terms

It is important not to provide too much information or detail when you answer these questions. This command word is often combined with another word, such as 'explain' or 'suggest'. As you work through the questions in this chapter, make sure you include answers to both command words in your answer to these questions.

11.1 Physical properties of Group 2 elements

1   Which physical properties show a general increase as you go down Group 2 (increasing atomic number)?

2   State and explain the trend in metallic radius going down Group 2.   **[Total: 3]**

> **《 RECALL AND CONNECT 1 《**
>
> What block of the Periodic Table do Group 2 elements belong to?

11.2 Reactions of Group 2 elements

1   What is the trend in reactivity going down Group 2?

2   When calcium is added to dilute sulfuric acid, bubbles are initially seen but the stream of bubbles quickly stops.

   Give an equation for the reaction, including state symbols, and explain the experimental observations.   **[Total: 3]**

11.3 Reactions with oxygen

1   What is the pH character of Group 2 oxides?

2   Group 2 metals give characteristic colours in flame tests. State the colour of the flame for barium and write an equation, including state symbols, for the reaction occurring.   **[Total: 2]**

11.4 Reactions with water

1   Give the equation for the formation of hydroxide ions from the oxide ion and water.

2   Magnesium reacts very slowly with cold water, forming very small bubbles of flammable gas and a solution with a pH of 10. Hot magnesium with steam reacts more vigorously, producing a white solid and a flammable gas. Barium reacts vigorously with cold water, producing bubbles of flammable gas and a cloudy solution with a pH of 14.

   Using your knowledge of the chemistry of Group 2, explain the observations stated. Include appropriate equations, including state symbols.   **[Total: 9]**

> **UNDERSTAND THESE TERMS**
> - saturated solution
> - thermal decomposition

REFLECTION

How well did you organise your answer to question 11.4.2? Do you think an examiner would find it easy to award you marks for it? How could you improve your answer so that you are confident you have covered all the relevant points?

SELF-ASSESSMENT CHECKLIST

Let's revisit the Knowledge focus and Exam skills focus for this chapter.

Decide how confident you are with each statement.

Now I can:	Show it	Needs more work	Almost there	Confident to move on
describe and write equations for the reactions of Group 2 elements with oxygen, water and dilute acids	Write equations for the reaction of calcium with: a oxygen b water c dilute hydrochloric acid.			
describe and write equations for the reactions of Group 2 oxides, hydroxides and carbonates with water and with dilute acids	Write equations for the reaction of magnesium oxide, hydroxide and carbonate with: a water b dilute sulfuric acid.			
describe and write equations for the thermal decomposition of Group 2 nitrates and carbonates	Name the products of decomposition of: a magnesium carbonate b calcium nitrate.			
describe, and make predictions from, the trends in properties of Group 2 elements and their compounds which are covered in this chapter	State the trend in the following properties going down Group 2: a melting point b density c metallic radius d reactivity.			
state the variation in the solubilities of Group 2 hydroxides and sulfates	Give the general trend in solubilities of Group 2 hydroxides and sulfates as you go down the group.			
show that I understand the 'state' command word and answer 'state' questions	Write a sentence to explain what the command word 'state' means.			

12 Group 17

Questions with a higher number of marks can be difficult to answer. You may find it difficult to write a well-developed explanation, not cover all the marking points in your answer or repeat yourself. In this chapter pay attention to the number of marks for each exam skills question and make sure you have included enough information and detail in your answers to produce high-quality responses.

12.1 Physical properties of Group 17 elements

1   What is the trend in the melting points of the elements with increasing atomic number in Group 17?

2   State and explain the trend in volatility of the elements going down Group 17.   [Total: 4]

UNDERSTAND THESE TERMS
• halogens
• volatility
• vigorous
• thermal stability

12.2 Reactions of Group 17 elements

1   What is the change in oxidation state when chlorine goes from its elemental form to its ionic form?

2   Describe an experiment to show that chlorine has a greater oxidising power than bromine.   [Total: 6]

12.3 Reactions of the halide ions

1   Copy and complete the table to show the properties of silver halide salts.

Halide ion	Colour of silver halide precipitate on addition of silver nitrate solution	Effect on precipitate of adding dilute ammonia solution	Effect on precipitate of adding concentrated ammonia solution chloride
chloride, Cl^- aq)		dissolves	dissolves
bromide, Br^-(aq	cream		
iodide, I^-(aq)		remains insoluble	

2   The equations below show some of the products formed when concentrated sulfuric acid reacts with sodium iodide. Equation 2 is unbalanced.

Equation 1: $NaI(s) + H_2SO_4(l) \rightarrow NaHSO_4(s) + HI(g)$

Equation 2: .....$HI(g)$ + ...$HSO_4(l) \rightarrow$ .....$I_2(g)$ + ...$H_2S(g)$ + ...$H_2O(l)$

Balance Equation 2.   [1]

State the types of reaction occurring in each equation, and two observations that indicate the formation of particular products.   [4]

[Total: 5]

REFLECTION
Are you able to draw conclusions from experimental observations and give observations that would illustrate given conclusions as, for example, in question 12.3.2? How can you organise your answers to make it easy for the examiner to see your thinking?

12.4 Disproportionation reactions

1   Give the formula of the compound produced when chlorine reacts with water which is responsible for its antibacterial properties.

2   Give equations for the reactions of chlorine with cold sodium hydroxide and hot sodium hydroxide. Label them with the oxidation numbers of chlorine in each substance. Summarise the redox reactions occurring.   **[Total: 6]**

CONTINUED

Now I can:	Show it	Needs more work	Almost there	Confident to move on
describe and explain the relative thermal stabilities of the hydrides (in terms of bond strengths)	Give the trend in relative thermal stabilities of Group 17 hydrides and explain why this trend is observed.			
describe and explain the reactions of halide ions with aqueous silver ions, followed by addition of aqueous ammonia	Construct a table showing the reaction of Cl⁻, Br⁻ and I⁻ with silver ions and the observations shown by the silver halides and dilute and concentrated ammonia.			
describe and explain the reactions of halide ions with concentrated sulfuric acid	Give all the equations for the reactions of the halide ions with concentrated sulfuric acid. Colour-code them for each halide and annotate with oxidation states.			
describe and interpret the disproportionation reactions of chlorine with cold, and with hot, aqueous sodium hydroxide	Write the equations for disproportion reactions of chlorine with cold and hot sodium hydroxide. Annotate your equations with oxidation states.			
explain the use of chlorine in water purification	Write two equations that show how chlorine in water is able to act as an antibacterial agent.			
write high-quality responses to questions with higher marks	Choose one of the questions. Write the answer in a paragraph of continuous prose and then compare your answer to the answer given online.			

13 Nitrogen

KNOWLEDGE FOCUS

In this chapter you will answer questions on:

- nitrogen gas
- ammonia and ammonium compounds
- nitrogen oxides in the atmosphere.

EXAM SKILLS FOCUS

In this chapter you will:

- recognise the level of depth required when writing short answers and extended responses.

Recognising different question types and understanding how much detail they need is an important exam skill. Short answer questions normally require one or two facts or calculation steps, while extended response questions require a greater depth of knowledge or feature longer calculations with many steps.

Chemistry has a diverse language consisting of words, chemical equations, symbols, formulae and maths. You will therefore need to carefully structure your answers to longer questions so that you use the right language to clearly communicate your understanding to the examiner.

As you work through the longer questions in this chapter, make sure you are including the correct scientific terms and symbols to show your understanding of this topic. The Exam skills chapter will give you more support in learning and understanding how to do this.

13.1 Nitrogen gas

1 This question is about nitrogen and its compounds. Nitrogen exists as the diatomic molecule, N_2, which contains a triple covalent bond.

    a What is meant by a triple covalent bond?

    b Draw a dot-and-cross diagram of nitrogen.

    c How does the triple bond in nitrogen contribute to its lack of reactivity?

    d Give the oxidation state of nitrogen in the following species:

        i N_2

        ii NH_3

        iii HNO_3

        iv NO

        v NO_2

        vi $NaCN$

2 **a** Describe, with the aid of chemical equations, how atmospheric nitrogen is converted into soluble nitrate ions that can be absorbed from soil by plants. Include state symbols. [4]

    b Nitrogen and phosphorus are both Group 15 elements. Phosphorus forms the compound phosphorus(V) pentafluoride (PF_5), but the analogous compound, nitrogen(V) pentafluoride (NF_5), does not exist.

        i Explain why phosphorus is described as having an expanded octet in PF_5. [1]

        ii State the full electron configuration of nitrogen. [1]

        iii Using your answer to part **bii**, suggest why nitrogen is unable to form compounds such as NF_5. [3]

[Total: 9]

13.2 Ammonia and ammonium compounds

1 **a** What is the shape of the ammonia molecule?

    b Explain the bond angles in ammonia.

    c What is meant by a *weak Brønsted–Lowry base*?

    d How is ammonia able to act as a Brønsted–Lowry base?

    e Write an equation to show ammonia acting as a weak base in its reaction with water. Include state symbols.

    f Ammonia reacts with phosphoric acid, H_3PO_4, to produce the important fertiliser, diammonium hydrogen phosphate, $(NH_4)_2HPO_4$.

        i Why are ammonium compounds important fertilisers?

        ii Write a balanced chemical equation for the reaction between ammonia and phosphoric acid. Include state symbols.

g   '880 ammonia' is a concentrated solution of ammonia in water that contains 35% ammonia by mass. Its name is derived from its density, which is $0.88\,\mathrm{g\,cm^{-3}}$. What is the concentration of 880 ammonia in $\mathrm{mol\,dm^{-3}}$?

2   Ammonia is one of the most important industrial chemicals, with a worldwide production of 235 million tonnes in 2021. 80% of ammonia is used to make fertilisers, such as $(NH_4)HCO_3$. It is manufactured by the reaction between ammonia, carbon dioxide and water.

a   Name the compound with formula $(NH_4)HCO_3$.   [1]

b   Construct a balanced chemical equation for the production of $(NH_4)HCO_3$. State symbols are not required.   [1]

c   Explain this reaction in terms of the Brønsted–Lowry theory.   [2]

d   The ammonia used to manufacture $(NH_4)HCO_3$ comes from the Haber process:

$$N_2(g) + 3H_2(g) \rightarrow 2NH_3(g)$$

Given that annual production of $(NH_4)HCO_3$ is $100\,000$ tonnes, calculate the mass of hydrogen used in its manufacture.
1 tonne $= 1\times10^6$g   [3]

e   Describe how you could use a chemical test to distinguish between a sample of $(NH_4)HCO_3$ and $NaHCO_3$. In your answer, you should describe any necessary reagents and conditions, and give any relevant chemical equations.   [4]

[Total: 11]

13.3 Nitrogen oxides in the atmosphere

≪ RECALL AND CONNECT 1 ≪

Nitrogen has many different oxidation numbers, so you can't use it to work out the oxidation numbers of other elements. Which are the important elements that have fixed oxidation states?

1   a   Which two conditions cause the formation of nitrogen(II) oxide in the atmosphere?

b   What is a catalyst and how do they work?

c   Write chemical equations to describe how sulfuric acid is formed from the sulfur found in fossil fuels, showing the role played by nitrogen oxides.

d   Which species acts as a catalyst in these reactions and why?

e   Write an equation to show how catalytic converters break down harmful nitrogen oxides into harmless nitrogen.

f   Explain, using oxidation numbers, why this is an example of a redox reaction.

2   Photochemical smog is a harmful mixture of smoke and fog, produced by the reactions of car exhaust gases in the presence of sunlight. Sunlight causes the photochemical decomposition of nitrogen(IV) oxide:

$$NO_2(g) \rightarrow NO(g) + O(g)$$

The highly reactive atoms produced combine with oxygen molecules to form ozone:

$$O_2(g) + O(g) \rightarrow O_3(g)$$

Figure 13.1 shows how the concentrations of NO, NO_2 and O_3 changed during a summer's day in a large city.

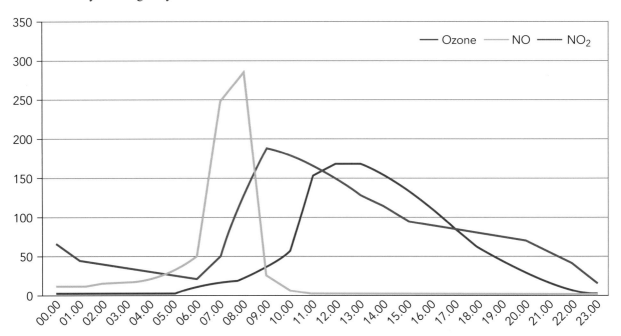

Figure 13.1

a   Explain why the concentrations of these three gases peak at different times of the day. [3]

b   Ozone is a harmful component of photochemical smog because it acts as an oxidising agent, reacting with unburnt hydrocarbons in exhaust gas to produce aldehydes and water. Aldehydes cause breathing difficulties.

   i   Explain what is meant by the term oxidising agent. [1]

   ii   Construct a chemical equation to show how unburnt hydrocarbons are oxidised by ozone, using RCH_3 to represent the hydrocarbon. [1]

   iii   Suggest why ozone is classed as a secondary pollutant. [1]

[Total: 6]

> **UNDERSTAND THESE TERMS**
>
> - hydrocarbon
> - PAN
> - photochemical reactions

« RECALL AND CONNECT 2 «

The nitrogen-based compounds in this chapter show acid and base properties. Ammonia is a base and dissolves in water to form an alkaline solution, whereas many nitrogen oxides are acidic. Can you recall the trend in the acid–base properties of Period 3 oxides?

REFLECTION

This chapter requires you to learn several chemical equations. How are you going to remember them? You will have faced this challenge before, during IGCSE chemistry and in earlier chapters. Are there similarities and differences between the way you learn chemical equations and mathematical equations?

SELF-ASSESSMENT CHECKLIST

Let's revisit the Knowledge focus and Exam skills focus for this chapter.

Decide how confident you are with each statement.

Now I can:	Show it	Needs more work	Almost there	Confident to move on
describe and explain the lack of reactivity of nitrogen gas	Draw the structure of nitrogen, showing the strong bond that makes it unreactive.			
describe and explain the basicity of ammonia, and the formation and structure of the ammonium ion	Write an equation showing how the lone pair on ammonia enables it to act as a base.			
describe and explain the displacement of ammonia from its ammonium salts	Write an equation for the reaction between an ammonium salt and calcium hydroxide.			
state and explain the natural and human-made occurrences of oxides of nitrogen and their catalytic removal from the exhaust gases of internal combustion engines	Write an equation, including key conditions, summarising how nitrogen oxides are formed in the atmosphere.			
state and explain why atmospheric oxides of nitrogen are pollutants, including their role in the formation of photochemical smog and the catalytic oxidation of atmospheric sulfur dioxide	Write the chemical equations that show the catalytic role of nitrogen(II) monoxide in the formation of atmospheric sulfuric acid.			

CONTINUED

Now I can:	Show it	Needs more work	Almost there	Confident to move on
understand that atmospheric oxides of nitrogen (NO and NO_2) can react with unburned hydrocarbons to form peroxyacetyl nitrate, PAN, which is a component of photochemical smog	Draw a flow diagram to show the photochemical reactions linking NO_x and PAN.			
recognise the level of depth required when writing short answers or oxtondod rosponsos	Identify the short answer and extended response questions in this chapter, and compare the knowledge and skills required.			

Exam practice 3

This section contains past paper questions from previous Cambridge exams which draw together your knowledge on a range of topics that you have covered up to this point. These questions give you the opportunity to test your knowledge and understanding. Additional past paper practice questions can be found in the accompanying digital material.

The following question has an example student response and commentary provided. Work through the question first, then compare your answer to the sample response and commentary. Are your answers different to the sample responses? How are they different?

1   Some of the common chlorides of Period 3 elements are shown in the list.

$$NaCl \quad MgCl_2 \quad AlCl_3 \quad SiCl_4 \quad PCl_5$$

a   From this list, identify:

   i   all the chlorides that have giant ionic structures in the solid state   [1]

   ii   all the chlorides that react vigorously with water to form strongly
        acidic solutions   [1]

   iii the chloride that dissolves in water to form a neutral solution   [1]

   iv   the chloride formed from the **element** with the highest melting point.   [1]

   [Total: 4]

Cambridge International AS & A Level Chemistry (9701) Paper 23 Q3a
November 2022

Example student response	Commentary
a i $NaCl$, $MgCl_2$, $AlCl_3$	The student has chosen all of the formulae which contain both metal and non-metal atoms, assuming that this would mean they are giant ionic lattices. However, aluminium chloride is an exception to this rule. However, aluminium chloride is an exception to this rule because it shows covalent characteristics under certain conditions. Reference to aluminium chloride as covalent is accepted but is an oversimplification. When this question was marked the reference to $AlCl_3$ was ignored. *This answer is awarded 1 out of 1 mark.*

Example student response	Commentary
ii PCl$_5$	The student has chosen the phosphorus pentachloride because it is the one that seems to have an analogous acid, phosphoric acid. However, all of the covalent Period 3 chlorides form acidic solutions. *This answer is awarded 0 out of 1 mark.*
iii NaCl	This is correct. When sodium chloride dissolves in water the water simply separates the ions. *This answer is awarded 1 out of 1 mark.*
iv SiCl$_4$	This is correct. The question asks for the Period 3 element with the highest melting point. This is silicon, which has a giant covalent lattice structure. *This answer is awarded 1 out of 1 mark.*

2 Now that you've gone through the commentary, attempt writing a full mark scheme for question **1**.

The following question has an example student response and commentary provided. Work through the question first, then compare your answer to the sample response and commentary. Are your answers different to the sample responses? How are they different?

3 Suggest why there is a general **decrease** in the melting points of the elements down Group 2. **[Total: 3]**

Cambridge International AS & A Level Chemistry (9701) Paper 22 Q1b iv June 2018

Example student response	Commentary
Down Group 2, the atoms get bigger because a new full principal quantum shell is added each time. So, the distance between the bonding electrons and the positive nucleus gets larger and there is less of an attraction between them. Hence, less energy is needed for melting.	This answer begins well using good subject-specific language; however, the statement about principal quantum shells does not gain credit because it is not relevant to the question asked. The answer then gets less detailed and does not show the examiner that the student understands metallic bonding. The term 'bonding electrons' is too vague. The comparison part of the sentence is also vague, referring to an 'attraction between them'. The student fails to discuss other factors that affect the strength in metallic bonding. *This answer is awarded 1 out of 3 marks.*

4 Write an improved answer to question **1**, for any part where you did not score highly. Use the commentary to help you.

The following question has an example student response and commentary provided. Work through the question first, then compare your answer to the sample response and commentary. Are your answers different to the sample responses? How are they different?

5 Group 17 elements are commonly referred to as the halogens.

a State and explain the trend in volatility of chlorine, bromine and iodine down the group. [3]

Hydrogen gas reacts with the different halogens under different conditions.

b **i** State the conditions required for chlorine to react with hydrogen at room temperature. [1]

  ii On heating, iodine reacts with hydrogen in a reversible reaction.

  Give the equation for this reaction. Include state symbols. [2]

[Total: 6]

*Cambridge International AS & A Level Chemistry (9701) Paper 22 Q2a, b
June 2019*

Example student response	Commentary
a Volatility decreases going down the group. Chlorine is a gas, but iodine is a solid. This is because the halogens lower in group 17 are bigger molecules and so there are greater forces between the molecules.	The student has correctly identified the trend in volatility. However, the remainder of the response lacks scientific detail. The type of intermolecular force between the molecules needs to be mentioned as there are three types of intermolecular forces. They also attribute the difference in strength of intermolecular forces to the size of the molecules. This part of the answer should be written in terms of the electrons in the molecules. *This answer is awarded 1 out of 3 marks.*
b **i** UV light	This is correct. *This answer is awarded 1 out of 1 mark.*
ii $I_2(g) + H(g) \rightarrow 2HI$	The equation is correct and balanced and the student has remembered to include the state symbols. However, the question says that the reaction is reversible so an equilibrium arrow $\rightleftharpoons$ needs to be used rather than a straight arrow $\rightarrow$. *This answer is awarded 1 out of 2 marks.*

6 Now write an improved answer to the parts of question **5** where you lost marks.

The following question has an example student response and commentary provided. Work through the question first, then compare your answer to the sample response and commentary. Are your answers different to the sample responses? If they are, what information does that give you about your understanding of the topic?

7 A sample of a fertiliser was known to contain ammonium sulfate, $(NH_4)_2SO_4$, and sand only.

A 2.96 g sample of the solid fertiliser was heated with 40.0 cm³ of NaOH(aq), an excess, and all of the ammonia produced was boiled away.

After cooling, the remaining NaOH(aq) was exactly neutralised by 29.5 cm³ of 2.00 mol dm⁻³ HCl.

In a separate experiment, 40.0 cm³ of the original NaOH(aq) was exactly neutralised by 39.2 cm³ of the 2.00 mol dm⁻³ HCl.

a Write balanced equations for the following reactions.

  i NaOH with HCl [1]

  ii $(NH_4)_2SO_4$ with NaOH [1]

b Calculate the amount, in moles, of NaOH present in the 40.0 cm³ of the original NaOH(aq) that was neutralised by 39.2 cm³ of 2.00 mol dm⁻³ HCl. [1]

c Calculate the amount, in moles, of NaOH present in the 40.0 cm³ of NaOH(aq) that remained after boiling the $(NH_4)_2SO_4$. [1]

d Use your answers to **b** and **c** to calculate the amount, in moles, of NaOH that reacted with the $(NH_4)_2SO_4$. [1]

e Use your answers to **a** and **b** to calculate the amount, in moles, of $(NH_4)_2SO_4$ that reacted with the NaOH. [1]

f Hence, calculate the mass of $(NH_4)_2SO_4$ that reacted. [1]

g Use your answer to **f** to calculate the percentage, by mass, of $(NH_4)_2SO_4$ present in the fertiliser.

Write your answer to a suitable number of significant figures. [2]

[Total: 9]

Adapted from Cambridge International AS & A Level Chemistry (9701) Paper 21 Q1a June 2013

Example student response	Commentary
a **i** $OH^- + H^+ \rightarrow H_2O$	**i** This is the correct balanced equation. *This answer is awarded 1 out of 1 mark.*
ii $(NH_4)_2SO_4 + 2NaOH \rightarrow 2NH_3 + Na_2SO_4 + H_2O$	**ii** This is the correct equation, but it is not balanced correctly, so the mark is not awarded. *This answer is awarded 0 out of 1 mark.*
b Moles of HCl = (39.2/1000) × 2 = 0.078 Moles of NaOH = 0.078	This is correct. *This answer is awarded 1 out of 1 mark.*
c Moles of HCl = (40/1000) × 2 = 0.08 Moles of NaOH is also 0.08	This is incorrect as the student has confused the volumes in the question. *This answer is awarded 0 out of 1 mark.*
d Moles of NaOH reacting with the salt = 0.08 − 0.078 = 0.0016	The student has clearly lost their way in this challenging multistep calculation – this response is incorrect. *This answer is awarded 0 out of 1 mark.*
e Moles of salt = 0.0016 moles	This answer is incorrect. *This answer is awarded 0 out of 1 mark.*
f Mass of the salt = 0.0016 × 132.1 = 0.211 g	The error-carried-forward rule is applied here as the approach is correct. *This answer is awarded 1 out of 1 mark.*
g Percentage of salt = (0.211/2.96) × 100 = 7%	The error-carried-forward rule could have been applied here, but the student overlooked the instruction about significant figures and no marks are awarded. *This answer is awarded 0 out of 2 marks.*

For multistep calculations based on experiments, a simple flow diagram of the procedure can help you better understand how to use the data and prevent you getting lost in the steps.

14 Introduction to organic chemistry

Organic chemistry is communicated in lots of different ways, using multiple representations. This includes different types of formulae, names and diagrams. Drawing organic molecules is a key exam skill and the term 'draw' is commonly used in questions. It is different to the 'sketch' command word because you need to use a pencil to produce a labelled, accurate diagram or graph. You focused on 'sketch' in Chapter 9. In this chapter you will practise answering questions containing 'draw'.

14.1 Representing organic molecules

1 Draw the missing skeletal formulae and give the missing names to complete the table of structural isomers.

Name	Skeletal formula
pent-1-en-1-ol	
	OH
pent-1-en-2-ol	

[Total: 3]

> UNDERSTAND THESE TERMS

- functional group
- nucleophile
- electrophile
- chiral centre
- carbocation
- inductive effect

« RECALL AND CONNECT 1 «

What is the electronic configuration of carbon?

14.2 Homologous series of organic compounds

1 Copy the table and tick the boxes to show whether the feature given is the same, similar or different for members of a homologous series.

	Same	Similar	Different
functional group			
general formula			
chemical properties			
physical properties			

2 Alkanes have the general formula C_nH_{2n+2}. Using this convention, give the general formulas for the halogenoalkane and alcohol homologous series. In each case, you should assume there is only one of the required functional group in each molecule of the homologous series. [Total: 2]

14.3 Naming organic compounds

1   What does the stem of the name of each organic compound show?

2   A skeletal formula for compound **X** is shown in Figure 14.2. Name **X**.   **[Total: 1]**

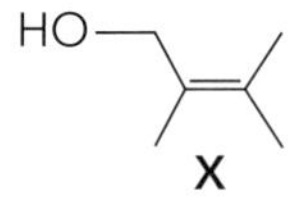

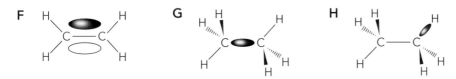

Figure 14.2

14.4 Bonding in organic molecules

1   A covalent bond is the electrostatic attraction between the nuclei of two atoms and a shared pair of electrons. In Figure 14.3, the diagrams **F**, **G** and **H** show the overlap of orbitals in two different molecules, each with two carbon atoms. State the type of bond, sigma (σ) or pi (π), that is depicted in each diagram **F–H**.

Figure 14.3: Diagrams of the overlap of orbitals in molecules

2   A covalent bond can be defined as the electrostatic attraction between the nuclei of two atoms and a shared pair of electrons. Explain how this shared pair of electrons is held in a sigma bond.   **[Total: 2]**

14.5 Structural isomerism

1   Name the three types of structural isomerism.

2   Pentane is an example of a hydrocarbon with the molecular formula C_5H_{12}. Draw two structural isomers of pentane.   **[Total: 2]**

14.6 Stereoisomerism

1   Name the two classes of organic compounds that show geometrical isomerism.

2   2-Bromobutane exists as optical isomers. Draw the two enantiomers of 2-bromobutane, clearly marking the chiral centre with an asterisk*.   **[Total: 3]**

14.7 Types of organic reaction and reaction mechanisms

1   There are two types of bond breaking, homolytic and heterolytic fission. Write a short description of what happens to the electrons in each type of bond breaking and state the type of reactive intermediate formed.

2   Equations **A**, **B** and **C** can be used to describe the process of converting butane to 2-bromobutane. Identify each equation as an initiation, propagation or termination step, or as none of these.   **[Total: 3]**

   A $CH_3CH_2CH_2CH_3 + Br_2 \longrightarrow CH_3CH_2CHBrCH_3 + HBr$
   B $CH_3CH_2\dot{C}HCH_3 + Br_2 \longrightarrow CH_3CH_2CHBrCH_3 + B\dot{r}$
   C $2\,CH_3CH_2\dot{C}HCH_3 \longrightarrow CH_3CH_2CH(CH_3)CH(CH_3)CH_2CH_3$

3   Outline the mechanism for the heterolytic fission of the C–Br bond in CH_3Br, clearly indicating the structure of the products.   **[Total: 3]**

≪ RECALL AND CONNECT 2 ≪

What feature of structure and bonding is represented by a dot on a molecular structure?

14.8 Types of organic reaction

1   Equations **a–d** show different types of organic reactions. Classify each equation as addition, substitution, elimination, oxidation, reduction or condensation. You may use each label once, more than once or not at all.

   a $C_2H_5OH + [O] \longrightarrow CH_3CHO + H_2O$
   b $C_2H_4 + Br_2 \longrightarrow C_2H_4Br_2$
   c $CH_4 + Cl_2 \longrightarrow CH_3Cl + HCl$
   d $C_2H_5OH \longrightarrow C_2H_4 + H_2O$

2   **a**   State suitable reagents and conditions for the oxidation of ethanol.

   b   Write equations for both partial oxidation and full oxidation using [O] to represent the oxidising agent.   **[Total: 3]**

REFLECTION

There were three opportunities to draw structures in this chapter. Were your diagrams correct? Go back and check for common mistakes, like having carbon atoms with five bonds.

SELF-ASSESSMENT CHECKLIST

Let's revisit the Knowledge focus and Exam skills focus for this chapter.

Decide how confident you are with each statement.

Now I can:	Show it	Needs more work	Almost there	Confident to move on
define the term *hydrocarbon* and describe how alkanes are simple hydrocarbons with no functional group	Draw an alkane molecule and describe how it fits the definition of a hydrocarbon.			
deduce the molecular and/or empirical formula of a compound, given its structural, displayed or skeletal formula	Make a spider diagram showing how the structural, displayed, or skeletal, molecular and empirical formula are related to each other.			
interpret, name and use the general, structural, displayed and skeletal formulae of the alkanes, alkenes, halogenoalkanes, alcohols (including primary, secondary and tertiary), aldehydes, ketones, carboxylic acids, esters, amines (primary only) and nitriles	Make a one-page summary of all the functional groups listed, showing their general, structural, displayed and skeletal formulae.			
explain and use the following terminology associated with organic reactions and their mechanisms: • functional group • homolytic and heterolytic fission • free radical, initiation, propagation, termination • nucleophile, electrophile, nucleophilic, electrophilic • addition, substitution, elimination, hydrolysis, condensation • oxidation and reduction	Make a one-page summary of the terminology listed in this objective. Make sure your summary includes lots of diagrams as they will help you to remember key information.			

CONTINUED

Now I can:	Show it	Needs more work	Almost there	Confident to move on
explain and identify isomerism, including chiral centres and geometrical isomers	Divide a page in two and on each side compare and contrast chiral molecules with geometrical isomers.			
deduce possible isomers from a given molecular formula	Draw all the possible isomers of C_7H_{14}.			
describe, give bond angles and explain the shape of molecules in terms of their sp, sp^2 and sp^3 hybridised atomic orbitals, and their σ bonds and π bonds	Draw the simple hydrocarbons C_2H_6, C_2H_4 and C_2H_2, give bond angles and explain the shape of these molecules in terms of their hybridised atomic orbitals and their σ and π bonds.			
describe and explain the different types of structural isomerism and stereoisomerism	Draw a flow diagram to show how the different types of structural and stereoisomerism relate to each other.			
show that I understand that questions asking you to 'draw' are different to questions with the 'sketch' command word	Check all the drawings of molecules you have made in studying this chapter to make sure they are correct and more accurate than a sketch.			

15 Hydrocarbons

KNOWLEDGE FOCUS

In this chapter you will answer questions on:

- the homologous group of alkanes
- reactions of alkanes
- the alkenes
- oxidation of the alkenes
- addition polymerisation
- addition polymers.

EXAM SKILLS FOCUS

In this chapter you will:

- understand and answer more questions using the 'explain' command word.

It is important to revisit command words in different topics so that you gain practice answering questions across many different topics in Chemistry. In this chapter you will practice your understanding of the command word 'explain', which you practised in Chapter 1. As you work through the chapter, compare your answers to the 'explain' questions in this chapter to the answers you gave in Chapter 1. Do you feel you have improved your understanding approach to these questions?

| Explain | give reasons, often using relevant evidence |

15.1 The homologous group of alkanes

1 What type of hybridisation is displayed by the carbon atoms in alkanes?

2 Figure 15.1 shows the 3D displayed formula of an alkane. The black circles show carbon atoms and the white circles show hydrogen atoms.

Figure 15.1

Give the IUPAC systematic name, molecular and skeletal formulae for the alkane in Figure 15.1 and describe the key feature of the 3D displayed formula.   **[Total: 5]**

≪ RECALL AND CONNECT 1 ≪

Carbon can form four identical single bonds. What is the shape and bond angle in a molecule with four bonding electron pairs?

15.2 Reactions of alkanes

1 Briefly describe why alkanes are unreactive.

2 a Write equations for the complete and incomplete combustion of butane.   [2]

   b Identify the environmental problems caused by the products of combustion.   [2]

                                                                   [Total: 4]

15.3 The alkenes

1 What is the dominant reaction type shown by alkenes?

2 When hydrogen bromide is reacted with propene, two possible halogenoalkane isomers can be formed.

   a Explain this observation with reference to the structure and bonding in the reactive intermediates formed in the mechanism.   [2]

   b Give the name of the major isomer formed and explain why it is formed preferentially.   [3]

                                                                   [Total: 5]

UNDERSTAND THESE TERMS

- alkanes
- saturated hydrocarbon
- electrophile

15.4 Oxidation of the alkenes

1   Give the formula of the oxidising agent used to oxidise alkenes to diols, ketones, aldehydes, carboxylic acids or carbon dioxide gas.

2   When 2-methylpropene is treated with an oxidising agent, bubbles of gas are seen.

   a   State what conditions cause this observation.

   b   Identify the gas.

   c   Write an equation for the reaction occurring using [O] to represent the oxidising agent.   **[Total: 3]**

15.5 Addition polymerisation

1   What is the formula of the monomer used to make poly(chloroethene)?

2   The polymer with the common name PVA, polyvinyl alcohol, is made from the monomer ethenol. Write an equation for the formation of PVA.   **[Total: 2]**

15.6 Tackling questions on addition polymers

1   What is the major difference between a diagram showing a monomer molecule and a diagram showing the same molecule when it is a repeating unit in the polymer chain of an addition polymer?

2   Draw the structure of the monomer used to make the polymer shown in Figure 15.2.

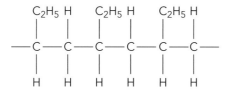

Figure 15.2   **[Total: 1]**

> **UNDERSTAND THESE TERMS**
>
> • monomers
> • polymer
> • addition polymerisation
> • repeat unit

> **REFLECTION**
>
> When you are studying a new topic, think about the possible links to previous topics. For example, you may find this topic more straightforward to understand if you understand oxidation reactions. What techniques could you use to help identify links between topics?

SELF-ASSESSMENT CHECKLIST

Let's revisit the Knowledge focus and Exam skills focus for this chapter.

Decide how confident you are with each statement.

Now I can:	Show it	Needs more work	Almost there	Confident to move on
explain the general unreactivity of alkanes, and describe their complete and incomplete combustion	Write equations for the complete and incomplete combustion of the second member of the homologous group of alkanes.			
explain the free-radical substitution of alkanes by chlorine and by bromine, as shown by their three-step mechanism	Sketch out the general mechanistic steps for the free-radical substitution of alkanes by chlorine and bromine. Add hints on how many equations to provide for each step and the positions of the radicals.			
suggest how cracking can be used to obtain more useful alkanes and alkenes of lower relative molecular mass from larger hydrocarbon molecules	Give an example of cracking a longer chain alkane.			
describe the environmental consequences of burning hydrocarbon fuels in vehicles and the removal of pollutants by catalytic converters	Draw a spider diagram of the pollutant gases formed from burning hydrocarbon fuels. Add details of how they can be reduced by catalytic converters in vehicles.			
describe the reactions of alkenes as shown by their addition, oxidation and polymerisation	Give examples of the addition, oxidation and polymerisation of alkenes using propene as the starting material.			
describe the mechanism of electrophilic addition in alkenes, and explain the inductive effects of alkyl groups on the stability of cations formed	Outline the mechanism for the electrophilic addition of but-1-ene. Add explanations to each step and explain the formation of the product in terms of cation stability.			

CONTINUED

Now I can:	Show it	Needs more work	Almost there	Confident to move on
describe the difficulty of disposing of waste poly(alkene)s	Write 2 or 3 bullet points explaining why it is difficult to dispose of poly(alkene) waste.			
understand and answer more questions using the 'explain' command word	Select some questions from a past exam paper and compare your answers to the answers given.			

16 Halogenoalkanes

Sometimes it can be difficult to distinguish command words from other instructional text. In this chapter you will respond to a variety of command words and practise including all the required information in an answer.

More support and advice on recognising command words within questions is given in the Exam skills chapter.

16.1 Making halogenoalkanes

1 Why is it necessary to synthesise halogenoalkanes?

2 Give equations for the synthesis of chloroethane from ethane, ethanol and ethene. State any necessary conditions. **[Total: 3]**

《 RECALL AND CONNECT 1 《

What is the polarity of the C–X bond when X is a halogen?

16.2 Nucleophilic substitution reactions

1 The reaction of bromoethane with hydroxide is a nucleophilic substitution:

$$CH_3CH_2Br + OH^- \rightarrow CH_3CH_2OH + Br^-$$

How is the hydroxide ion acting as a nucleophile in this reaction?

2 Halogenoalkanes undergo nucleophilic substitution at different rates. This can be determined by adding aqueous silver nitrate to a solution of the halogenoalkane in ethanol.

The table shows some results from an investigation into the rate of hydrolysis of halogenoalkanes containing different halogen atoms.

Halogenoalkane	Time taken for reaction / s
1-iodobutane	52
1-bromobutane	87
1-chlorobutane	606

a Explain why silver nitrate can be used to determine the rate of hydrolysis. Use equations to illustrate your answer. [2]

b Explain the results shown in the table above. [3]

[Total: 5]

UNDERSTAND THESE TERMS

- nucleophilic substitution
- heterolytic fission
- S_N2 mechanism
- S_N1 mechanism
- positive inductive effect

REFLECTION

Did you notice the questions that included instructional text in addition to command words? Did you take note of these and apply them in your answers? What strategies might ensure you don't miss any instructional text in an exam?

16.3 Mechanism of nucleophilic substitution in halogenoalkanes

1   What do the letters and numbers in the abbreviations S_N1 and S_N2 stand for?

2   a   Outline the mechanism for the reaction of aqueous sodium hydroxide with 2-bromo-2-methylbutane.   [4]

   b   Identify the rate-determining step in the mechanism.   [1]

   c   State the name of the product.   [1]

[Total: 6]

16.4 Elimination reactions

1   What role does the hydroxide ion have in an elimination reaction?

2   Draw the two alkenes that can be formed from the elimination of 2-bromobutane with ethanolic sodium hydroxide.   **[Total: 2]**

REFLECTION

How well did your answers match those given in the Answers section? Did your answers follow the command words? Make sure your answers to 'draw' questions are clear and unambiguous. If you are asked to 'outline' a reaction mechanism, make sure you show a clear curly arrow mechanism including all lone pairs, charges and dipoles.

SELF-ASSESSMENT CHECKLIST

Let's revisit the Knowledge focus and Exam skills focus for this chapter.

Decide how confident you are with each statement.

Now I can:	Show it	Needs more work	Almost there	Confident to move on
write equations for the main reactions that can produce halogenoalkanes, including the reagents and conditions used	Draw a spider diagram of the main reactions that produce halogenoalkanes, including the reagents and conditions used. Extend this to the synthesis of specific halogenoalkanes.			

CONTINUED

Now I can:	Show it	Needs more work	Almost there	Confident to move on
write equations for the reactions of halogenoalkanes when they undergo: • nucleophilic substitution such as hydrolysis, formation of nitriles and the formation of primary amines by reaction with ammonia • elimination of hydrogen bromide (for example, from 2-bromopropane)	Draw a spider diagram of the reactions of halogenoalkanes; for each reaction include an example equation.			
describe and explain the S_N1 and S_N2 mechanisms of nucleophilic substitution in halogenoalkanes	Produce a one-page summary of the S_N1 and S_N2 mechanisms of nucleophilic substitution in halogenoalkanes.			
interpret the different reactivities of halogenoalkanes	Write some bullet points to explain the trend in reactivities of the different halogenoalkanes.			
distinguish command words from other instructional text	Find a past paper. Choose a full question and list the command words and identify other instructional text.			

17 Alcohols, esters and carboxylic acids

KNOWLEDGE FOCUS

In this chapter you will answer questions on:

- the homologous series of alcohols
- reactions to make alcohols
- reactions of the alcohols
- carboxylic acids.

EXAM SKILLS FOCUS

In this chapter you will:

- develop an awareness of the mark scheme when writing equations for reactions in organic chemistry.

AS & A Level Chemistry questions commonly ask for the equation for an organic reaction. The structures you write in your answers need to be completely clear about the structural formula of the organic substances. In this chapter you will answer a number of these types of questions and see which answers are valid and which would result in lost marks.

17.1 The homologous series of alcohols

1 What is the general formula for the homologous series of alcohols?

2 Alcohols have hydrogen bonding as their strongest intermolecular force. Which two properties are influenced by this?

3 Using the molecular formula $C_4H_{10}O$, give the names of examples of primary, secondary and tertiary alcohols. **[Total: 3]**

UNDERSTAND THESE TERMS

- primary alcohol
- secondary alcohol
- tertiary alcohol

⟪ RECALL AND CONNECT 1 ⟪

How many covalent bonds does oxygen usually form?

17.2 Reactions to make alcohols

1 How are alcohols made in nature?

2 Give equations for the formation of ethanol from:

   a ethene [1]

   b ethanal [1]

   c ethanoic acid. [1]

   [Total: 3]

17.3 Reactions of the alcohols

1 State the reagent(s) for the oxidation of alcohols.

2 Give the equation for the formation of ethyl propanoate from an appropriate combination of alcohol and acid. **[Total: 2]**

UNDERSTAND THESE TERMS

- esterification
- dehydration

17.4 Carboxylic acids

1 Carboxylic acids undergo the same reactions as other acids. Give equations for the reaction of ethanoic acid with:

   a sodium hydroxide

   b magnesium

   c sodium carbonate.

2   Propan-1-ol can be made in a two-step reaction sequence from propanenitrile as shown below.

$$CH_3CH_2CN \rightarrow X \rightarrow CH_3CH_2CH_2OH$$

   a   Name the intermediate X.   [1]
   b   Name the two reactions occurring.   [2]
   c   Give reagents and conditions for each reaction.   [2]

   [Total: 5]

REFLECTION

How well did the equations you wrote in your answers fulfil the requirements of the mark scheme? Did you make sure that you used formulae with appropriate detail to show an understanding of the functional groups?

SELF-ASSESSMENT CHECKLIST

Let's revisit the Knowledge focus and Exam skills focus for this chapter.

Decide how confident you are with each statement.

Now I can:	Show it	Needs more work	Almost there	Confident to move on
explain the acidity of alcohols compared with water	Use a series of equations to explain why alcohols are less acidic than water.			
recall the reactions (reagents and conditions) by which alcohols can be produced	Summarise the reactions to produce alcohols from alkenes, halogenoalkanes, aldehydes/ketones, carboxylic acids and esters.			
recall the reactions of alcohols in combustion, substitution to give halogenoalkanes, reaction with sodium, oxidation to carbonyl compounds and carboxylic acids, and dehydration to alkenes	Sketch a spider diagram to show the reactions of alcohols in combustion and substitution. Include reagents and conditions.			
classify hydroxy compounds into primary, secondary and tertiary alcohols	Give examples of primary, secondary and tertiary alcohols and suggest how samples of these could be distinguished from each other.			
suggest characteristic distinguishing reactions, e.g., mild oxidation				

CONTINUED

Now I can:	Show it	Needs more work	Almost there	Confident to move on
describe the acid and base hydrolysis of esters	Write equations for the hydrolysis of methyl ethanoate in acid and in base.			
describe the formation of carboxylic acids from alcohols, aldehydes and nitriles	Draw a spider diagram showing the different methods of formation of carboxylic acids.			
describe the reactions of carboxylic acids in the formation of: • salts, by the use of reactive metals, alkalis or carbonates • alkyl esters, by reaction with alcohols • primary alcohols, by reduction using $LiAlH_4$	Draw a spider diagram showing the reactions of carboxylic acids to form salts, alkyl esters and primary alcohols.			
understand the mark scheme when writing equations for reactions in organic chemistry	Look back at the questions you have attempted. Make a list of the key aspects of the mark schemes that you need to remember in the exam.			

18 Carbonyl compounds

Organic chemistry exam questions often test the skill of writing 'curly arrow' mechanisms. In these questions, marks are typically awarded for correctly drawn curly arrows (which should start either at a lone pair, or a bond, and go towards the relevant atom), intermediates (together with any relevant charges), and for correctly drawn products and by-products. This chapter will provide you with different opportunities for answering questions with writing mechanisms.

Always check the number of available marks against your answer to ensure you do not miss out something important.

18.1 The homologous series of aldehydes and ketones

1 **a** What is the systematic name of the following carbonyl compounds?

   i $(CH_3)_2CO$

   ii $CH_3CH_2CH_2CHO$

   iii $CH_3COCH_2CH_2CH_3$

   iv CH_2CHCHO

b Write the structural formula of:

   i ethanal

   ii hexan-3-one

c Draw the displayed formula of 3-methylbutan-2-one.

d Draw the skeletal formula for (E)-hex-2-enal.

2 **a** The systematic name of the compound in Figure 18.1 is 4-hydroxy-5-methylhexan-2-one. Explain the rules that are used to deduce this name.   [5]

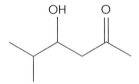

Figure 18.1

b State and explain the geometry of carbon atom 2 in this compound.   [2]

[Total: 7]

≪ RECALL AND CONNECT 1 ≪

Aldehydes and ketones form a homologous series. What are the characteristics of members of a homologous series?

18.2 Preparation of aldehydes and ketones

1 **a** Using [O] to represent the oxidising agent, write chemical equations for the following reactions:

   i The oxidation of ethanol to ethanal.

   ii The oxidation of propan-2-ol to propan-2-one.

b Figure 18.2 shows a diagram of the distillation apparatus used in the oxidation of ethanol to ethanal. Ethanol boils at 78 °C, while ethanal boils at 22 °C.

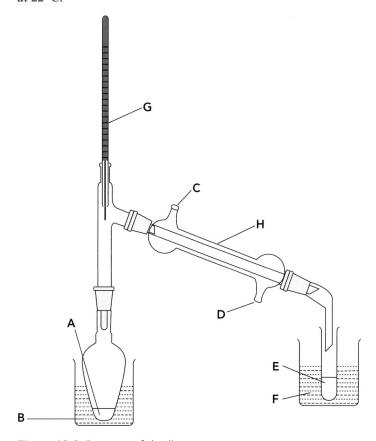

Figure 18.2: Diagram of distillation apparatus

i Explain why ethanol and ethanal have different boiling points.

ii Copy and complete the table with the correct labels.

Description	Label
hot water bath	
ice-water bath	
water in	
water out	
thermometer	
condenser	
ethanol, $K_2Cr_2O_7$ and H_2SO_4	
distillate (ethanal)	

iii Describe how this apparatus is used to obtain a pure sample of ethanal from ethanol.

iv Why is an ice-water bath used?

2 Butane-2,3-dione, $(CH_3CO)_2$, is used as an artificial flavouring in many food and drink products. It can be prepared in the lab by oxidation of butane-2,3-diol using acidified potassium dichromate(VI). The relevant half-equations are shown.

$$C_4H_{10}O_2 \rightarrow C_4H_6O_2 + 4e^- + 4H^+$$

$$Cr_2O_7^{2-} + 14H^+ + 6e^- \rightarrow 2Cr^{3+} + 7H_2O$$

  a State the overall reaction between dichromate(VI) and butane-2,3-diol. [2]

  b Name the reducing agent in this reaction. [1]

  c Describe one observation that would be made during the reaction. [1]

  d Give the average oxidation state of carbon in butane-2,3-dione. [1]

[Total: 5]

18.3 Reduction of aldehydes and ketones

1 **a** Give the systematic names for:

  i Sodium borohydride, $NaBH_4$.

  ii Lithium aluminium hydride, $LiAlH_4$.

  iii Describe how reductions are carried out using these reagents.

  iv What is the oxidation number of hydrogen in both of these compounds?

  b Using [H] to represent the reducing agent, write chemical equations for the following reduction reactions:

  i Methanal to methanol.

  ii 2-Butanone to 2-butanol.

  iii Ethanoic acid to ethanol.

  iv Pentane-2,3-dione to pentane-2,3-diol.

2 3,5-Dimethylcyclopentane-1,2-dione is called 'caramel dione' due to its creamy, sugary aroma. Its structure is shown in Figure 18.3. It can be reduced to a single organic product, X, by adding it to a solution of lithium aluminium hydride in dry ether.

  a Deduce the molecular formula of caramel dione. [1]

  b Draw the displayed formula of the organic product X. [1]

  c Using molecular formula and [H] to represent the reducing agent, write a chemical equation for the reduction reaction. [1]

  d Explain why it is important to use dry ether. [1]

  e In an experiment, 2.29 g of caramel dione produced 1.58 g of X. Calculate the percentage yield for the reaction. [3]

[Total: 7]

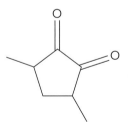

Figure 18.3

18.4 Nucleophilic addition with HCN

1 Aldehydes and ketones undergo nucleophilic addition reactions with hydrogen cyanide in the presence of an acid, such as H_2SO_4, and potassium cyanide, KCN.

   a Explain the role of KCN in this reaction.

   b Why is CN^- in this reaction described as a *nucleophile*?

   c Why are aldehydes and ketones susceptible to attack by nucleophiles?

   d Why is this reaction of value in organic synthesis?

   e Name the following products of nucleophilic addition reactions:

   i $CH_3CH_2CH(OH)CN$

   ii $CH_3CH_2CH_2C(OH)(CH_2CH_3)CN$

   f Show the mechanism for the nucleophilic addition reaction between propanone and hydrogen cyanide. Include relevant dipoles.

18.5 Testing for aldehydes and ketones

1 a i Describe how 2,4-DNPH could be used to confirm the identity of an aldehyde thought to be propanal.

   ii Write a chemical equation using structural formulae for this reaction.

   iii Why can this reaction be described as a condensation?

   iv Name the class of organic compounds formed when 2,4-DNPH reacts with carbonyl compounds.

   b i Which chemicals are used to prepare Tollens' reagent?

   ii What is the chemical formula for Tollens' reagent?

   iii Describe how Tollens' reagent could be used to distinguish between butanal and butan-2-one. What is the organic product formed?

   iv The general equation for a positive Tollens' test is shown.

   $$2Ag^+ + RCHO + 3OH^- \rightarrow 2Ag + RCOO^- + 2H_2O$$

   How does this show that the test involves a redox reaction?

   v Why does Tollens' test not give a positive result with ketones?

   c i Describe how Fehling's solution could be used to distinguish propanal from propanone.

   ii Name the organic product formed in this test.

   iii What is responsible for the red precipitate in a positive Fehling's test?

UNDERSTAND THESE TERMS
• nucleophilic addition
• 2-hydroxynitrile

2 The table lists some oxygen-containing organic compounds and some common laboratory reagents. Copy and complete the table. If no reaction occurs, write 'no reaction' for the structural formulae.

Reaction	Compound	Reagent	Structural formulae of organic compound formed
A	$CH_3CHC(CH_3)_2$	Br_2 water	
B	$CH_3CH_2C(OH)(CH_3)_2$	$H^+/Cr_2O_7^{2-}$	
C	$CH_3CH_2COCH_3$	$NaBH_4$	
D	$CH_3CH(CH_3)CHO$	Tollens' reagent	
E	$CH_3C(CH_3)_2COCH_3$	Fehling's solution	
F	CH_3CH_2COOH	$LiAlH_4$	
G	CH_3CH_2CN	$HCl(aq)$	

[Total: 7]

18.6 Reactions to form tri-iodomethane

1 Tri-iodomethane, CHI_3, has the trivial name *iodoform* and is the product of the iodoform test.

  a Which types of compounds give positive iodoform tests?

  b Describe how an iodoform test is carried out, including any observations.

  c Write two chemical equations to describe the iodoform test for ethanal and name the reaction types occurring.

  d A branched alcohol with the molecular formula $C_5H_{12}O$ undergoes a positive iodoform test.

  i Name the alcohol.

  ii Give the structural formula of the organic compound formed.

2 There are many isomers with the molecular formula C_4H_8O.

  a Identify an isomer of C_4H_8O that gives a positive test with Tollens' reagent. [1]

  b Identify an isomer of C_4H_8O that gives a positive test with Fehling's solution. [1]

  c Identify an isomer of C_4H_8O that gives a positive test with 2,4-DNPH but not with either Tollens' reagent or Fehling's solution. [1]

  d Identify the isomer of C_4H_8O that can be oxidised to a carboxylic acid by acidified dichromate(VI) and which decolourises bromine water. [1]

  e Identify the isomer of C_4H_8O that gives a yellow precipitate when warmed with alkaline iodine solution but no visible change with 2,4-DNPH. [1]

[Total: 5]

18.7 Infrared spectroscopy

1   The infrared spectra of but-1-ene, butan-2-ol, butanone and butanoic acid are shown in Figure 18.5. Match each compound to its infrared spectrum **A–D**, stating the characteristic absorbance bands you used to identify the bonds present.

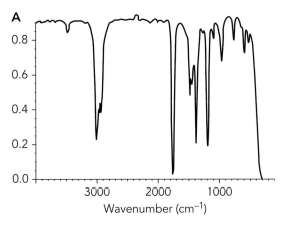

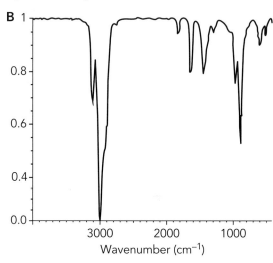

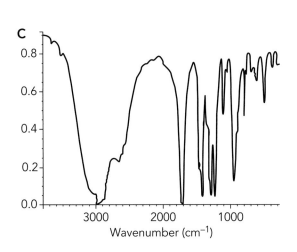

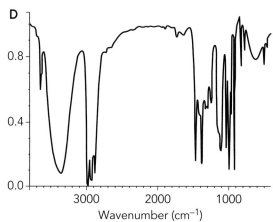

Figure 18.5: IR spectra of compounds A–D

2   Compound Z is branched and does not have geometric isomers. It contains 71.39% carbon, 9.59% hydrogen and 19.02% oxygen by mass. When warmed with an alkaline solution of iodine, Z gives a yellow precipitate. Its mass spectrum contains a molecular ion peak with a mass-to-charge ratio of 84. The infrared spectrum of compound Z is shown in Figure 18.6.

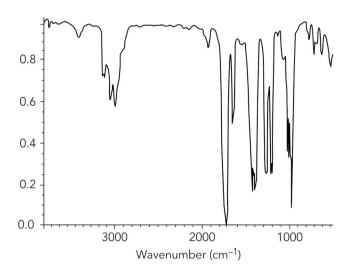

Figure 18.6

a   Explain how geometric isomerism arises.   [1]

b   Calculate the empirical formula of compound Z.   [2]

c   Hence, deduce the molecular formula of Z, explaining your answer.   [1]

d   Identify compound Z. You should explain how you have used the
    information provided to arrive at your answer.   [3]

[Total: 7]

UNDERSTAND THESE TERMS

- infrared spectroscopy
- resonance frequency

≪ RECALL AND CONNECT 2 ≪

a   What are the general formulae of these homologous series?

   i   Alkanes   ii   Alkenes   iii   Cycloalkanes

b   How would you name the following compounds?

   i $CH_3CH(CH_3)CH(CH_3)CH_3$ ii $CH_3CH(OH)CH_2CH_2CH_3$

   iii $CH_2CHC(CH_3)_3$

REFLECTION

Writing mechanisms is a key skill in organic chemistry and you will answer several mechanism questions in the exam. In mechanisms, curly arrows should start at a lone pair or the middle of a bond and move towards an atom or the middle of a bond. Common mistakes usually involve curly arrows starting or finishing in the wrong place. Try writing the mechanisms for electrophilic addition, nucleophilic substitution and nucleophilic addition, and, for each step, think about the common 'curly arrow' mistakes students might make. Are you confident you will avoid similar errors?

SELF-ASSESSMENT CHECKLIST

Let's revisit the Knowledge focus and Exam skills focus for this chapter.

Decide how confident you are with each statement.

Now I can:	Show it	Needs more work	Almost there	Confident to move on
describe the formation of aldehydes from the oxidation of primary alcohols	Draw a labelled diagram to show the apparatus used to oxidise ethanol to ethanal and include the chemical equation.			
describe the formation of ketones from the oxidation of secondary alcohols	Draw a labelled diagram to show the apparatus used to oxidise propan-2-ol to propanone and include the chemical equation.			
describe the reduction of aldehydes and ketones, e.g., using $NaBH_4$ or $LiAlH_4$	Write balanced chemical equations for the reduction of propanone using $NaBH_4$, and of ethanoic acid using $LiAlH_4$.			
describe the reaction of aldehydes and ketones with HCN (hydrogen cyanide) and KCN (potassium cyanide)	Write an equation for the reaction of HCN/KCN with ethanal and explain the role of KCN.			
describe the mechanism of the nucleophilic addition reactions of hydrogen cyanide with aldehydes and ketones	Write out the 'curly arrows' mechanism for the reaction of HCN with butanone and with propanal.			
describe the detection of carbonyl compounds using 2,4-dinitrophenylhydrazine (2,4-DNPH) reagent	Write the step-by-step procedure describing how 2,4-DNPH is used to detect and identify carbonyl compounds, including observations.			
distinguish between aldehydes and ketones by testing with Fehling's and Tollens' reagents	Write the step-by-step procedure describing how Fehling's and Tollens' reagents are used to distinguish aldehydes and ketones, including key observations.			

CONTINUED

Now I can:	Show it	Needs more work	Almost there	Confident to move on
describe the reaction of CH_3CO- compounds with alkaline aqueous iodine to give tri-iodomethane, CHI_3, and a carboxylate ion, $RCOO^-$	Write two equations using structural formulae to show how ethanal and methyl ketones containing the CH_3CO- group react with alkaline aqueous iodine, and state the key observation.			
devise a synthetic route (series of reactions) using any of the reactions from Chapters 14–18 to make a named organic product	Construct a flowchart showing the reactions that link the functional groups from Chapters 14–18, writing the reaction conditions over the arrows.			
deduce the presence of a $CH_3CH(OH)-$ group in an alcohol from its reaction with alkaline aqueous iodine to form tri-iodomethane	Write three chemical equations to show the steps occurring when propan-2-ol reacts with alkaline aqueous iodine and state the key observation that allows detection of the $CH_3CH(OH)-$ group.			
analyse an infrared spectrum of a simple molecule to identify functional groups	Annotate the infrared spectra of ethanol, ethanal and ethanoic acid to show the important absorption frequencies and bonds.			
become familiar with the breakdown of marks in questions on organic chemistry	Answer exam questions on organic mechanisms without referring to the mark scheme. Try to work out how marks are allocated. Once you have finished, check your mark allocation against the mark scheme.			

Exam practice 4

This section contains past paper questions from previous Cambridge exams which draw together your knowledge on a range of topics that you have covered up to this point. These questions give you the opportunity to test your knowledge and understanding. Additional past paper practice questions can be found in the accompanying digital material.

The following question has an example student response and commentary provided. Work through the question first, then compare your answer to the sample response and commentary. Are your answers different to the sample responses? How are they different?

1 Methylpropane, $(CH_3)_2CHCH_3$, is an isomer of butane, $CH_3(CH_2)_2CH_3$.

    a   Explain why methylpropane and butane are a pair of isomers.   [2]

    b   Identify the type of isomerism shown by methylpropane and butane.   [1]

                                                                             [Total: 3]

Cambridge International AS & A Level Chemistry (9701) Paper 22 Q1a June 2019

Example student response	Commentary
a They have the same number of atoms of each element.	This answer is underdeveloped. The statement the student has made is correct in identifying the similarities between the compounds, but they have not mentioned the differences. *This answer is awarded 0 out of 2 marks.*
b Structural isomers.	This answer is not specific enough. There are three types of structural isomerism. *This answer is awarded 0 out of 1 mark.*

2 Now that you've gone through the commentary, try to write an improved answer to any part of question **1** where you did not score highly. Use the commentary to help you.

The following question has an example student response and commentary provided. Work through the question first, then compare your answer to the sample response and commentary. Are your answers different to the sample responses?

3   The table compares the reactivity of alkanes and alkenes with chlorine.

	alkanes	alkenes
name of the type of reaction with chlorine	substitution	addition and substitution
name of the type of reacting species	free radical	electrophile and free radical

a   During the first stage in the substitution reaction chlorine forms chlorine free radicals. Explain what is meant by the term *free radical*.   [1]

b   Name and explain the type of bond breaking which occurs to form chlorine free radicals.   [2]

c   Name the stage of the reaction mechanism which occurs when a methane molecule reacts with a chlorine free radical.   [1]

d   Complete the equation for the reaction which occurs when a methane molecule reacts with a chlorine free radical.

$$H-\overset{\displaystyle H}{\underset{\displaystyle H}{\overset{|}{\underset{|}{C}}}}-H \ + \ \bullet Cl \ \rightarrow \qquad\qquad + $$

---------   ---------   [1]

e   Carbon atoms can form σ and π bonds within hydrocarbon molecules.

Explain the following statement with reference to σ and π bonds.

Alkenes react with electrophiles but alkanes do not.   [2]

[Total: 7]

Adapted from Cambridge International AS & A Level Chemistry (9701) Paper 22 Q4d June 2019

Example student response	Commentary
a A free radical is a species that contains one or more unpaired electrons.	This is correct. However, the student does not need to repeat the question in their answer or write in full sentences. All that was required was the phrase 'unpaired electron'. Cutting down on writing full sentences may save you time in an examination. *This answer is awarded 1 out of 1 mark.*
b Homolytic bond breaking forms free radicals.	The statement is correct and answers the first part of the question, gaining one mark. The student has failed to address the command word 'explain' so the answer is incomplete. *This answer is awarded 1 out of 2 marks.*

Example student response	Commentary
c $CH_4 + Cl\bullet \rightarrow \bullet CH_3 + HCl$	The question asked for the name of the stage in a mechanism – the student has just written an equation. It is acceptable to do this as part of your working out but make sure you respond to the question asked. Here, the response should identify a stage in the free-radical substitution mechanism: initiation, propagation or termination. *This answer is awarded 0 out of 1 mark.*
d (structural equation showing H—C(H)(H)—H + $\bullet Cl$ → HCl + $\bullet C$(H)(H)—H)	This is correct, the student shows that they understand that the free radical on the chlorine is used to make a HCl molecule and this results in a methyl free radical being formed. *This answer is awarded 1 out of 1 mark.*
e Alkenes react with electrophiles because electrophiles like electrons and alkenes are electron rich.	The statements here are correct but don't address the question fully, and so gain no marks. This question contains cued recall, it is asking for an answer in terms of σ and π bonds, which the student has not used in their response. *This answer is awarded 0 out of 2 marks.*

4   Now that you have read the sample response, rewrite your answer to any part of question **3** where you did not score highly. Use the commentary to help you.

The following question has an example student response and commentary provided. Work through the question first, then compare your answer to the sample response and commentary. Are your answers different to the sample responses? How are they different?

5   Fig. 5.1 shows three reactions of 2-bromopropane, $CH_3CH(Br)CH_3$.

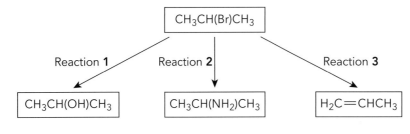

Fig. 5.1

a   Complete Table 5.1 for each reaction, by:

   •   stating the reagent and conditions used

   •   identifying the type of reaction that occurs.

reaction	reagent and conditions	type of reaction
1		
2		
3		

[6]

Table 5.1

b   A sample of 2-iodopropane, $CH_3CH(I)CH_3$, reacts under the same conditions as reaction **1** to produce $CH_3CH(OH)CH_3$.

Explain why 2-iodopropane reacts at a faster rate than 2-bromopropane.   [2]

c   Fig. 5.2 shows how butan-1-ol can be made from 1-bromopropane in three steps.

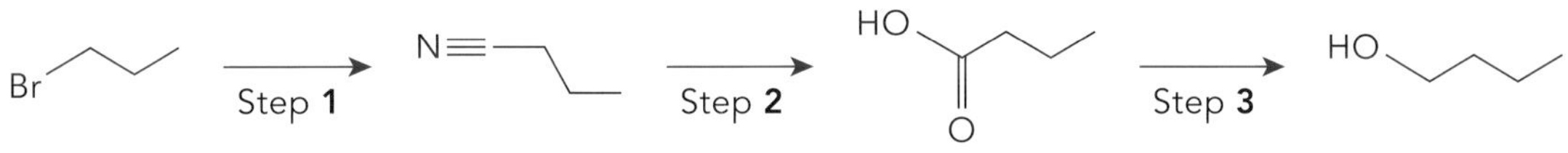

Fig. 5.2

i   In step **1**, 1-bromopropane reacts with CN^- to form butanenitrile.

Complete Fig. 5.3 to show the mechanism for step **1**. Include charges, dipoles, lone pairs of electrons and curly arrows as appropriate.

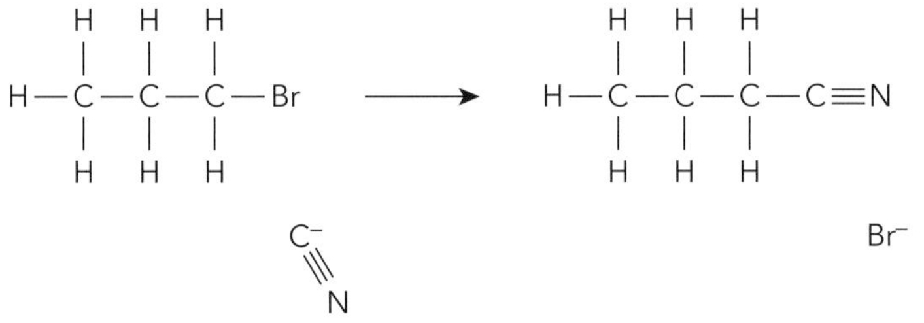

[2]

Fig. 5.3

ii   In step **2**, butanenitrile is heated with HCl (aq).

A hydrolysis reaction occurs.

Construct an equation for the reaction in step **2**.   [1]

[Total: 11]

Cambridge International AS & A Level Chemistry (9701) Paper 22 Q5a, b, c i–ii June 2022

Example student response	Commentary
a Reaction 1 NaOH(aq) substitution. Reaction 2 NH$_3$ substitution. Reaction 3 NaOH in ethanol, elimination.	The student has correctly identified the reaction types for all of the reactions; this gains 2 marks. For reaction 1 the answer should include 'heat' for full conditions. For reactions 2 and 3, the reagents are correct; however, the conditions are incomplete. A mark is gained for the NH$_3$, but the second mark for the conditions is lost. In reaction 3, both the reagent, solvent and reference to heat were required, so this mark is lost. *This answer is awarded 4 out of 6 marks.*
b The C–I bond is weaker because there is not much difference in electronegativity between C and I.	The first statement the student makes is correct and gains 1 mark. The second statement is also correct, but not relevant in the context of the question. To get the second mark, the student needs to make a statement about the activation energy or the reaction, or about the S$_N$1 mechanism or the reason why the C–I bond is weaker in terms of attraction of the halogen nucleus for the bonding pair of electrons (including the reasons). *This answer is awarded 1 out of 2 marks.*
c i	The arrows here are correct, the mechanism is an S$_N$2 substitution. The student has forgotten to include the lone pair on the C of the CN⁻ ion and the dipole on the C–Br bond. As each of these details is important for the arrows, this means neither arrow gains a mark. *This answer is awarded 0 out of 2 marks.*
ii CN(CH$_2$)$_2$CH$_3$ + 2H$_2$O + HCl → HOOC(CH$_2$)$_2$CH$_3$ + NH$_4$Cl	This is correct and the structural formulae are unambiguous. *This answer is awarded 1 out of 1 mark.*

6 Now that you've gone through the commentary, try to write an improved answer to any part of question **5** where you did not score highly. This will help you check if you've understood exactly why each mark has (or has not) been allocated.
In your new answers, make sure you read the question and address the scope of the question.

The following question has an example student response and commentary provided. Work through the question first, then compare your answer to the sample response and commentary. Are your answers different to the sample responses? How are they different?

7 Glycerol, $CH_2(OH)CH(OH)CH_2OH$, is widely used in the food industry and in pharmaceuticals.

A series of reactions starting from glycerol is shown.

a Suggest the reagent(s) and conditions for reaction 1. [2]

b Name the reaction mechanism for reaction 2. [1]

c Give the observation you would make when 2,4-dinitrophenylhydrazine is added to **P**. [1]

d **Q** does **not** show optical isomerism.

Explain why. [1]

e When **Q** is heated with excess aqueous ethanoic acid in the presence of a catalytic amount of sulfuric acid, two reactions take place to form compound **R**.

Identify the two types of reaction that occur. [2]

[Total: 7]

Adapted from Cambridge International AS & A Level Chemistry (9701) Paper 22 Q3a March 2020

Example student response	Commentary
a Potassium dichromate.	The student has given the correct reagent; however, they have failed to include crucial conditions. The potassium dichromate must be acidified and the reaction must be heated under reflux. *This answer is awarded 1 out of 2 marks.*
b Nucleophilic addition reaction.	This is correct. *This answer is awarded 1 out of 1 mark.*

Example student response	Commentary
c An orange precipitate would form when 2,4-DNP is added to substance P because there is a carbonyl group.	This is correct; however, students are advised not to add additional detail where it is not needed. The question here only asked for the result, not the reason. The student has wasted time here. *This answer is awarded 1 out of 1 mark.*
d Q does not have a carbon atom with 4 different groups attached to it.	This is correct. There are lots of other possible ways to explain this, including in terms of the absence of a chiral centre or having two identical functional groups. *This answer is awarded 1 out of 1 mark.*
e Esterification and hydrolysis.	The student has correctly identified the two reactions that take place. *This answer is awarded 2 out of 2 marks.*

Now you have read the commentary to the previous question, here is a similar question which you should attempt. Use the information from the previous response and commentary to guide you as you answer.

8 The reaction sequence below begins with an alcohol **X**.

Alcohol **X** ⟶ [structure with H_3C–C(=O)–C(CH_3)(CH_3)(CH_3)] labelled **Y** → NaCN and HCN → **Z**

a State the systematic name of the alcohol **X**. [1]

b Write an equation for the oxidation of **X** to form **Y**. Use [O] to represent your oxidising agent. [1]

c State the reagents and conditions for the oxidation of alcohol **X** and the key observation of the reaction. [2]

d State the type of stereoisomerism that is observed in the product **Z** and explain, with reference to the product's structure, why this arises. [3]

[Total: 7]

Author's own question

The following question has an example student response and commentary provided. Work through the question first, then compare your answer to the sample response and commentary. Are your answers different to the sample responses? How are they different?

9 a Triphenylphosphine is used in a type of reaction known as a *Wittig reaction*.

triphenylphosphine

where ⬡ = $-C_6H_5$

i   Give the empirical formula of triphenylphosphine.   [1]

In a Wittig reaction, an aldehyde reacts with a halogenoalkane to form
an alkene. The conversion is shown in the following unbalanced equation.

Compound **H** can be made from propanal, C_2H_5CHO. Stage 3 in the reaction
scheme is a Wittig reaction.

stage 1 $C_2H_5CHO \xrightarrow{\quad NaBH_4 \quad}$ **G**

stage 2   **G** $\xrightarrow{\quad red\ phosphorus\ and\ I_2 \quad}$ $C_2H_5CH_2I$

stage 3 $C_2H_5CH_2I + C_2H_5CHO \xrightarrow[\text{strong base}]{\text{triphenylphosphine}}$ **H**
(Wittig reaction)

ii   State the types of reaction that occur in stages 1 and 2.   [2]

iii Draw the structures of **G** and **H** in the boxes provided.

G	H

[2]

b   Identify the organic products formed when compound **J**, shown below,
    is heated with hot concentrated acidified manganate(VII) ions.

J

$\xrightarrow[\text{H}_2\text{SO}_4]{\text{hot concentrated MnO}_4^-}$

[2]

[Total: 7]

Adapted from Cambridge International AS & A Level Chemistry (9701)
Paper 21 Q3c, d November 2021

Example student response	Examiner comments
a i $C_{18}H_{15}P$	This is correct. *This answer is awarded 1 out of 1 mark.*
ii Stage 1 is a reduction. Stage 2 is a halogenation.	Stage 2 is more correctly called a substitution reaction. *This answer is awarded 1 out of 2 marks.*

Example student response	Examiner comments
iii G is $C_2H_5CH_2OH$ H is $CH_3CH_2CH=CHCH_2CH_3$	Both structures are correct. *This answer is awarded 2 out of 2 marks.*
b CH_3CH_2CHO and CH_3CH_2COOH	Propanoic acid is correct, but the other product should be propanone, CH_3COCH_3. *This answer is awarded 1 out of 2 marks.*

Now answer an additional question.

10 **W** is $CH_3COCH_2CH_3$.

   a   The reaction between **W** and alkaline aqueous iodine produces a yellow precipitate.

   i   Give the name of the compound formed as a yellow precipitate in this reaction. [1]

   ii   Give the name of **W**. [1]

   b   There are two structural isomers of **W** that are also carbonyl compounds.

   Draw the structures of these two isomers of **W**. [2]

Two reactions of **W** are shown.

   c   **i**   Identify the type of reaction occurring in reaction **1**. [1]

   ii   Identify the reagent for reaction **1**. [1]

   d   Reaction **2** is carried out by adding a mixture of HCN and NaCN to **W**.

   The product, **X**, is formed as a mixture of two isomers.

   i   Complete the mechanism for this reaction.

   Include the structure of the intermediate formed and all necessary charges, dipoles, lone pairs and curly arrows.

[4]

    ii   State the name of the type of isomerism shown by **X**.   [1]

    iii Explain fully why **X** shows this type of isomerism.   [2]

e If **X** is treated with ammonia and the product hydrolysed, a compound, **Y**, is obtained that contains 51.3% C, 9.40% H, 12.0% N and 27.3% O by mass.

    i   Show that the empirical formula of **Y** is $C_5H_{11}NO_2$.   [2]

    ii The empirical formula of **Y** is $C_5H_{11}NO_2$ and the M_r of **Y** is 117.
        Deduce the molecular formula of **Y**. You **must** explain
        your reasoning.   [1]

                                                          [Total: 16]

Cambridge International AS & A Level Chemistry (9701) Paper 22 Q4 June 2018

Practical skills for AS Level

Chemistry is a practical subject, and everything observed and measured in a laboratory can be linked to the background theory. Observations and measurements operate in the macroscopic domain, whereas much of the theory is in the microscopic and symbolic domain.

In this chapter you will practise questions that link practical work to the theory in your course.

P1.1 Introduction

1 What is an anomalous result?

2 What kind of variable is displayed using a bar chart?

3 A student was investigating the rate of hydrolysis of halogenoalkanes. They used three halogenoalkanes: 1-chloropropane, 1-bromopropane and 1-iodopropane, dissolved in ethanol and added drops of aqueous silver nitrate. They measured the time taken for a precipitate of silver halide to form.

    a Write equations for the two reactions occurring in this investigation, using 1-chloropropane as the starting halogenoalkane. [2]

    b State the independent and dependent variables in this investigation. Suggest two control variables. [4]

                                                        [Total 6]

≪ RECALL AND CONNECT 1 ≪

What is the SI unit of temperature?

P1.2 Manipulation, measurement and observation

1 Carbon dioxide gas is bubbled through limewater.
How should the cloudy appearance be described?

2 What is the name for two titration results within $0.10\,cm^3$?

3 A student carried out a titration four times and got results for the titre of 26.50, 25.15, 25.20 and then $25.35\,cm^3$. Determine the most accurate value of the titre to use in any calculations. **[Total: 2]**

4 A student carried out a titration and wrote the value of the titre in their lab book as $25.73\,cm^3$. Explain why this value cannot be correct. **[Total: 2]**

P1.3 Presentation of data and observations

1 In questions using experimental data, how many significant figures should the answer be quoted to?

2 A student calculated the concentration of an acid using the results from a titration. The student used $25.0\,cm^3$ of the acid and $23.45\,cm^3$ of an alkali with a concentration of $0.100\,mol\,dm^{-3}$. The calculated concentration showed on the calculator screen was 0.988745712. State the value the student should quote as the final answer. **[Total: 1]**

P1.4 Analysis, conclusions and evaluation

1 What are systematic errors?

2 Figure P1.1 shows a graph obtained from some experimental data.

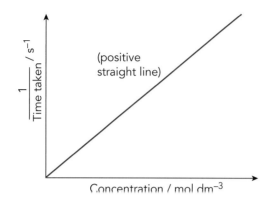

Figure P1.1

a State the independent and dependent variable in this experiment. [2]

b Describe how the gradient of the line could be determined. [3]

[Total: 5]

3 A student weighed a quantity of solid using a two-decimal place balance. They weighed a weighing bottle, added some solid and reweighed the bottle. They then transferred the solid to the reaction flask and reweighed the weighing bottle with any residue. The mass transferred to the reaction flask was calculated by subtracting the mass of the weighing bottle and residue from the mass of the weighing bottle and solid. The mass transferred to the reaction flask was 1.57 g. Calculate the percentage error from weighing. Explain your working. **[Total: 3]**

UNDERSTAND THESE TERMS
• independent variable
• dependent variable
• control variables
• random errors
• systematic errors

REFLECTION

How well have you linked the theory with the practical skills in the questions you have attempted in this chapter? The practical context can make questions appear more difficult than they actually are. In each case, were you able to identify the key information needed to attempt the question?

SELF-ASSESSMENT CHECKLIST

Let's revisit the Knowledge focus and Exam skills focus for this chapter.

Decide how confident you are with each statement.

Now I can:	Show it	Needs more work	Almost there	Confident to move on
plan for successful collection of data and observations	Consider the experiment to find the enthalpy change of combustion of propan-1-ol. Make a list of all the data that you would collect in this experiment.			
assess the quality of measurements or observations	Consider a titration experiment. How many decimal places should the burette readings be quoted to? If you did four titrations, how would you treat the results?			
make decisions relating to measurements or observations	What is the minimum number of titrations that could be carried out and give a useful result? Justify your answer.			
display calculation and reasoning	Use bullet points to outline the steps needed in calculating the concentration of a substance from a series of titre values and the volume and concentration of a reacting substance.			
lay out data	Design a table to collect data for a class practical and once the data is collected, plot the data as a suitable graph.			
interpret data or observations	Complete three data analysis questions from a past practical Paper 3.			
draw conclusions	Write a conclusion for all practical experiments you have conducted in class. Link to statistical data when it has been calculated.			

CONTINUED

Now I can:	Show it	Needs more work	Almost there	Confident to move on
identify sources of error and suggest improvements	Review the method of three practicals you have conducted in class and consider the limitations that might result in sources of error.			
link practical chemistry and background theory	Make a list of the practicals you have carried out and, beside each one, list the topics that are related.			

19 Lattice energy

When responding to questions you will need to judge whether your answer needs to be short, detailed, or structured; if you need to include calculations; or if you need to include specific units. Understanding what is a good answer is very important for questions on this topic. Any equations written need to be balanced and must completely fit the definition, including state symbols. This takes practice. You will also see how using a Hess cycle or Born–Haber cycle can be helpful to make sure your working is correct, even though it might not be directly credited in mark schemes. This chapter will provide opportunities for you to practise answering questions on thermodynamics, including specific symbols and states.

19.1 Defining lattice energy

1 What sign does lattice energy always have?

2 Write an equation to describe the lattice energy of lithium oxide. **[Total: 1]**

≪ RECALL AND CONNECT 1 ≪

Why are ionic bonds strong?

19.2 Enthalpy change of atomisation and electron affinity

1 What sign does the standard enthalpy change of atomisation, $\Delta H_{at}^{\ominus}$, always have? Explain your answer.

2 Write equations for the standard enthalpy change of atomisation, $\Delta H_{at}^{\ominus}$, and the first electron affinity, EA_1, for bromine. **[Total: 2]**

3 The table shows data for the first electron affinities for some elements in Group 17.

Explain the trend. **[Total: 4]**

Element	Electron affinity / kJ mol^{-1}
Cl	−348.8
Br	−324.6
I	−295.4

19.3 Born–Haber cycles

1 Draw a simple energy cycle that can be used to calculate lattice energy.

2 The table shows some thermodynamic data. Use these data to calculate the lattice energy of magnesium oxide. **[Total: 3]**

	Enthalpy change / kJ mol^{-1}
enthalpy of formation for magnesium oxide	−602
enthalpy of atomisation for magnesium	+150
first ionisation energy for magnesium	+736
second ionisation energy for magnesium	+1450
bond dissociation enthalpy for oxygen	+496
first electron affinity for oxygen	−142
second electron affinity for oxygen	+844

UNDERSTAND THESE TERMS

- lattice energy, ΔH_{latt}
- standard enthalpy change of atomisation, ΔH_{at}
- first electron affinity, EA_1
- second electron affinity, EA_2
- ion polarisation
- polarising power

---

3   The table shows some thermodynamic data. Construct a Born–Haber
cycle diagram and use these data to calculate the standard enthalpy
of atomisation of iodine.   **[Total: 5]**

	Enthalpy change / kJ mol⁻¹
enthalpy of atomisation of caesium	+79
first ionisation energy of caesium	+376
electron affinity of iodine	−314
enthalpy of formation of caesium iodide	−337
lattice energy of caesium iodide	−585

4   CaO and NaCl have similar ionic radii. Which compound will have
the higher lattice energy? Explain your answer.   **[Total: 1]**

5   Explain why some ionic compounds may be considered to have
a degree of covalent character.   **[Total: 3]**

19.4 Enthalpy changes in solution

1   Draw a series of labelled diagrams to show how an ionic compound dissolves
in water. Include relevant ionic charges and dipoles.

2   The table shows some thermodynamic data for magnesium chloride.

	Enthalpy change / kJ mol⁻¹
lattice enthalpy of formation of magnesium chloride	−2493
enthalpy of hydration of Mg^{2+} ions	−1920
enthalpy of hydration of Cl^- ions	−364

Use these data to calculate a value for the enthalpy of solution
of magnesium chloride.   **[Total: 2]**

REFLECTION

In this chapter you have written a lot of equations that represent
thermodynamic data. Go back and check them all against the answers
provided. Did they all include state symbols? State symbols are essential
when writing equations in this topic as you cannot completely represent
the definition of a particular enthalpy change without them.

SELF-ASSESSMENT CHECKLIST

Let's revisit the Knowledge focus and Exam skills focus for this chapter.

Decide how confident you are with each statement.

Now I can:	Show it	Needs more work	Almost there	Confident to move on
define and use the terms *enthalpy change of atomisation, lattice energy* and *first electron affinity*	Write definitions for *enthalpy change of atomisation, lattice energy* and *first electron affinity.* Write example equations fulfilling these definitions.			
explain the factors affecting the electron affinities of the elements	Explain why the first electron affinity of the halogens (Group 17) is greater than the first electron affinity of Group 16 elements by comparing the nuclear charge, atomic radius and electron configuration.			
describe and explain the trends in the electron affinities of Group 16 and Group 17 elements				
construct and use Born–Haber cycles for ionic solids	Sketch a Born–Haber cycle for a Group 1 oxide and perform a calculation using data from the data booklet.			
carry out calculations involving Born–Haber cycles				
explain the effect of ionic charge and ionic radius on the magnitude (big or small) of the lattice energy	Use bullet points to explain the effect of ionic charge and ionic radius on the magnitude of the lattice energy.			
define and use the terms *enthalpy change of hydration* and *enthalpy change of solution*	Define the terms *enthalpy change of hydration* and *enthalpy change of solution,* and write examples of equations fulfilling these definitions.			
construct and use an energy cycle involving enthalpy change of solution, lattice energy and enthalpy changes of hydration	Construct an example energy cycle including enthalpy change of solution, lattice energy and enthalpy changes of hydration. Show the two routes in the cycle with equal energy according to Hess's law.			

CONTINUED

Now I can:	Show it	Needs more work	Almost there	Confident to move on
carry out calculations using an energy cycle involving enthalpy change of solution, lattice energy and enthalpy changes of hydration	The hydration enthalpies for calcium and chloride ions are −1650 and −364 kJ mol^{-1}, respectively. The lattice energy of calcium chloride is −2258 kJ mol^{-1}. Use these values to prove that the enthalpy of solution of calcium chloride is −120 kJ mol^{-1}.			
explain the effect of ionic charge and ionic radius on the magnitude (big or small) of the enthalpy change of hydration	Use bullet points to explain the effect of ionic charge and ionic radius on the magnitude of the enthalpy change of hydration.			
describe and explain qualitatively the trend in the thermal stability of nitrates and carbonates of Group 2 elements, including the effect of ionic radius on the polarisation of the large anion	The relative stabilities of carbonates and nitrates of Group 2 elements increase down the group. Use bullet points to explain this.			
describe and explain qualitatively the variation in solubility and enthalpy change of solution of hydroxides and sulfates of Group 2 in terms of relative magnitudes of enthalpy change of hydration and the lattice energy	Group 2 hydroxides increase in solubility down the group but Group 2 sulfates decrease in solubility down the group. Explain this in terms of enthalpy change of hydration and the lattice energy.			
understand what good answers look like for questions involving thermodynamics	Check all the equations you have written in your revision of this chapter. Make sure they contain state symbols.			

20 Electrochemistry

KNOWLEDGE FOCUS

In this chapter you will answer questions on:

- redox reactions revisited
- electrolysis
- quantitative electrolysis
- electrode potentials
- combining half-cells
- using E values
- more about electrolysis.

EXAM SKILLS FOCUS

In this chapter you will:

- practise evaluating your progress and identifying areas where more work is needed.

Completing the Self-assessment checklists at the end of each chapter is essential so that you can evaluate your progress. It is very important that you do this based on evidence. You should not tick a 'Confident to move on' box just because the topic makes sense when you read through your notes. Reading notes is a passive process that simply tests your familiarity with the basic ideas. In the exam, you will be tested on your ability to apply understanding and skills, so you need to ensure your revision is active and focused on answering questions. Only when you can confidently answer questions on a topic will you be ready to move on. As you work your way through the Exam skills questions in this chapter, compare your answers to those provided in order to evaluate your progress and identify any areas where more revision is required. The Exam skills chapter at the back of this book will show you how to evaluate your progress and make sure your revision is the most effective it can be.

20.1 Redox reactions revisited

1   In the following redox reactions:

   a $O_2(g) + 4Mn^{2+}(aq) + 8OH^-(aq) + 2H_2O(l) \rightarrow 4Mn(OH)_3(s)$

   b $5V^{2+}(aq) + 3MnO_4^-(aq) + 3H_2O(l) \rightarrow 5VO_3^-(aq) + 3Mn^{2+}(aq) + 6H^+(aq)$

     i Identify the element undergoing oxidation and reduction by referring to oxidation number changes.

     ii Identify the oxidising and reducing agents, explaining your answer.

2   Balance the following chemical reactions by considering oxidation number changes:

   a $....H_2O(l) + ...H_3AsO_3(aq) + ...I_3^-(aq) \rightarrow ....I^-(aq) + ...H_3AsO_4(aq) + ...H^+(aq)$

   b $....C_6H_6(l) + ...H_2O_2(aq) \rightarrow ....CO_2(g) + ...H_2O(l)$

≪ RECALL AND CONNECT 1 ≪

This chapter builds on Chapter 7 Redox reactions, so it is important to be familiar with some of the key ideas from that chapter. Can you recall the definitions for the following key terms?

a oxidation

b reduction

c redox reaction

d half-equation

e oxidising agent

f reducing agent

g disproportionation

20.2 Electrolysis

1   Draw a labelled diagram of an electrolytic cell. Label the following: positive electrode (anode), negative electrode (cathode), electrodes, electrolyte, direct current power supply.

2   Write half-equations for the reactions occurring at the anode and cathode during electrolysis of the following electrolytes, followed by the overall equation for electrolysis. You do not need to include state symbols.

   a molten zinc iodide

   b molten aluminium oxide

   c molten iron(III) sulfide

   d molten titanium(IV) chloride

UNDERSTAND THESE TERMS

- electrolysis
- electrolyte
- electrode
- cathode
- anode

20.3 Quantitative electrolysis

1 a Which equations relate the following variables?

   i The Faraday constant, F, the charge on the electron, e, and the Avogadro constant, L.

   ii The charge, Q, the current passed, I, and the time the current passes, t.

   b Calculate the mass of magnesium deposited at the cathode when molten magnesium chloride is electrolysed for 4.5h using a current of 2A. ($F = 96\,500\,C\,mol^{-1}$)

   c Calculate the volume of H_2 and O_2 formed, in cm^3, when a current of 0.5A passes through a solution of dilute sulfuric acid for 45 minutes. ($F = 96\,500\,C\,mol^{-1}$; 1 mole of gas occupies $24\,dm^3$ at r.t.p.)

2 A value for the Avogadro constant can be determined by passing a known current for a known time period through an electrolytic cell containing copper sulfate, and weighing the mass of copper lost from the anode.

   a Sketch a diagram of the apparatus used. Label the following: dc power supply, + and – terminals, copper anode, copper cathode, aqueous copper sulfate, variable resistor, ammeter. [4]

   b Write a half-equation to show the reaction occurring at the anode. [1]

   The table shows the results obtained in one experiment.

current passed	0.25A
time current was passed	38.0min
initial mass of copper anode	49.771g
final mass of copper anode	49.579g

   c Using these data, calculate a value for the Avogadro constant, L, to three significant figures. (The charge on an electron, e, is $1.60 \times 10^{-19}\,C$). [5]

   [Total: 10]

≪ RECALL AND CONNECT 2 ≪

Write equations to show the disproportionation reactions of:

a chlorine and water

b chlorine with cold sodium hydroxide

c chloride and hot sodium hydroxide.

20.4 Electrode potentials

1   Some electrode potentials are shown in the table.

Half-cell reaction	Electrode potential / V
$0.5I_2(aq) + e^- \rightarrow I^-(aq)$	+0.54
$Ba^{2+}(aq) + 2e^- \rightarrow Ba(s)$	−2.90
$0.5F_2(g) + e^- \rightarrow F^-(aq)$	+2.87
$Co^{3+}(aq) + e^- \rightarrow Co^{2+}(aq)$	+1.92
$Fe^{3+}(aq) + e^- \rightarrow Fe^{2+}(aq)$	+0.77
$K^+(aq) + e^- \rightarrow K(s)$	−2.93
$Cr^{3+}(aq) + e^- \rightarrow Cr^{2+}(aq)$	−0.41

   a   Which species is the most powerful oxidising agent? Explain your answer.
   b   Which species if the most powerful reducing agent? Explain your answer.
   c   Identify all the species capable of oxidising iodide ions to iodine.
   d   Identify all the species capable of reducing iron(III) to iron(II).

2   a   Sketch a diagram of the standard hydrogen electrode. Label the following:
        platinum wire, platinum electrode, glass jacket, supply of H_2, HCl(aq).   [3]
   b   State the conditions used with the standard hydrogen electrode.   [3]

[Total: 6]

20.5 Combining half-cells

1   a   Draw a labelled diagram of the apparatus that would be used to measure
        the standard electrode potential of a F_2 / F^- half-cell. Include any relevant
        conditions.

   b   The standard electrode potential of the F_2 / F^- half-cell is +2.87 V.
        Add an arrow to your diagram to show the direction of electron flow.
   c   Write an equation, including state symbols, to show the reaction occurring
        at the negative electrode in this cell.
   d   Explain the function of the salt bridge.

20.6 Using $E^\ominus$ values

1 a Draw a labelled diagram to show the electrochemical cell created when a half-cell containing vanadium and aqueous vanadium(II) sulfate is connected to a half-cell containing aqueous potassium iodide and solid iodine. The relevant electrode potentials are shown.

$$0.5I_2(s) + e^- \rightarrow I^-(aq) \qquad E^\ominus = +0.54\,V$$
$$V^{2+}(aq) + 2e^- \rightarrow V(s) \qquad E^\ominus = -1.20\,V$$

b Show the direction of electron flow with an arrow.

c Write the equation for the feasible reaction that would occur in this cell.

d Calculate the standard cell potential for this cell.

e How would the $E^\ominus_{cell}$ value change if $[V^{2+}(aq)]$ was increased? Explain your answer.

> **UNDERSTAND THESE TERMS**
> - standard cell potentials
> - feasible

2 The table shows some standard electrode potentials.

Use the data in the table to answer the questions.

Half-cell reaction	$E^\ominus$/ V
$Cu^+(aq) + e^- \rightarrow Cu(s)$	+0.52
$Fe^{3+}(aq) + e^- \rightarrow Fe^{2+}(aq)$	+0.77
$Cr^{3+}(aq) + 3e^- \rightarrow Cr(s)$	−0.74
$0.5Cl_2(g) + e^- \rightarrow Cl^-(aq)$	+1.36
$Cu^{2+}(aq) + e^- \rightarrow Cu^+(aq)$	+0.15
$Cr_2O_7^{2-}(aq) + 14H^+(aq) + 6e^- \rightarrow 2Cr^{3+}(aq) + 7H_2O(l)$	+1.36
$Al^{3+}(aq) + 3e^- \rightarrow Al(s)$	−1.66
$0.5Br_2(l) + e^- \rightarrow Br^-(aq)$	+1.09
$Li^+(aq) + e^- \rightarrow Li(s)$	−3.04
$Co^{3+}(aq) + e^- \rightarrow Co^{2+}(aq)$	+1.92

a Identify the weakest oxidising agent in the table, explaining your answer.

b Identify the species that can reduce Cr^{3+} ions to Cr but cannot reduce Li^+ ions to Li.

c Identify the species that can oxidise Cu to Cu^+ but cannot oxidise Br^- to Br_2.

d Explain why solutions containing Cu^+ ions are unstable and disproportionate.

e Identify the half-cell that, when combined with the Cl_2/Cl^- half-cell, produces a voltage of +0.56 V.

f Can chromium(III) ions reduce bromine? Explain your answer.

3 The Ni/Ni^{2+} half-cell has a standard electrode potential of –0.26 V, while the Mn^{2+}/MnO_4^- half-cell has a standard electrode potential of +1.51 V.

    a Calculate the electrode potential of the Ni/Ni^{2+} half-cell when [Ni^{2+}] is 0.05 mol dm^{-3}.

    b Calculate the electrode potential of the Mn^{2+}/MnO_4^- half-cell when [MnO_4^-] is 5×10^{-2} mol dm^{-3} and [Mn^{2+}] is 5×10^{-5} mol dm^{-3}.

    c How would the cell potential produced when these two half-cells are connected compare to the standard cell potential?

4 Under certain conditions, potassium manganate(VI) can oxidise chloride ions. The relevant standard electrode potentials are shown:

$$0.5Cl_2(aq) + e^- \rightarrow Cl^-(aq) \qquad\qquad E^\ominus = +1.36\,V$$

$$MnO_4^-(aq) + 8H^+(aq) + 5e^- \rightarrow Mn^{2+}(aq) + 4H_2O(l) \quad E^\ominus = +1.52\,V$$

    a Write an equation for the feasible reaction that occurs when the MnO_4^-/Mn^{2+} half-cell is connected to the Cl_2/Cl^- half-cell. [1]

    b Calculate the standard cell potential for this reaction. [1]

    c Suggest why no reaction occurs when these standard half-cells are combined. [1]

    d In an experiment, the amount of iron(II) in an iron tablet was determined by titration against potassium manganate(VI). The reaction mixture was acidified using hydrochloric acid. In a typical titration, [$Cl_2(aq)$] was 1.2×10^{-5} mol dm^{-3} and [$Cl^-(aq)$] was 0.3 mol dm^{-3}.

        i Calculate the electrode potential for the Cl_2/Cl^- half-cell in the titration. [2]

        ii Explain why this redox titration would be hazardous and suggest how the hazard can be avoided. [3]

[Total: 8]

20.7 More about electrolysis

1 **a** A dilute aqueous solution of magnesium sulfate is electrolysed. Predict the product formed:

        i at the negative electrode and write a half-equation to show its formation.

        ii at the positive electrode and write a half-equation to show its formation.

    b Write half-equations for the reactions occurring at the anode and cathode when the following substances are electrolysed.

        i Molten lithium chloride.

        ii Very dilute potassium bromide, KBr(aq). Explain your choice of products by referring to standard electrode potentials.

        iii Concentrated sodium chloride solution. Explain your choice of products by referring to standard electrode potentials.

UNDERSTAND THIS TERM
• discharged

REFLECTION

Mnemonics are useful tools to help remember key facts and trends. OILRIG (Oxidation Is Loss, Reduction Is Gain) is probably the best-known mnemonic in chemistry. Another useful redox mnemonic is OATRAG: Oxidising Agents Take, Reducing Agents Give. Try to come up with a mnemonic to help you remember some of the important facts and trends related to electrochemical cells, such as the order of increasing ease of ion discharge in electrolysis: SO_4^{2-}, NO_3^-, Cl^-, OH^-, Br^-, I^-.

SELF-ASSESSMENT CHECKLIST

Let's revisit the Knowledge focus and Exam skills focus for this chapter.

Decide how confident you are with each statement.

Now I can:	Show it	Needs more work	Almost there	Confident to move on
predict the identity of the substance liberated during electrolysis from the state of electrolyte (molten or aqueous)	Create a table showing the products formed at the anode and cathode from a range of electrolytes in molten and aqueous states.			
predict the identity of the substance liberated during electrolysis from the position of the ions (in the electrolyte) in the redox series (electrode potential)	Create a table showing the products formed at the anode and cathode from a range of electrolytes containing metals from the reactivity series and the following ions: SO_4^{2-}, NO_3^-, Cl^-, Br^-, I^- and OH^-.			
predict the identity of the substance liberated during electrolysis from the concentration of the ions in the electrolyte	Create a table showing the products formed at the anode and cathode from a range of electrolytes having different concentrations of ions.			
state and apply the relationship $F = Le$ between the Faraday constant, F, the Avogadro constant, L, and the charge on the electron, e	Write this equation from memory and explain what each of its terms means.			

CONTINUED

Now I can:	Show it	Needs more work	Almost there	Confident to move on
calculate the quantity of charge passed during electrolysis using $Q = It$	Devise two cells that would produce solid and gaseous products and, for each one, calculate how long a current of 1 A would need to flow for it to discharge 1 g of product.			
calculate the mass and/or volume of substance liberated during electrolysis				
describe the determination of a value of the Avogadro constant by an electrolytic method	Draw the apparatus used and describe step-by-step how the data obtained from it is used to calculate the Avogadro constant.			
define the term *standard electrode (reduction) potential*	Add this definition to a flashcard and practise writing it out from memory.			
define the term *standard cell potential*	Add this definition to a flashcard and practise writing it out from memory.			
describe the standard hydrogen electrode	Draw a labelled diagram of the standard hydrogen electrode, including conditions.			
describe the methods used to measure the standard electrode potentials of metals or non-metals in contact with their ions in aqueous solution	Draw a labelled diagram to show a half-cell containing a metal/non-metal in contact with their ions connected to the standard hydrogen electrode.			
describe the methods used to measure the standard electrode potentials of ions of the same element in different oxidation states	Draw a labelled diagram to show a mixed ion half-cell connected to the standard hydrogen electrode.			
calculate a standard cell potential by combining two standard electrode potentials	Write the equation used to calculate standard cell potentials and use it to calculate standard cell potentials for different half-cells from the electrochemical series.			

CONTINUED

Now I can:	Show it	Needs more work	Almost there	Confident to move on
use standard cell potential to deduce the polarity of each electrode and hence explain/ deduce the direction of electron flow in the external circuit of a simple cell	Draw a diagram of a cell constructed from two half-cells and label the polarity of each electrode, marking the electron flow direction with an arrow.			
use standard cell potential to predict the feasibility of a reaction	Calculate some standard cell potential values from common half-cells and use them to state which reactions are feasible.			
deduce from standard electrode potential values the relative reactivity of elements, compounds and ions as oxidising agents or reducing agents	Write out a typical reactivity series (such as the one you learned for IGCSE chemistry) and identify the strongest oxidising and reducing agents.			
construct redox equations using the relevant half-equations	Select a halogen disproportionation reaction equation and split it into two half-equations.			
qualitatively predict how the value of an electrode potential varies with the concentration of the aqueous ion	Calculate a standard electrode potential for two metal-metal ion half cells, then predict how the value would change when the metal ion concentration varies.			
use the Nernst equation $E = E^{\ominus} + \dfrac{0.059}{z} \log_{10} \dfrac{[\text{oxidised species}]}{[\text{reduced species}]}$ to quantitatively predict how the value of an electrode potential varies with the concentration of the aqueous ions	Calculate the standard cell potential from a given pair of standard electrode potentials, then use the Nernst equation to calculate a new cell potential when the concentration of aqueous ions are changed by a factor of 10.			

CONTINUED

Now I can:	Show it	Needs more work	Almost there	Confident to move on
evaluate my progress and identify areas where more work is needed	Work out how many marks you gained for the questions in this chapter and use your scores to complete the Self-assessment checklist.			

21 Further aspects of equilibria

Equilibrium constants are mathematical relationships that summarise a range of chemistry concepts. Practising the calculations themselves is helpful but, to get a full understanding, it is essential to link the mathematical relationships with the chemistry concepts. In this chapter you will practise linking mathematical relationships with chemistry concepts through a range of Knowledge recall and Exam skills questions.

21.1 Conjugate acids and conjugate bases

1 Which theory of acids and bases defines acidity in terms of donation of protons?

2 Give the expression for the ionic product of water, K_w.

3 Consider the equation below. Label each species as acid/base and identify the conjugate pairs.

$$HNO_3 + H_2O \rightleftharpoons H_3O^+ + NO_3^-$$ **[Total: 2]**

4 The ionic product of water, K_w, at 50 °C is 5.476×10^{-14}.

Calculate a value for the concentration of hydrogen ions, and hence pH, at this temperature. Show your working. **[Total: 2]**

> **≪ RECALL AND CONNECT 1 ≪**
>
> What element is present in all Brønsted–Lowry acids?

21.2 pH calculations

1 State the expression for calculating pH.

2 Calculate the pH of a solution with a H^+ ion concentration of $5.21 \times 10^{-4}\,mol\,dm^{-3}$. **[Total: 1]**

3 Calculate the pH of a solution of KOH of concentration $0.045\,mol\,dm^{-3}$. $K_w = 1.00 \times 10^{-14}\,mol^2\,dm^{-6}$ (at 298 K) **[Total: 3]**

21.3 Weak acids: using the acid dissociation constant, K_a

1 State the expression for the acid dissociation constant for a generic acid, HA, and the rearranged expression that can be used to calculate the pH of a pure weak acid.

2 a State the expression for calculating pK_a. [1]

   b Give the reason why pK_a values are often used instead of K_a values to compare the strength of weak acids. [1]

   [Total: 2]

3 a State the expression for K_a for ethanoic acid. [2]

   b Calculate the pH of $0.110\,mol\,dm^{-3}$ ethanoic acid, CH_3COOH. ($K_a = 1.74 \times 10^{-5}\,mol\,dm^{-3}$) [2]

   [Total: 4]

21.4 Buffer solutions

1   State the two types of mixtures that can make up a buffer solution.

2   Calculate the pH of a buffer solution made from $0.0450\,mol\,dm^{-3}$ methanoic acid and $0.110\,mol\,dm^{-3}$ sodium methanoate. (K_a of methanoic acid $= 1.60 \times 10^{-4}\,mol\,dm^{-3}$)   **[Total: 2]**

3   Calculate the number of moles of sodium ethanoate that must be added to $1.00\,dm^3$ of $0.100\,mol\,dm^{-3}$ ethanoic acid to produce a buffer solution of pH 4.96. (K_a of ethanoic acid $= 1.74 \times 10^{-5}\,mol\,dm^{-3}$)   **[Total: 3]**

4   Explain how a buffer solution containing ethanoic acid and sodium ethanoate is able to resist a pH change when a small amount of H^+ is added to it.   **[Total: 5]**

21.5 Equilibrium and solubility

1   State the general expression for the solubility product of an ionic substance containing x moles of cations (C^+) and y moles of anions (A^-).

2   Write equilibrium expressions for the solubility product of $Al(OH)_3$ and state its units.   **[Total: 3]**

3   Cobalt sulfide, CoS, has a solubility product $2.0 \times 10^{-26}\,mol^2\,dm^{-6}$. Calculate the solubility in $mol\,dm^{-3}$ of cobalt sulfide.   **[Total: 3]**

> ### « RECALL AND CONNECT 2 «
> What does the small 'p' in front of a symbol related to acids and bases mean?

21.6 Partition coefficients

1   How is the partition coefficient K_{pc} related to the polarity of the substances in the mixture?

2   A solution of butanedioic acid (BDA) in ether (an organic solvent) contains $0.030\,mol$ of BDA in $20\,cm^3$ of ether. This solution is shaken with $50\,cm^3$ of water in a separating funnel. After shaking, the aqueous layer contained $0.028\,mol$.

   a   Calculate the concentration of BDA in the water layer and the concentration of BDA in the ether layer after shaking.   [3]

   b   Determine the value of the partition coefficient, K_{pc}, and comment on the significance of the constant.   [2]

   [Total: 5]

> ### UNDERSTAND THESE TERMS
> - buffer solution
> - solubility product, K_{sp}
> - common ion effect
> - partition coefficient, K_{pc}

The calculations in this chapter may have many steps depending on how the information is presented in the question; however, the concepts are all related by the equilibrium concept. Can you see how the constants used here are related to K_c, the equilibrium constant, discussed in Chapter 8?

SELF-ASSESSMENT CHECKLIST

Let's revisit the Knowledge focus and Exam skills focus for this chapter.

Decide how confident you are with each statement.

Now I can:	Show it	Needs more work	Almost there	Confident to move on
define and use the terms *conjugate acid* and *conjugate base*	Define the terms *conjugate acid* and *conjugate base* and give examples of pairings.			
define mathematically the terms pH, K_a, pK_a and K_w, and use them in calculations	Define mathematically the terms pH, K_a, pK_a and K_w. Illustrate how they can be used in calculations using bullet points.			
calculate [H⁺(aq)] and pH values for strong acids, strong alkalis and weak acids	Write a flashcard showing how to calculate [H⁺] and pH for strong acids, strong alkalis and weak acids.			
define a buffer solution and explain how a buffer solution can be made	Define a buffer solution and write a series of bullet points to explain how a buffer solution can be made.			
explain how buffer solutions control pH, using chemical equations in these explanations	Explain how buffer solutions control pH when small amounts of acid or alkali are added. Illustrate your explanations with equations using HX as the formula of the weak acid in the buffer solution.			
describe and explain the uses of buffer solutions, including the role of HCO_3^- in controlling pH in the blood	Make a flash card that describes and explains the uses of buffer solutions, including the role of HCO_3^- in controlling pH in the blood.			

CONTINUED

Now I can:	Show it	Needs more work	Almost there	Confident to move on
calculate the pH of buffer solutions, given appropriate data	Attempt a question on calculating the pH of a buffer solution.			
describe and use the term solubility product, K_{sp}	Define the term solubility product, K_{sp}, and give the expression used in calculations.			
write an expression for K_{sp}				
calculate K_{sp} from concentrations and vice versa	A saturated solution of magnesium fluoride, MgF_2, has a solubility of $1.22 \times 10^{-3}\,mol\,dm^{-3}$. Prove that the solubility product K_{sp} is $7.26 \times 10^{-9}\,mol^3\,dm^{-9}$.			
describe and use the common ion effect to explain the different solubility of a compound in a solution containing a common ion	Describe and use the common ion effect to explain the different solubility of a compound in a solution containing a common ion.			
perform calculations using K_{sp} values and concentration of a common ion	The solubility of barium sulfate, $BaSO_4$, in water is $1.0 \times 10^{-5}\,mol\,dm^{-3}$ and the solubility of barium sulfate in $0.100\,mol\,dm^{-3}$ sulfuric acid, H_2SO_4, is only $1.0 \times 10^{-9}\,mol\,dm^{-3}$. Use calculations to explain these solubilities.			
state what is meant by the term *partition coefficient*, K_{pc}	Define the term *partition coefficient*, K_{pc}.			
calculate and use a partition coefficient for a system in which the solute is in the same physical state in the two solvents	A substance X has a concentration of $0.15\,mol\,dm^{-3}$ in a water layer and of $0.05\,mol\,dm^{-3}$ in an organic layer. Calculate the partition coefficient, K_{pc}.			

CONTINUED

Now I can:	Show it	Needs more work	Almost there	Confident to move on
understand the factors affecting the numerical value of a partition coefficient in terms of the polarities of the solute and the solvents used	Write some bullet points summarising the factors affecting the numerical value of a partition coefficient.			
understand how to link mathematical relationships with chemistry concepts	Draw a mind map showing how the various equilibrium constants in this chapter are related.			

Exam practice 5

This section contains past paper questions from previous Cambridge exams which draw together your knowledge on a range of topics that you have covered up to this point. These questions give you the opportunity to test your knowledge and understanding. Additional past paper practice questions can be found in the accompanying digital material.

The following question has an example student response and commentary provided. Work through the question first, then compare your answer to the sample response and commentary. Are your answers different to the sample responses? How are they different?

1 a Define the term *standard cell potential*. [2]

b i Draw a fully labelled diagram of the experimental set-up you could use to measure the standard electrode potential of the $Pb^{2+}(aq)/Pb(s)$ electrode. Include the necessary chemicals. [4]

ii The $E^{\ominus}$ for a $Pb^{2+}(aq)/Pb(s)$ electrode is -0.13 V.

Suggest how the E for this electrode would differ from its $E^{\ominus}$ value if the concentration of $Pb^{2+}(aq)$ ions is reduced. Indicate this by placing a tick (✓) in the appropriate box in the table.

more negative	no change	less negative

Explain your answer. [2]

c Car batteries are made up of rechargeable lead-acid cells. Each cell consists of a negative electrode made of Pb metal and a positive electrode made of PbO_2. The electrolyte is $H_2SO_4(aq)$.

When a lead-acid cell is in use, Pb^{2+} ions are precipitated out as $PbSO_4(s)$ at the negative electrode.

$$Pb(s) + SO_4^{2-}(aq) \rightarrow PbSO_4(s) + 2e^-$$

i Calculate the mass of Pb that is converted to $PbSO_4$ when a current of 0.40 A is delivered by the cell for 80 minutes. [2]

ii Complete the half-equation for the reaction taking place at the positive electrode.

$PbO_2(s) + SO_4^{2-}(aq) +$ .... + ... $\rightarrow PbSO_4(s) +$ .... [1]

[Total: 11]

Cambridge International AS & A Level Chemistry (9701) Paper 41 Q3a–c November 2017

Example student response	Commentary
a The voltage of a half-cell when connected to the standard hydrogen electrode measured at 298K and 1 atm.	Unfortunately, the student has given the definition for the standard electrode potential. *This answer is awarded 0 out of 2 marks.*
b i 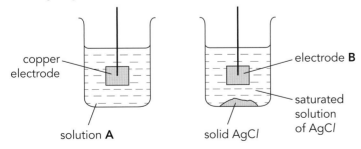	This is an accurate labelled sketch of the required cell showing the voltmeter, salt bridge, electrodes, electrolytes and hydrogen delivery system. *This answer is awarded 4 out of 4 marks.*
ii More negative; because the equilibrium for the reaction $Pb^{2+} + 2e^- \rightarrow Pb$ shifts to the left.	This is the correct answer. *This answer is awarded 2 out of 2 marks.*
c i Charge = 80 × 60 × 0.4 = 1920 C Charge needed for 207.2 g Pb = 193 000 C Mass of lead = (1920/193 000) × 207.2 = 2.06 g	This is the correct approach and solution. *This answer is awarded 2 out of 2 marks.*
ii $PbO_2(s) + SO_4^{2-}(aq) + 4H^+ + 2e^- \rightarrow PbSO_4(s) + 2H_2O$	This is the correctly balanced redox equation. *This answer is awarded 1 out of 1 mark.*

Now you have read the commentary to the previous question, here is a similar question which you should attempt. Use the information from the previous response and commentary to guide you as you answer.

2 a The diagram below shows an incomplete experimental set-up needed to measure the E_{cell} of a cell composed of the standard Cu^{2+}/Cu electrode and an Ag^+/Ag electrode.

copper electrode — solution **A**

electrode **B**

solid AgCl — saturated solution of AgCl

   i   State the chemical composition of

      solution **A**: .... [1]

      electrode **B**: .... [1]

   ii Complete the diagram to show the whole experimental set-up. [2]

b The above cell is not under standard conditions, because the $[Ag^+]$ in a saturated solution of AgCl is much less than 1.0 mol dm^{-3}. The $E_{electrode}$ is related to $[Ag^+]$ by the following equation.

  equation 1 $\qquad\qquad E_{electrode} = E^{\ominus}_{electrode} + 0.06 \log[Ag^+]$

  In the above experiment, the E_{cell} was measured at +0.17V.

   i   Calculate the value of $E_{electrode}$ for the Ag^+/Ag electrode in this experiment. [1]

   ii Use equation 1 to calculate $[Ag^+]$ in the saturated solution. [1]

c i   Write an expression for K_{sp} of silver sulfate, Ag_2SO_4, including units. [2]

  Using a similar experimental set-up to that illustrated opposite, it is found that $[Ag^+]$ in a saturated solution of Ag_2SO_4 is 1.6×10^{-2} mol dm^{-3}.

   ii Calculate the value of K_{sp} of silver sulfate. [1]

d Describe how the colours of the silver halides, and their relative solubilities in $NH_3(aq)$, can be used to distinguish between solutions of the halide ions Cl^-, Br^- and I^-. [4]

e Describe and explain the trend in the solubilities of the sulfates of the elements in Group II. [4]

[Total: 17]

Cambridge International AS & A Level Chemistry (9701) Paper 42 Q2 November 2012

The following question has an example student response and commentary provided. Work through the question first, then compare your answer to the sample response and commentary. Are your answers different to the sample responses? What does this tell you about your understanding of the topic?

3 Iodine is found naturally in compounds in many different oxidation states.

   Iodide ions, I^-, react with acidified $H_2O_2(aq)$ to form iodine, I_2, and water.

   This reaction mixture is shaken with cyclohexane, C_6H_{12}, to extract the I_2.

   Cyclohexane is immiscible with water.

  a Identify the role of $H_2O_2(aq)$ in its reaction with I^- ions in acidic conditions.

     Write an ionic equation for the reaction. [2]

b 15.0 cm³ of C_6H_{12} is shaken with 20.0 cm³ of an aqueous solution containing I_2 until no further change is seen.

It is found that 0.390 g of I_2 is extracted into the C_6H_{12}.

The partition coefficient of I_2 between C_6H_{12} and water, K_{pc}, is 93.8.

Calculate the mass of I_2 that remains in the aqueous layer.

Show your working. [2]

c Suggest how the value of K_{pc} of I_2 between hexan-2-one, $CH_3(CH_2)_3COCH_3$, and water compares to the value given in **a ii**.

Explain your answer. [2]

[Total: 6]

Adapted from Cambridge International AS & A Level Chemistry (9701)
Paper 42 Q1a March 2022

Example student response	Commentary
a H_2O_2 is an oxidising agent in the reaction.	The student has correctly identified the role of the H_2O_2 in the reaction; however, they have failed to give the equation. *This answer is awarded 1 out of 2 marks.*
b $K_{pc} = [I_2(cyclohexane)]/[I_2(aq)]$ $93.8 = (0.390/15)/(X/20)$ $93.9 = 0.026/(X/20)$ $X/20 = 0.026/93.9$ $X/20 = 2.77 \times 10^{-4}$ $X = 5.53 \times 10^{-3}$ g	The student has taken a systematic approach to the calculation. They have used g cm⁻³ as the concentration, there is no need to go to the effort of calculating mol dm⁻³ for this constant as it is effectively a ratio, so as long as the units match it does not matter that they are not the standard units of concentration. Each step in the working is well set out. *This answer is awarded 2 out of 2 marks.*
c Hexan-2-one is a ketone and cyclohexane is an alkane. Hexan-2-one has a C=O bond, cyclohexane only contains C-C and C-H bonds, so is non-polar. Iodine is non-polar so iodine would be more soluble in cyclohexane.	The student includes rather too much information in their answer, the description of the bonding in hexan-2-one and cyclohexane is not needed and uses up time in an exam situation. The student has not written a statement comparing the polarity of cyclohexane and hexan-2-one and has not discussed how K_{pc} will be affected by the change in solvent. *This answer is awarded 0 out of 2 marks.*

4 Now that you have read the sample response, rewrite your answer to any part of question **3** where you did not score highly. Use the commentary as a guide.

22 Reaction kinetics

Questions that ask you to analyse experimental data and then present a conclusion will often require you to justify your conclusion. This usually means explaining exactly how you have used the data to reach your conclusion. If the question asks you to give an answer and justify it, you must provide the explanation; otherwise, you will lose some marks. You must also ensure that the justification you provide is clear and logically presented; otherwise, the examiner will not be able to follow it. 'Justify' can also be used in a similar way to the phrase 'Show your working' in order to limit the number of marks that could be gained by simply guessing.

| Justify | support a case with evidence/argument |

22.1 Factors affecting reaction rate

Refresh your understanding of the factors affecting reaction rate by referring
to the questions in Chapter 9 Rates of reaction.

22.2 Rate of reaction

Refresh your understanding of the rate of reaction by referring to the questions
in Chapter 9 Rates of reaction.

22.3 Rate equations

≪ RECALL AND CONNECT 1 ≪

What are the central ideas behind collision theory and how does it explain
the effect of temperature on reaction rates?

1   Sucrose ($C_{12}H_{22}O_{11}$), commonly called table sugar, undergoes hydrolysis in the
presence of hydrochloric acid to produce glucose and fructose, both of which
have the molecular formula $C_6H_{12}O_6$. The reaction is known to be first order
with respect to both sucrose and hydrochloric acid. The chemical equation
for the reaction may be written as:

$$C_{12}H_{22}O_{11}(aq) + H_2O(l) \rightarrow 2C_6H_{12}O_6(aq)$$

**UNDERSTAND
THESE TERMS**

- rate constant
- rate equation
- order of reaction

a   What is meant by '*first order with respect to both sucrose and hydrochloric acid*'?
b   Write the rate equation for hydrolysis of sucrose.
c   What is the overall order for the reaction?
d   Why does HCl appear in the rate equation, but not in the chemical equation?

Some initial rate data for the hydrolysis reaction is shown in the table.

Experiment	[$C_{12}H_{22}O_{11}$(aq)] / mol dm^{-3}	[HCl(aq)] / mol dm^{-3}	Initial rate / mol dm^{-3} s^{-1}
1	0.05	0.050	0.06
2	0.10	0.050	
3	0.05	0.125	
4	0.20	0.200	

e   What is meant by the initial rate of a reaction and how can it be determined?
f   Copy and complete the table to show the initial rates in experiments 2, 3, and 4.
g   Calculate a value for the rate constant, k, and state its units.

2   The reaction between ozone and unburnt hydrocarbons produces aldehydes, which are respiratory irritants and one of the main components of photochemical smog. The equation for ozone reacting with ethene is shown below.

$$2C_2H_4(g) + 2O_3(g) \rightarrow 4CH_2O(g) + O_2(g)$$

    a   Show, using oxidation numbers, that the reaction between ozone and ethene is a redox reaction.   [2]

    b   In an experiment to investigate the kinetics of this reaction, it was found that the reaction rate was a quarter of its initial value when the concentration of both ozone and ethene were halved.

         i   Determine the orders of reaction with respect to ozone and ethene. Justify your answer.   [2]

        ii   Write the rate equation for the reaction.   [1]

    c   It was found experimentally that the initial rate of reaction was $4.21 \times 10^{-13}\,\text{mol}\,\text{dm}^{-3}\,\text{s}^{-1}$ when the concentration of ozone was $0.29 \times 10^{-7}\,\text{mol}\,\text{dm}^{-3}$ and that of ethene was $0.77 \times 10^{-8}\,\text{mol}\,\text{dm}^{-3}$. Calculate the value for the rate constant and state its units.   [3]

                                                      [Total: 8]

3   In the 'vanishing cross' experiment, sodium thiosulfate and hydrochloric acid react to produce a precipitate of sulfur that gradually causes the solution to become opaque:

$$Na_2S_2O_3(aq) + 2HCl(aq) \rightarrow 2NaCl(aq) + S(s) + SO_2(aq) + H_2O(l)$$

The time taken for a cross drawn on a piece of paper and placed beneath the reaction flask to disappear is used as a measure of rate (see Figure 22.1).

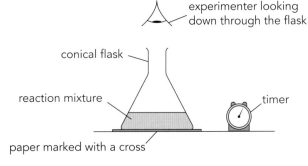

Figure 22.1

Use these data to answer the following questions.

Experiment	Volume of $Na_2S_2O_3$ / cm^3	Volume of HCl / cm^3	Volume of distilled water / cm^3	Time for cross to vanish / s
1	50	25	25	7.7
2	40	25	35	9.6
3	30	25	45	12.5
4	20	25	55	19.4
5	10	25	65	38.4
6	10	30	60	31.9
7	10	35	55	27.6
8	10	40	50	23.8
9	10	45	45	21.2
10	10	50	40	19.3

a Give two reasons why the total volume in each experiment was kept constant by the addition of distilled water. [2]

b Suggest another variable that must be kept constant during the experiment. [1]

c Using these data, determine the orders of reaction with respect to sodium thiosulfate and hydrochloric acid. Justify your choices. [2]

d Write the rate equation for the reaction. [1]

e $1/t$ can be used as a measure of rate in the experiment, where t is the time taken for the cross to vanish. Explain the reason for this. [1]

f The initial concentrations of sodium thiosulfate and hydrochloric acid used were $0.25 \, mol \, dm^{-3}$ and $1.0 \, mol \, dm^{-3}$, respectively.

   i Calculate the concentrations of sodium thiosulfate and hydrochloric acid in experiment 5. [2]

   ii Using $1/t$ as the rate, determine the value of the rate constant for experiment 5. Give its units. [2]

[Total: 11]

22.4 Which order of reaction?

1 a In which two situations is the rate of reaction equal to the rate constant?

   b Sketch concentration versus time graphs for zero order, first order and second order reactions.

   c Sketch rate versus concentration graphs for zero order, first order and second order reactions.

> **UNDERSTAND THIS TERM**
> - half-life, $t_{1/2}$

2 Calcium reacts with propanoic acid as shown by the following equation:

$$Ca(s) + CH_3CH_2COOH(aq) \rightarrow (CH_3CH_2COO)_2Ca(aq) + H_2(g)$$

a Briefly outline an experiment to show the reaction is first order with respect to propanoic acid using a titration approach.

b Explain, with the aid of sketch graphs, how the half-lives of a reactant vary for zero order, first order and second order reactions.

3 Dinitrogen pentoxide decomposes as shown below.

$$N_2O_5(g) \rightarrow 2NO_2(g) + 0.5O_2(g)$$

To deduce the rate equation for this reaction, an experiment was carried out using different initial concentrations of N_2O_5. The experimental data is shown in the table.

Time / s	$[N_2O_5] \times 10^{-3}$ / mol dm^{-3}
0	6.67
30	5.42
66	4.23
96	3.43
132	2.68
198	1.70
312	0.77
402	0.42
528	0.17

a Plot a concentration–time graph using the data in the table. [3]

b Use your graph to determine three successive half-lives for this reaction and calculate the mean half-life. Show your working on the graph. [2]

c Write the rate equation for the decomposition of N_2O_5. [1]

d Calculate a value for k using your answer to part **b** and state its units. [2]

e The experiment was repeated using double the initial concentration of N_2O_5. State and explain what effect this would have on the half-life of the reaction. [2]

[Total: 10]

22.5 Calculations involving the rate constant, k

1 Use the initial rate data in the table to answer the questions.

Experiment	[A] / mol dm⁻³	[B] / mol dm⁻³	[C] / mol dm⁻³	Initial rate / mol dm⁻³ s⁻¹
1	0.125	0.125	0.0125	1.88×10^{-3}
2	0.125	0.375	0.0125	5.63×10^{-3}
3	0.625	0.125	0.0125	9.38×10^{-3}
4	0.125	0.125	0.1250	1.88×10^{-2}
5	0.625	0.625	0.1250	4.69×10^{-1}

   a Determine the orders with respect to reactants **A**, **B** and **C**.
   b Write the rate equation for the reaction.
   c Determine the value of the rate constant and state its units.

2 The kinetics of the reaction between iodate(V) ions and iodide was studied using the initial rates method. The equation for the reaction is shown below.

$$IO_3^-(aq) + 6H^+(aq) + 5I^-(aq) \rightarrow 3I_2(aq) + 3H_2O(l)$$

The experimental data is shown in the table.

Experiment	[I⁻(aq)] / mol dm⁻³	[H⁺(aq)] / mol dm⁻³	[IO₃⁻(aq)] / mol dm⁻³	Initial rate / 10^{-3} mol dm⁻³ s⁻¹
1	0.075	0.075	0.075	0.9
2	0.075	0.075	0.150	1.8
3	0.225	0.075	0.075	2.7
4	0.075	0.150	0.150	7.2

   a Show, using oxidation numbers, that iodate(V) acts as an oxidising agent in the reaction. [1]
   b The initial rates in the table above were determined by measuring the change in concentration of iodine over time. Suggest a suitable experimental technique for this. [1]
   c Using the data in the table above:
   i Determine the orders of reaction with respect to I⁻, H⁺ and IO_3^-. Justify your choices. [3]
   ii Write the rate equation for the reaction. [1]
   iii Calculate the rate constant for the reaction and state its units. [2]

   [Total: 8]

REFLECTION

How well do you feel you answered the three 'justify' questions in this chapter? Are you confident you know what is required from this command word?

22.6 Deducing order of reaction from raw data

1 Use the initial rate data in the table to answer the questions.

Experiment	[A] / mol dm⁻³	[B] / mol dm⁻³	[C] / mol dm⁻³	Initial rate / mol dm⁻³ s⁻¹
1	1.10	1.65	0.275	1.49×10^{-3}
2	2.20	1.65	0.275	2.97×10^{-3}
3	3.30	3.30	0.275	1.78×10^{-2}
4	4.40	4.40	2.750	4.22×10^{-2}
5	5.50	5.50	4.125	8.25×10^{-2}

a Determine the orders with respect to reactants **A**, **B** and **C**.

b Write the rate equation for the reaction.

c Determine the value of the rate constant and state its units.

2 Nitrogen dioxide decomposes according to the following equation:

$$2NO_2 \rightarrow 2NO + O_2$$

The table shows the rate–concentration data for the reaction, obtained by measuring the change in NO_2 concentration over time.

$[NO_2] \times 10^{-3}$ / mol dm⁻³	Rate / mol dm⁻³ s⁻¹
6.67	0.0325
4.72	0.0163
3.33	0.0081
2.87	0.0060
2.17	0.0034
1.57	0.0018

a Explain how the data in the table above could be obtained from a plot of NO_2 concentration against time. [1]

b Use the data in the table above to plot a graph and hence determine the order of reaction with respect to NO_2 concentration. [3]

c Write the rate equation for the reaction. [1]

d Suggest another graphical method that could be used to verify the order of reaction. [1]

[Total: 6]

22.7 Kinetics and reaction mechanisms

1 **a** Consider the following reaction mechanism:

Step 1: $A + B \rightarrow X$ (fast)

Step 2: $X + A \rightarrow C$ (slow)

Overall: $2A + B \rightarrow C$

   i What is the rate the equation for the mechanism? Explain your answer.

   ii What could be the role of X in the mechanism? Explain your answer.

b Given that rate = $k[A]^2[B]$, which step is the slow step in the following mechanism? Explain your answer.

Step 1: $A + B \rightarrow C + D$

Step 2: $A + D \rightarrow E$

Step 3: $B + E \rightarrow F$

Overall: $2A + 2B \rightarrow C + F$

c In the following mechanism, XY* represents a reactive intermediate. What is the overall equation and which is the rate-determining step?

Step 1: $X + Y \rightarrow XY^*$

Step 2: $XY^* + X \rightarrow X_2Y$

Step 3: $X_2Y + Y \rightarrow Z + X$

The rate equation is rate = $k[X]^2[Y]^2$.

UNDERSTAND THIS TERM

- rate-determining step

2 Iodine monochloride reacts with hydrogen as shown in the following equation:

$$2ICl + H_2 \rightarrow 2HCl + I_2$$

The rate is found experimentally to be first order with respect to both iodine monochloride and hydrogen.

a Write the rate equation for the reaction.

b Explain how it is possible to deduce that an intermediate is likely to be involved in the mechanism.

c Propose a two-step mechanism for the reaction, identifying the rate-determining step.

3 Hydrogen peroxide undergoes catalytic decomposition by iodide in acidic conditions. The equation for the reaction is given below:

$$H_2O_2(aq) + 2I^-(aq) + 2H^+(aq) \rightarrow I_2(aq) + 2H_2O(l)$$

The reaction is known to proceed via a four-step mechanism, in which:

- The first step is the slow step
- Step 3 of the mechanism produces OH^-
- There are two intermediates, IO^- and HIO.

a A student finds an online article that states this reaction is catalysed by acid. Explain whether or not you agree with this. [1]

b Suggest equations for the four steps of the mechanism, clearly identifying the rate-determining step. State symbols are not required. [4]

[Total: 5]

22.8 Catalysis

≪ RECALL AND CONNECT 2 ≪

What is shown on a Boltzmann distribution and how does it explain the effect of adding a catalyst to a reaction?

UNDERSTAND THESE TERMS

- homogeneous catalysis
- heterogeneous catalysis
- adsorption (in catalysis)
- desorption

1 a The Haber process involves the reaction between hydrogen and nitrogen in the presence of an iron metal catalyst.

  i Write the chemical equation for the Haber process, including state symbols.

  ii What type of catalyst is iron in the Haber process? Explain your answer.

  iii Explain the mode of action of the iron catalyst in the Haber process.

b The equations below show the formation of sulfuric acid from sulfur present in fossil fuels:

$S(s) + O_2(g) \rightarrow SO_2(g)$

$SO_2(g) + NO_2(g) \rightarrow SO_3(g) + NO(g)$

$NO(g) + 0.5O_2(g) \rightarrow NO_2(g)$

$SO_3(g) + H_2O(l) \rightarrow H_2SO_4(aq)$

  i Write the overall equation for the reaction.

  ii How do the equations shown demonstrate the catalytic role of nitrogen oxides in the formation of acid rain?

2 Peroxodisulfate ions, $S_2O_8^{2-}$, slowly oxidise iodide ions, forming sulfate ions and iodine as shown by the following equation:

$$S_2O_8^{2-}(aq) + 2I^-(aq) \rightarrow 2SO_4^{2-}(aq) + I_2(aq)$$

Some relevant standard electrode potentials are given in the table.

Half-equation	$E^\ominus$ / V
$S_2O_8^{2-}(aq) + 2e^- \rightarrow 2SO_4^{2-}(aq)$	+2.01
$I_2(aq) + 2e^- \rightarrow 2I^-(aq)$	+0.54
$Fe^{3+}(aq) + e^- \rightarrow Fe^{2+}(aq)$	+0.77

a Explain why the reaction between peroxodisulfate ions and iodide ions is slow. [1]

b Define the term *standard electrode potential*. [3]

c Explain, using data from the table, how both Fe^{2+} and Fe^{3+} can catalyse the oxidation of iodide ions by peroxodisulfate. You should include relevant equations and calculations in your answer. [3]

d The standard electrode potential for the reduction of V^{3+} ions is given below:

$$V^{3+}(aq) + e^- \rightarrow V^{2+}(aq) \quad E^\ominus = -0.26\,V$$

Explain why it is not possible for V^{3+} to catalyse the reaction between peroxodisulfate ions and iodide ions. [2]

[Total: 9]

SELF-ASSESSMENT CHECKLIST

Let's revisit the Knowledge focus and Exam skills focus for this chapter.

Decide how confident you are with each statement.

Now I can:	Show it	Needs more work	Almost there	Confident to move on
define and explain the terms *rate equation*, *order of reaction*, *overall order of reaction*, *rate constant*, *half-life*, *rate-determining step* and *intermediate*	Create flashcards for each of these key terms and practise recalling the definitions.			
construct and use rate equations of the form rate = $k[A]^m[B]^n$, for which m and n are 0, 1 or 2	Find an example of a first, second and zero order reaction and write their rate equations.			
deduce the order of a reaction from concentration–time graphs or from experimental data relating to the initial rate method or half-life method	Answer questions that require deduction of orders from raw data and graphs.			
interpret experimental data in graphical form, including concentration–time and rate–concentration graphs	Answer questions that require you to analyse graphs of concentration data.			
calculate initial rates using concentration data	Answer questions that require you to use concentration data and rate equations to calculate initial rates.			
demonstrate that the half-life of a first-order reaction is independent of concentration	Draw half-lives on a graph starting with different initial concentrations to show the value is unchanged.			
calculate the numerical value of a rate constant by using initial rates and the rate equation	Analyse some initial rate data, deduce the reaction orders and rate equation, and then calculate a value for k.			
calculate the numerical value of a rate constant by using the half-life and the equation: $$k = \frac{0.693}{t_{1/2}}$$	Use the half-life from a first order reaction to calculate its rate constant.			

CONTINUED

Now I can:	Show it	Needs more work	Almost there	Confident to move on
suggest a multistep reaction mechanism that is consistent with the rate equation and the equation for the overall reaction	Answer questions that require you to deduce mechanisms from rate equations and an overall reaction.			
predict the order that would result from a given reaction mechanism and rate-determining step	Answer questions that require you to predict the order from a given mechanism or reaction kinetics data.			
deduce a rate equation given a reaction mechanism and rate-determining step for a given reaction	Draw the mechanisms for the S_N1 and S_N2 reactions and write their rate equations, labelling the slow and fast steps.			
identify an intermediate or catalyst from a given reaction mechanism	Write out the mechanisms for the nitration of benzene, and the reaction between bromine and ethene, and identify the intermediates/catalysts.			
identify the rate-determining step from a rate equation and a given reaction mechanism	Answer questions where you are given a rate equation and mechanism and need to label the slow step.			
describe catalysts as homogeneous or heterogeneous	Construct a table that classifies catalysts used in some common reactions as homogeneous or heterogeneous.			
describe heterogeneous catalysis in terms of adsorption of reactants, bond weakening and desorption of products (with reference to iron in the Haber process, and palladium, platinum and rhodium in the catalytic removal of oxides of nitrogen from the exhaust gases of car engines)	Write a description for the mode of action of the iron catalyst in the Haber process.			

CONTINUED

Now I can:	Show it	Needs more work	Almost there	Confident to move on
describe homogeneous catalysis in terms of being used in one step and reformed in a later step (with reference to atmospheric oxides of nitrogen in the oxidation of atmospheric sulfur dioxide and Fe^{2+} or Fe^{3+} in the $I^-/S_2O_3^{2-}$ reaction)	Write the chemical equations for oxidation of SO_2 by NO_x in the atmosphere, and for the catalysis of the peroxodisulfate–iodine reaction by Fe^{2+}/Fe^{3+}, explaining the role of the catalysts.			
describe qualitatively the effect of temperature on the rate constant and therefore on rate of reaction	Explain for a given rate equation how the increase in rate with temperature is due to the relationship between temperature and the rate constant.			
show that I understand the 'justify' command word and answer 'justify' questions	Find and answer 'justify' questions and ensure you clearly describe how you have used the information given to reach your conclusion.			

23 Entropy and Gibbs free energy

The command word in a question is the key to getting a good answer and efficiently. It can be easy to get them mixed up, especially when working under pressure in an exam situation. Focused practice helps you to do this automatically.
In this chapter you will practise answering questions with the command words 'describe' and 'explain'.

| Describe | state the points of a topic/give characteristics and main features |
| Explain | set out purposes or reasons/make the relationships between things evident/provide why and/or how and support with relevant evidence |

23.1 Introducing entropy

1   Entropy is a measure of the dispersal of energy at a specific temperature. How else can entropy be thought of?

2   The system of magnesium reacting with sulfuric acid in a test-tube to form magnesium sulfate and hydrogen releases energy to the surroundings. List everything that makes up the surroundings in this system.

23.2 Chance and spontaneous change

1   What are the standard conditions used when measuring entropy values?

2   Write an equation for the formation of ammonia from nitrogen and hydrogen with all substances in the gaseous phase. Use this to predict the sign of the change in entropy for this reaction and explain your answer.   **[Total: 3]**

3   Figure 23.1 shows the change of entropy as a substance is heated up. Describe and explain the relative size of the vertical points on the graph at the melting and boiling points.   **[Total: 4]**

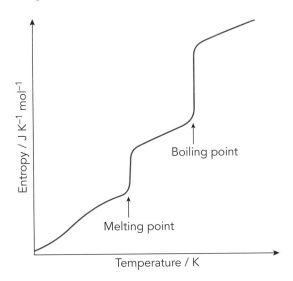

Figure 23.1

23.3 Calculating entropy changes

1 State the equation needed to calculate the entropy change of a reaction system.

2 The table shows some entropy data. Use these data to answer the questions that follow.

Substance	$S^{\ominus}$ / $J\,K^{-1}\,mol^{-1}$
$Al_2O_3(s)$	51
$Al(s)$	28
$C(s)$	6
$CO_2(g)$	214

    a Explain the difference between the entropy values for aluminium
    and carbon [2]

    b Calculate the entropy change for the reaction
    $2Al_2O_3(s) + 3C(s) \rightarrow 4Al(s) + 3CO_2(g)$. [2]

                                              [Total: 4]

23.4 Entropy, enthalpy changes and Gibbs free energy

1 Consider the reaction $Mg(s) + 0.5O_2(g) \rightarrow MgO(s)$, which has $\Delta G_f^{\ominus}$ of $-569.4\,kJ\,mol^{-1}$. Comment on the feasibility and completion of the formation of magnesium oxide.

2 The decomposition of calcium carbonate has $\Delta H^{\ominus}$ of $+178\,kJ\,mol^{-1}$ and $\Delta S^{\ominus}$ of $+160\,J\,K^{-1}\,mol^{-1}$.

    a Calculate $\Delta G^{\ominus}$ of the reaction at $30\,°C$. [2]

    b The reaction is not feasible at this temperature. Explain why. [2]

    c Calculate the temperature at which the reaction becomes feasible. [2]

                                              [Total: 6]

≪ RECALL AND CONNECT 1 ≪

The Faraday (F) has the value $96\,500\,C\,mol^{-1}$. What is a Faraday?

23.5 Gibbs free energy

1   What is the equation for calculating ΔG from E_{cell} values?

2   Why are the values for $\Delta G^\ominus$ of $O_2(g)$ and $H_2(g)$ zero?

3   a   Calculate $\Delta G^\ominus$ for the reaction $C_3H_8(g) + 5O_2(g) \rightarrow 3CO_2(g) + 4H_2O(l)$

   b   Suggest whether the reaction is feasible.   **[Total: 4]**

   Values for $G^\ominus$ in $kJ\,mol^{-1}$: $C_3H_8(g) = -23.4$, $CO_2(g) = -394.4$, $H_2O(l) = -273.2$.

4   a   Calculate the standard free energy change for the reaction of iron with copper(II) ions.

   b   Suggest whether the reaction is feasible. Explain your answer.
      ($F = 96\,500\,C\,mol^{-1}$)   **[Total: 5]**

	$E^\ominus$ / V
$Cu^{2+}(aq) + 2e^- \rightleftharpoons Cu(s)$	+0.34
$Fe^{2+}(aq) + 2e^- \rightleftharpoons Fe(s)$	−0.44

REFLECTION

In this chapter you focused on the command words 'describe' and 'explain' in the questions. Look back at your answer to question 23.2.3. Did you include all the description and explanation points? It can be easy to forget to cover all parts of the question for higher-mark questions. In question 23.5.4, did you remember to explain your answer?

SELF-ASSESSMENT CHECKLIST

Let's revisit the Knowledge focus and Exam skills focus for this chapter.

Decide how confident you are with each statement.

Now I can:	Show it	Needs more work	Almost there	Confident to move on
define the term *entropy* as being the number of possible arrangements of the particles and their energy in a given system	Draw a pictorial representation of entropy to illustrate the definition.			

CONTINUED

Now I can:	Show it	Needs more work	Almost there	Confident to move on
predict and explain the sign of the entropy changes that occur during a change in state, during a temperature change and during a reaction in which there is a change in the number of gaseous molecules	Consider the following physical and chemical changes: • $H_2O(g) \rightarrow H_2O(l)$ • $2Mg(s) + O_2(g) \rightarrow 2MgO(s)$ • $2H_2O_2(l) \rightarrow 2H_2O(l) + O_2(g)$ • $0.5H_2(g) + 0.5I_2(s) \rightarrow HI(g)$ • $N_2(g) + 3H_2(g) \rightarrow 2NH_3(g)$ For each predict and explain the sign of the entropy changes that occur.			
calculate the entropy change for a reaction using standard entropy values of the reactants and products	$4HCl(g) + O_2(g) \rightleftharpoons 2Cl_2(g) + 2H_2O(g)$ Calculate the entropy change for this reaction given the following entropy data: HCl(g) 187, O_2(g) 205, Cl_2(g) 223 and H_2O(g) 189, all in $J\,K^{-1}\,mol^{-1}$.			
perform calculations using the Gibbs equation $\Delta G^{\ominus} = \Delta H^{\ominus} - T\Delta S^{\ominus}$	A reaction has a $\Delta S^{\ominus}$ value of $129\,J\,K^{-1}\,mol^{-1}$ and a $\Delta H^{\ominus}$ value of $-116\,kJ\,mol^{-1}$. Calculate the $\Delta G^{\ominus}$ at a temperature of 50 °C.			
determine if a reaction is feasible by referring to the sign of $\Delta G^{\ominus}$	Using the calculation above, comment on the feasibility of the reaction at this temperature.			
predict the effect of temperature change on the feasibility of a reaction when given standard enthalpy and entropy changes	Summarise the feasibility of reactions for each of the following: 		$\Delta H^{\ominus}$ positive	$\Delta H^{\ominus}$ negative
---	---	---
$\Delta S^{\ominus}$ positive		
$\Delta S^{\ominus}$ negative						

CONTINUED

Now I can:	Show it	Needs more work	Almost there	Confident to move on
predict the feasibility of a reaction using the equation $\Delta G^\ominus = -nFE^\ominus_{cell}$	A two-electron transfer cell has an $E^\ominus_{cell}$ of +0.22 V. Calculate the $\Delta G^\ominus$ and predict the feasibility of the reaction.			
show that I understand the 'describe' and 'explain' command words and the difference between them	Go back to your answers to the questions in this chapter. Highlight the descriptions using one colour highlighter and use a different colour to highlight the explanations. Compare the length and organisation of your answers to the answers provided.			

24 Transition elements

KNOWLEDGE FOCUS

In this chapter you will answer questions on:

- what transition elements are

- physical and chemical properties of the transition elements

- ligands and complex formation.

EXAM SKILLS FOCUS

In this chapter you will:

- evaluate your progress and know what to do to improve.

Using the end-of-chapter self-assessment checklists will give you a better understanding of your strengths and weaknesses. You then need to develop an action plan to improve your understanding of a topic.

Ways you can improve include doing further questions to increase familiarity with exam language, ensuring keywords are thoroughly understood and learned, or asking someone to explain a topic in a different way if you realise you have knowledge gaps. The Exam skills chapter at the end of this book provides different strategies for you to identify where you need extra support and how to improve your revision to make it much more effective.

24.1 What is a transition element?

1 a Why are transition elements referred to as d-block elements?

   b Why are scandium and zinc not considered transition elements?

   c Give the abbreviated electron configurations of the following transition elements and ions:

       i Ti^{2+} **ii** Cr **iii** Mn^{4+} **iv** Fe^{3+} **v** Cu^+

   d Why do transition metals have variable oxidation states?

2 A transition metal Z has the electronic configuration $[Ar]4s^2 3d^5$.

   a State the full electronic configuration of a Z^{5+} ion. [1]

   b Predict the highest possible oxidation state for Z. [1]

   c Give the systematic name for the compound whose formula is Z_2O_3. [1]

   d State two expected chemical properties of Z that are typical of transition elements. [2]

   [Total: 5]

> **≪ RECALL AND CONNECT 1 ≪**
>
> Transition metals undergo lots of redox chemistry, so you can expect exam questions about knowledge from other redox topics like electrochemistry. Can you recall the order of ease with which ions are discharged in electrolysis?

24.2 Physical and chemical properties of the transition elements

1 a Due to its chemical properties, iron can be described as a typical transition metal. Explain why, using specific examples to illustrate your answer.

   b Chromium has colourful redox chemistry. $Cr_2O_7^{2-}(aq)$ ions are orange, $Cr^{3+}(aq)$ ions are typically green, while $Cr^{2+}(aq)$ ions are blue. Using the standard electrode potentials in the table, explain the colour changes seen when zinc metal is added to a solution of sodium dichromate(VI). Illustrate your answer with relevant chemical equations and $E^{\ominus}_{cell}$ values.

Half-cell reaction	$E^{\ominus}$ / V
$Cr_2O_7^{2-}(aq) + 6e^- + 6H^+(aq) \rightarrow 2Cr^{3+}(aq) + 14H_2O(l)$	+1.36
$Cr^{3+}(aq) + e^- \rightarrow Cr^{2+}(aq)$	+0.34
$Cr^{3+}(aq) + 3e^- \rightarrow Cr(s)$	−0.74
$Cr^{2+}(aq) + 2e^- \rightarrow Cr(s)$	−0.89
$Zn^{2+}(aq) + 2e^- \rightarrow Zn(s)$	−0.76

2   The percentage of iron(II) in an iron tablet can be determined using redox titration. Five iron tablets were crushed and dissolved in distilled water to form a 250.0 cm³ solution. A 25.0 cm³ portion of this solution was acidified and titrated against a 0.005 mol dm⁻³ potassium manganate(VII) solution.

23.30 cm³ of the potassium manganate(VII) solution was required to completely react with the iron(II) present.

a   Balance the equation below to show the reaction between manganate(II) ions and iron(II) ions: [1]

$$....MnO_4^-(aq) + ...H^+(aq) + ...Fe^{2+}(aq) \rightarrow ....Mn^{2+}(aq) + ...H_2O(l) + ...Fe^{3+}(aq)$$

b   Calculate the number of moles of manganate(II) ions used in the titration. [1]

c   Calculate the number of moles of iron(II) ions reacting in the titration. [1]

d   Calculate the number of moles of iron(II) present in the five tablets. [1]

e   The mass of each iron tablet was 210 mg.
Calculate the percentage by mass of iron in each tablet. [3]

[Total: 7]

3   Ethanedioic acid is a poisonous dicarboxylic acid present in very low concentrations in food, such as spinach. It exists as a hydrated compound with the formula $C_2O_4H_2.xH_2O$. A student decided to use a redox titration to determine the number of waters of crystallisation, x.

1.225 g of hydrated ethanedioic acid was dissolved in water to form a 250.0 cm³ solution. A 25.0 cm³ sample of this solution was acidified and titrated against 0.02 mol dm⁻³ potassium manganate(VII) solution.

19.45 cm³ of the potassium manganate(VII) solution were needed to completely react with the ethanedioic acid in the titration.

Relevant standard electrode potentials are shown in the table.

Half-cell reaction	$E^\ominus$ / volts
$MnO_4^-(aq) + 8H^+(aq) + 5e^- \rightarrow Mn^{2+}(aq) + 4H_2O(l)$	+1.51
$2CO_2(g) + 2e^- \rightarrow C_2O_4^{2-}(aq)$	−0.43

a   Write a balanced chemical equation for the reaction between ethanedioate ions, $C_2O_4^{2-}$, and manganate(VII) ions, MnO_4^- [1]

b   Using the standard electrode potentials provided, show that the reaction between ethanedioate ions and manganate(VII) is a feasible reaction. [2]

c   Calculate the number of moles of manganate(II) ions used in the titration. [1]

d   Calculate the number of moles of ethanedioate ions reacting in the titration. [1]

e   Calculate the total moles of ethanedioate ions present in 1.225 g of the hydrated ethanedioic acid. [1]

f Calculate the relative formula mass of $C_2O_4H_2.xH_2O$ [1]

g The relative formula mass of $C_2O_4H_2$ is 90.

Calculate the value of x in $C_2O_4H_2.xH_2O$. [1]

[Total: 8]

4 'Copper' coins are made from brass, which is an alloy of copper and zinc. The percentage of copper in coins can be determined by redox titration. A 2.494 g coin was dissolved completely in nitric acid. After adding sodium carbonate to neutralise the excess acid, a precipitate of $CuCO_3$ was formed that was dissolved in ethanoic acid. The resulting solution containing Cu^{2+} ions was made up to $100.0\,cm^3$ with distilled water. A $25.0\,cm^3$ portion of this solution was pipetted into a conical flask and an excess of potassium iodide was added. The iodine liberated was titrated against $0.25\,mol\,dm^{-3}$ sodium thiosulfate solution. $18.40\,cm^3$ of sodium thiosulfate solution was needed for complete reaction.

The relevant chemical equations are given below:

$$2Cu^{2+}(aq) + 4I^-(aq) \rightarrow 2CuI(s) + I_2(aq)$$

$$2S_2O_3^{2-}(aq) + I_2(aq) \rightarrow 2I^-(aq) + S_4O_6^{2-}(aq)$$

Using the data provided, calculate the percentage by mass of copper in the coin. **[Total: 5]**

24.3 Ligands and complex formation

1 a Give the formulae of:

i A neutral (uncharged) monodentate ligand.

ii A charged monodentate ligand.

b Name and give the structural formulae of:

i A neutral bidentate ligand.

ii A charged bidentate ligand.

c Give the oxidation number of the transition metal in the following complex ions:

i $[Ti(H_2O)_6]^{3+}$

ii $[FeCl_4]^{2-}$

iii $[Ni(C_2O_4)_3]^{4-}$

iv $[VO(H_2O)_5]^{2+}$

v $Cr(H_2O)_3(OH)_3$

vi $Mn(SCN)_2(H_2O)_2$

2 Look at the reaction flowchart in Figure 24.1 and then answer the following questions:

   a What are the colours of complexes A, C, D and E?

   b What are the formulae of complexes B, C and D?

   c What reagents are used for reactions 1, 3 and 4?

   d Write balanced chemical equations for:

      i Reaction 1

      ii Reaction 2

      iii Reaction 3

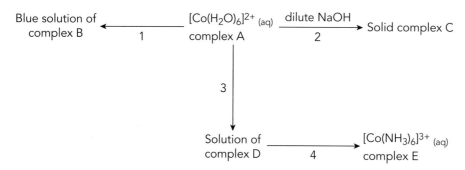

Figure 24.1: Cobalt aqueous chemistry reactions

3 **a** **i** Give the formula of the complex formed between silver(I) ions and ammonia ligands that has a coordination number of two.

      ii What is the geometry of this complex?

      iii What is this complex used for?

   b Draw a 3D diagram of the tetrahedral complex formed between iron(II) ions and chloride ligands.

   c Draw a 3D diagram of the square planar complex formed between nickel(II) ions and ammonia ligands.

   d Draw 3D diagrams of the two geometric isomers of $[Pt(NH_3)_2Cl_2]^{2+}$ and name the geometry.

   e Draw 3D diagrams of the two geometric isomers of $[V(NH_2CH_2CH_2NH_2)_2(CN)_2]^{3+}$ and name the geometry.

   f Draw the two optical isomers of $[Fe(C_2O_4)(en)Cl_2]^-$.

   g Draw 3D diagrams of the following complex ions:

      i The non-polar complex of $[Mn(H_2O)_4Cl_2]$

      ii The most polar complex of $[Mn(C_2O_4)_2(CN)_2]^{4-}$

4 **a** Sketch a diagram of the d orbitals, labelling the names of each orbital.

   b Draw 'electron in a box' diagrams to show the electron configuration of a Ni^{2+} ion when it is:

   i surrounded by six ligands

   ii surrounded by four ligands.

   c Why are solutions containing the complex $[Ni(H_2O)_6]^{2+}$ coloured?

   d Which factors affect the colour of a transition metal ion?

5 **a** State the difference between a transition element and a d-block element.   [2]

   b **i** State what is observed when dilute ammonia solution followed by concentrated hydrochloric acid is added to a solution of copper(II) sulfate.   [2]

   ii Write equations for the reactions that occur and give the geometry of complexes formed.   [4]

Some stability constant (K_{stab}) values for different ligand exchange reactions of hexaaquairon(III) ions, $[Fe(H_2O)_6]^{3+}$, are shown in the table.

Ligand exchange reaction	K_{stab}
$[Fe(H_2O)_6]^{3+}(aq) + 4Cl^-(aq) \rightarrow [FeCl_4]^-(aq) + 6H_2O(l)$	7.94×10^{-2}
$[Fe(H_2O)_6]^{3+}(aq) + 6CN^-(aq) \rightarrow [Fe(CN)_6]^{3-}(aq) + 6H_2O(l)$	3.98×10^{43}
$[Fe(H_2O)_6]^{3+}(aq) + SCN^-(aq) \rightarrow [Fe(SCN)(H_2O)_5]^{2+}(aq) + H_2O(l)$	1.05×10^2

   c Write an expression for the stability constant, K_{stab}, for the reaction between hexaaquairon(III) ions and chloride ions. Give the units.   [2]

   d Predict the reaction that would occur when a solution of sodium cyanide, NaCN, is added to a solution containing pentaaquathiocyanatoiron(III) ions, $[Fe(SCN)(H_2O)_5]^{2+}(aq)$.   [1]

   e Explain your prediction.   [2]

[Total: 13]

> **UNDERSTAND THESE TERMS**
>
> - ligand
> - complex ion
> - co-ordination number
> - bidentate ligand
> - monodentate ligand
> - geometric isomers
> - stability constant, K_{stab}
> - degenerate orbitals
> - non-degenerate orbitals

《 RECALL AND CONNECT 2 《

Geometric and optical isomers are also encountered in organic chemistry.

a What are the criteria for geometric isomerism in organic compounds?

b What are the criteria for optical isomerism in organic compounds?

REFLECTION

Transition metals are considered an inorganic chemistry topic, but you will notice it requires understanding of concepts from physical chemistry (redox, electron configuration, equilibria) and organic chemistry (stereoisomerism, structures of 'organic' ligands like ethanedioate and 1,2-diaminoethane). You can therefore expect to see synoptic questions featuring transition metals in the exam. Think about the strategies you can use to ensure the connections between different topics are reinforced as part of your exam preparation.

SELF-ASSESSMENT CHECKLIST

Let's revisit the Knowledge focus and Exam skills focus for this chapter.

Decide how confident you are with each statement.

Now I can:	Show it	Needs more work	Almost there	Confident to move on
explain what is meant by a transition element	On a Periodic Table, highlight the two 3d elements that are not transition elements and write a description of why.			
describe how transition elements have variable oxidation states, behave as catalysts, form complex ions and form coloured ions	Write an explanation of why iron is considered a typical transition metal.			
state the electronic configuration of a first-row transition element and of its ions	Write out the electron configurations of the first-row transition elements and their most common ions.			
describe the tendency of transition elements to have variable oxidation states	Create a table showing the most common ions for each first-row transition element.			
describe and explain the use of $MnO_4^-/C_2O_4^{2-}$, MnO_4^-/Fe^{2+} and Cu^{2+}/I^- as examples of redox systems	Write half-equations, then balanced redox equations for each of these systems.			

CONTINUED

Now I can:	Show it	Needs more work	Almost there	Confident to move on
predict, using $E^{\ominus}$ values, the feasibility of redox reactions involving transition metal compounds	Using a table of standard electrode potentials, calculate the E_{cell} value for the reduction of Fe^{3+} by I^- and explain why the reaction is feasible.			
define the terms *ligand* and *complex*	Write down the meaning of these terms in the context of the ion $[Co(NH_3)_6]^{2+}$.			
describe and explain the reactions of transition elements with ligands to form complexes, and describe the shapes and bond angles of complexes	Construct reaction flowcharts to show the aqueous chemistry of Cu^{2+} and Co^{2+} ions, adding the shapes and bond angles for each complex.			
describe the types of stereoisomerism (*cis/trans* and optical isomerism) shown by complexes, including those with bidentate ligands	Write a list of the different metal–ligand combinations that produce stereoisomers and give an example of each.			
deduce the overall polarity of complexes that show stereoisomerism	Draw 3D diagrams of some stereoisomeric complex ions containing Cu^{2+} with H_2O, NH_3 and/or Cl^- ligands, labelling them polar or non-polar.			
explain qualitatively how ligand exchange may occur	Describe, referring to the strengths of bonds broken and formed, why Cl^- ions displace H_2O ligands in $[Cu(H_2O)_6]^{2+}$.			
describe the term *stability constant*, K_{stab}, of a complex ion, and write an expression for the stability constant of a complex	Write K_{stab} for the reaction where ammonia ligands displace water ligands in a complex containing Co^{2+} ions.			

CONTINUED

Now I can:	Show it	Needs more work	Almost there	Confident to move on
explain ligand exchange in terms of stability constants	Look up K_{stab} values for three ligands and then write equations to show which ligands would displace the other using the complex ion $[Co(H_2O)_6]^{2+}$.			
sketch the general shape of atomic d orbitals	Label a diagram of the five sets of d orbitals.			
describe the splitting of degenerate d orbitals into two energy levels in octahedral and tetrahedral complexes	Label a diagram showing the arrangement of d orbitals and electrons in an octahedral and tetrahedral Fe^{3+} complex.			
explain the origin of colour in transition element complexes	Write a detailed explanation as to why $[Cu(H_2O)_6]^{2+}$(aq) is blue.			
describe, in qualitative terms, the effects of different ligands on the absorption of light, and hence the colour of a complex	Write an explanation for why $[CuCl_4]^{2-}$(aq) is yellow, whereas $[Co(H_2O)_6]^{2+}$(aq) is pink.			
evaluate my progress and know what to do to improve	When you have worked through this table, identify which topics you are less confident about and make a plan to improve your understanding of these topics.			

Exam practice 6

This section contains past paper questions from previous Cambridge exams which draw together your knowledge on a range of topics that you have covered up to this point. These questions give you the opportunity to test your knowledge and understanding. Additional past paper practice questions can be found in the accompanying digital material.

The following question has an example student response and commentary provided. Work through the question first, then compare your answer to the sample response and commentary. Are your answers different to the sample responses?

1 a The rate of reaction between 2-chloro-2-methylpropane, $(CH_3)_3CCl$, and methanol is investigated. When a large excess of methanol is used, the overall reaction is first order.

$$(CH_3)_3CCl + CH_3OH \rightarrow (CH_3)_3COCH_3 + HCl$$

Fig. 1.1 shows the results obtained.

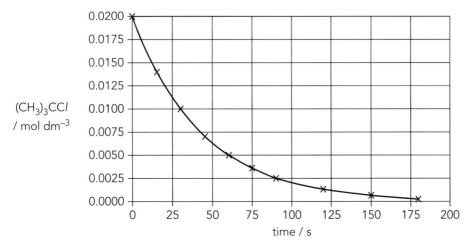

Fig. 1.1

   i   Use the graph to determine the rate of reaction at 40 s.
       Show all your working. [1]

   ii Use the graph to show that the overall reaction is first order.
       Explain your answer. [2]

   b In a different reaction, which is also a first order reaction,
      75% of the reactant is consumed in 320 s.

      Calculate the rate constant, k, for this reaction. State the units for k. [2]

[**Total: 5**]

Adapted from Cambridge International AS & A Level Chemistry (9701)
Paper 41 Q3a,b June 2022

Example student response	Commentary
a **i** Rate = 1.70×10^{-4} mol dm^{-3} s^{-1}	The student has correctly drawn a tangent to the curve at t = 40 s and calculated its gradient to find the rate. *This answer is awarded 1 out of 1 mark.*
ii The reaction is first order wrt 2-chloro-2-methylpropane because the half-life is constant.	The student has correctly demonstrated that the reaction is first order because the half-lives are constant. The working is clearly shown on the graph. *This answer is awarded 2 out of 2 marks.*
b 75% means two half-lives have elapsed. This happened in 320 s so each half-life is 160 s. Using $k = 0.693/160$ gives $k = 0.00433$ s^{-1}	The student has correctly interpreted that, in two half-lives, 75% of the reactant would be consumed. They have then correctly recalled and used the equation for calculating a rate constant from a half-life. *This answer is awarded 2 out of 2 marks*

Now answer an additional question.

2 **a** The oxidation of nitrogen(II) oxide is shown in the equation.

$$2NO(g) + O_2(g) \rightarrow 2NO_2(g)$$

The initial rate of this reaction was measured, starting with different concentrations of the two reactants. The following results were obtained.

experiment number	[NO] / mol dm^{-3}	[O$_2$] / mol dm^{-3}	initial rate / mol dm^{-3} s^{-1}
1	0.032	0.012	4.08×10^{-3}
2	0.032	0.024	8.15×10^{-3}
3	0.064	0.024	3.28×10^{-2}
4	0.096	0.036	

    i Use the data in the table to determine the order with respect to each reactant. Show your reasoning. [2]

    ii   Calculate the initial rate in experiment 4.
          Give your answer to **two** significant figures.   [1]

    iii   Write the rate equation for this reaction.   [1]

    iv   Use the results of experiment 1 to calculate the rate constant, k,
          for this reaction. Include the units of k.   [2]

b **i**   On the following axes:

- draw two Boltzmann distribution curves, at two different
temperatures, T_1 and T_2 $(T_2 > T_1)$;

- label the curves and the axes.   [3]

    ii   State and explain, using your diagram, the effect of increasing
          temperature on the rate of reaction.   [2]

c The compound nitrosyl fluoride, NOF, can be formed by the
following reaction.

$$2NO(g) + F_2(g) \rightleftharpoons 2NOF(g)$$

The rate is first order with respect to NO and F_2.

The reaction mechanism has **two** steps.

Suggest equations for the two steps of this mechanism,
stating which is the rate determining slower step.   [2]

[Total: 13]

*Cambridge International AS & A Level Chemistry (9701) Paper 42 Q1
November 2014*

The following question has an example student response and commentary provided.
Work through the question first, then compare your answer to the sample response and
commentary. Are your answers different to the sample responses? How are they different?

3   Silicon is the second most abundant element by mass in the Earth's crust.

    a   In industry, silicon is extracted from SiO_2 by reaction with carbon
        at over 2000 °C.

          reaction 1 $SiO_2(s) + 2C(s) \rightarrow Si(l) + 2CO(g)$

      i   Explain why the entropy change, $\Delta S^{\ominus}$, of reaction 1 is positive.   [1]

      ii   Reaction 1 is highly endothermic.

          Suggest the effect of an increase in temperature on the feasibility
          of this reaction.

          Explain your answer.   [2]

b Silicon is purified by first heating it in a stream of $HCl(g)$ to form $SiHCl_3$. The $SiHCl_3$ formed is then distilled to remove other impurities.

reaction 2 $Si(s) + 3HCl(g) \rightarrow SiHCl_3(g) + H_2(g)$

i Table 3.1 shows some standard entropy data.

compound	standard entropy, $S^{\ominus}$ / J K^{-1} mol^{-1}
$Si(s)$	19
$HCl(g)$	187
$SiHCl_3(g)$	314
$H_2(g)$	131

Table 3.1

Use the data in Table 3.1 to calculate $\Delta S^{\ominus}$ for reaction 2.   [2]

ii Reaction 3 is the reverse of reaction 2 and is used to obtain pure silicon.

reaction 3 $SiHCl_3(g) + H_2(g) \rightarrow Si(s) + 3HCl(g)$ $\Delta H = +219.3$ kJ mol^{-1}

Use this information and your answer to **bi** to calculate the temperature, in K, at which reaction 3 becomes feasible.

Show your working.

[If you were unable to answer **bi**, you should use $\Delta S^{\ominus} = -150$ J K^{-1} mol^{-1} for reaction 2. This is not the correct answer to **bi**.]   [2]

[Total: 7]

Adapted from Cambridge International AS & A Level Chemistry (9701)
Paper 42 Q2a,b March 2022

Example student response	Commentary
a **i** There are 3 moles of substance on the left of the equation and 2 moles on the right.	The answer should mention the state changes: 1 mol liquid and 2 mol gas are formed from 3 mol solid OR two solid compounds are converted to a liquid and a gas. *This answer is awarded 0 out of 1 mark.*
ii The reaction is endothermic so the sign of $\Delta H^{\ominus}$ is positive. So, to make $\Delta G^{\ominus}$ be zero or negative, the $-T\Delta S$ part of the equation would need to be larger than the value of $\Delta H^{\ominus}$. As T increases, the $-T\Delta S^{\ominus}$ value gets bigger so the reaction becomes more feasible.	The student has started the answer restating a piece of information that was given in the question. This wastes time but can be useful to help guide your thoughts when answering. They have answered in terms of the key expression $\Delta G^{\ominus} = \Delta H^{\ominus} - T\Delta S^{\ominus}$ but need to clearly state the reaction becomes more feasible because of the change in $\Delta G^{\ominus}$. *This answer is awarded 0 out of 2 marks.*
b **i** $\Delta S^{\ominus}_{system} = \Sigma S^{\ominus}_{products} - \Sigma S^{\ominus}_{reactants}$ $= (314 + 131) - (19 + 187)$ $= 445 - 206$ $= 239$ J K^{-1} mol^{-1}	The student has forgotten to include the stoichiometry of the equation into their calculation. This has meant that they have lost all the marks. *This answer is awarded 0 out of 2 marks.*

Example student response	Commentary
ii $\Delta G = 0$ so $T = \Delta H/\Delta S$ $T = 219.3/0.239$ $T = 917.6\ K$	The student has correctly rearranged the equation for ΔG when $\Delta G = 0$. They have used their value for ΔS from the previous question and, even though this is wrong, they are still able to access the marks for this question as an error carried forward. This answer is completely correct, they have remembered to match the units of ΔH and ΔS by dividing the value of ΔS by 1000 (alternatively they could have multiplied the ΔH value by 1000). *This answer is awarded 2 out of 2 marks.*

4   Now that you have read the sample response, rewrite your answer to any part of question **3** where you did not score highly. Use the commentary as a guide.

The following question has an example student response and commentary provided. Work through the question first, then compare your answer to the sample response and commentary. Are your answers different to the sample responses? Do you understand why the sample answer was given the marks?

5   **a**   Explain why chromium complexes are coloured.   [4]

   b   Four different compounds can be obtained when anhydrous chromium(III) chloride reacts with water under various conditions. When samples of each compound are reacted separately with aqueous silver nitrate, different amounts of silver chloride are precipitated. The precipitation leaves the complex ions **P**, **Q**, **R** and **S** in solution.

formula of compound	moles of AgCl precipitated per mole of complex ion	complex ion	property of complex ion
$CrCl_3(H_2O)_6$	3	P	non-polar
$CrCl_3(H_2O)_5$	2	Q	polar
$CrCl_3(H_2O)_4$	1	R	polar
$CrCl_3(H_2O)_4$	1	S	non-polar

   i   Draw three-dimensional diagrams for the structures of complex ions **P**, **Q**, **R** and **S**. Include the charges for each complex ion.

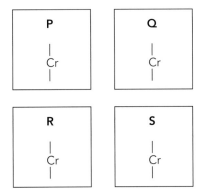

[4]

   ii   Suggest why complex ion **S** is non-polar.   [1]

c The structure of picolinic acid is shown.

picolinic acid

The conjugate base of picolinic acid is a bidentate ligand, **Z**.

i Define the term *bidentate ligand*. [2]

ii Draw the structure of **Z**. [1]

iii **Z** reacts with aqueous chromium(III) ions, $[Cr(H_2O)_6]^{3+}$, in a 3:1 ratio to form a new neutral complex.

State the coordination number and the geometry of the chromium(III) centre in the complex. [1]

d $(NH_4)_2Cr_2O_7$ decomposes readily on heating to form Cr_2O_3, steam and an inert colourless gas.

i Deduce the oxidation numbers of chromium in $(NH_4)_2Cr_2O_7$ and in Cr_2O_3. [1]

ii Construct an equation for the thermal decomposition of $(NH_4)_2Cr_2O_7$. [1]

[Total: 15]

Cambridge International AS & A Level Chemistry (9701) Paper 41 Q2 June 2021

Example student response	Commentary
a There is d splitting in the 3d sub-shell, so electrons get excited up to the higher energy orbitals, which causes light of a certain wavelength to be absorbed. The wavelengths of light that are transmitted produce the solution colour you see.	A good, accurate answer to a common question about origin of colour. Note that 'wavelength' of light can be substituted by 'colour' or 'frequency'. *This answer is awarded 4 out of 4 marks.*
b i	All four complexes have been correctly identified, but the question required 3D diagrams – dash and wedge bonds must be used to show the octahedral geometry. *This answer is awarded 3 out of 4 marks.*
ii The dipoles are symmetrically arranged so cancel out.	This is correct. *This answer is awarded 1 out of 1 mark.*

Example student response	Commentary
c i A bidentate ligand is a molecule that forms two dative covalent bonds to a metal ion.	This is partially correct – note that the central metal in a complex may be an atom rather than an ion. *This answer is awarded 1 out of 2 marks.*
ii	This is the correct structure. *This answer is awarded 1 out of 1 mark.*
iii 6 coordinate and octahedral.	This is correct. *This answer is awarded 1 out of 1 mark.*
d i $(NH_4)_2Cr_2O_7$: +6 Cr_2O_3: +3	This is correct. *This answer is awarded 1 out of 1 mark.*
ii $(NH_4)_2Cr_2O_7 \rightarrow N_2 + Cr_2O_3 + 4H_2O$	This is correct. *This answer is awarded 1 out of 1 mark.*

Now you have read the commentary to the previous question, here is a similar question which you should attempt. Use the information from the previous response and commentary to guide you as you answer.

6 Iodine is found naturally in compounds in many different oxidation states.

a The Group 1 iodides all form stable ionic lattices and are soluble in water.

   i Define enthalpy change of solution. [1]

   ii Use the data in Table 6.1 to calculate the enthalpy change of solution of potassium iodide, KI. [1]

process	process enthalpy change, ΔH / kJ mol^{-1}
$K^+(g) + I^-(g) \rightarrow KI(s)$	–629
$K^+(g) \rightarrow K^+(aq)$	–322
$I^-(g) \rightarrow I^-(aq)$	–293

Table 6.1

   iii Suggest the trend in the magnitude of the lattice energies of the Group 1 iodides, LiI, NaI, KI.

   Explain your answer. [2]

b The concentration of $Cu^{2+}(aq)$ in a solution can be determined by the reaction of Cu^{2+} ions with I^- ions.

   reaction 1 $2Cu^{2+} + 4I^- \rightarrow 2CuI + I_2$

The I_2 produced in reaction 1 is titrated against a solution containing thiosulfate ions, $S_2O_3^{2-}$, using a suitable indicator.

reaction 2 $2S_2O_3^{2-} + I_2 \rightarrow S_4O_6^{2-} + 2I^-$

i   A 25.0 cm^3 portion of a Cu^{2+}(aq) solution reacts with an excess of I^-(aq).

The end-point of the titration occurs when 22.30 cm^3 of 0.150 mol dm^{-3} $S_2O_3^{2-}$(aq) is added.

Calculate the concentration of Cu^{2+}(aq) in the original solution.   [2]

ii   Identify a suitable indicator for the titration.   [1]

iii   Copper(I) and copper(II) both contain electrons in all five 3d orbitals.

Sketch the shape of a $3d_{xy}$ orbital on the axes provided.

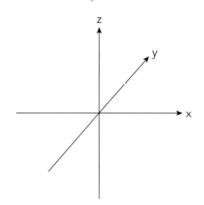

[1]

c   The reaction of I^- ions with persulfate ions, $S_2O_8^{2-}$, can be catalysed by Fe^{3+} ions.

$$2I^- + S_2O_8^{2-} \rightarrow I_2 + 2SO_4^{2-}$$

Write equations to show how Fe^{3+} catalyses this reaction.   [2]

d   An orange precipitate of HgI_2 forms when Hg^{2+} ions are added to KI(aq).

The solubility of HgI_2 at 25 °C is 1.00×10^{-7} g dm^{-3}.

Calculate the solubility product, K_{sp}, of HgI_2.

Include units in your answer.

[M_r: HgI_2, 454.4]   [3]

[Total: 13]

Adapted from Cambridge International AS & A Level Chemistry (9701) Paper 42 Q1 March 2022

25 Benzene and its compounds

The 'explain' command word is common in chemistry examinations. You have answered questions focused on the 'explain' command words in Chapters 1, 15 and 23. Explanation questions are usually between 3 and 6 marks so require some organisation to make sure all the points are covered. Look out for the 'explain' questions in this chapter and take care not to mix up descriptions with explanations.

Explain	set out purposes or reasons/make the relationships between things evident/provide why and/or how and support with relevant evidence

25.1 The benzene ring

1   Draw the skeletal formula of benzene.

2   There were two main models for the bonding in benzene, the delocalised model and the Kekulé model.

    a   Describe both models.   [2]

    b   Explain how the chemical reactivity of benzene provides evidence for the delocalised model of benzene.   [3]

                                                     [Total: 5]

> **UNDERSTAND THESE TERMS**
>
> - arene
> - electrophilic substitution
> - Friedel–Crafts reaction

25.2 Reactions of arenes

1   Aluminium chloride, $AlCl_3$, and aluminium bromide, $AlBr_3$, are commonly used as catalysts in reactions of benzene. By what term are these catalysts known?

2   Name and outline the mechanism for the reaction of benzene with bromine, Br_2, in the presence of a catalyst of $AlBr_3$.   **[Total: 5]**

25.3 Phenol

1   Compare the acidity of phenol and cyclohexanol.

2   **a**   Give the equation for the dissociation of phenol.   [1]

    b   Explain how the position of this equilibrium and the acidity of phenol are influenced by its bonding.   [3]

                                                     [Total: 4]

25.4 Reactions of phenol

1   State the conditions for the bromination of phenol.

2   Describe and explain the reactivity of phenol and benzene towards electrophiles.   **[Total: 4]**

« RECALL AND CONNECT 1 «

What is an sp^2 hybridised orbital?

REFLECTION

In this chapter you focused on the 'explain' command word. Compare your answers to the ones provided in the Answer section. Did your explanations for questions in this chapter have the right amount of detail, including relevant keywords?

SELF-ASSESSMENT CHECKLIST

Let's revisit the Knowledge focus and Exam skills focus for this chapter.

Decide how confident you are with each statement.

Now I can:	Show it	Needs more work	Almost there	Confident to move on
interpret, name and use the general, structural, displayed and skeletal formulae of benzene and simple aryl compounds	Find five simple compounds containing benzene rings from a suitable resource such as a textbook or revision guide. Copy the structures and give the name, general, structural, displayed and skeletal formulae for each.			
describe and explain the shape of, and bond angles in, benzene molecules in terms of σ and π bonds	Create a flashcard summarising the shape of, and bond angles in, benzene molecules in terms of σ and π bonds.			
describe the reactions of arenes, such as benzene and methylbenzene, in: • substitution reactions with chlorine and with bromine • nitration • Friedel–Crafts alkylation and acylation • complete oxidation of the side-chain to give a benzoic acid • hydrogenation of the benzene ring to form a cyclohexane ring	Draw a spider diagram of the reactions of arenes, including halogenation, Friedel–Crafts reactions, oxidation of side-chains and hydrogenation.			

CONTINUED

Now I can:	Show it	Needs more work	Almost there	Confident to move on
describe the mechanism of electrophilic substitution in arenes and the effect of the delocalisation of electrons in such reactions, as well as the directing effects of electron-donating and electron-withdrawing groups on further substitutions	Draw the mechanism of electrophilic substitution in arenes with a general electrophile E^+. Annotate the drawing with explanations of each arrow and intermediate structure. Include detail on directing effects of electron-donating and electron-withdrawing groups on further substitutions.			
interpret the difference in reactivity between benzene and chlorobenzene	Explain why chlorobenzene is less reactive than benzene.			
predict whether halogenation will occur in the side-chain or in the benzene ring in arenes, depending on reaction conditions	Give the conditions for: i halogenation of the benzene ring ii halogenation of an alkyl side-chain.			
apply knowledge relating to position of substitution in the electrophilic substitution of arenes and aryl compounds such as phenol	Explain why chlorobenzene substitutes at positions 2 or 4.			
describe the reactions (reagents and conditions) by which phenol can be prepared	Write equations for the preparation of phenol from phenylamine.			
describe the reactions of phenol with bases and with Na(s)	Draw a spider diagram to describe the reactions of phenol with bases and with Na(s).			
describe the nitration and bromination of phenol's aromatic ring and compare these reactions with those of benzene	Construct a table to compare the nitration and bromination of the aromatic rings in benzene and phenol.			

CONTINUED

Now I can:	Show it	Needs more work	Almost there	Confident to move on
explain the acidity of phenol and the relative acidities of water, phenol and ethanol	Write a few bullet points to summarise why phenol is more acidic than ethanol and water.			
apply knowledge of the reactions of phenol to those of other phenolic compounds such as naphthol	Draw the structure of napthol and explain why the bonded benzene ring is more open to electrophilic substitution, directing attack to the 2 and/or 4 positions.			
show that I understand the 'explain' command word and answer 'explain' questions	Look through the exam syllabus for this topic and write yourself some questions using the 'explain' command word.			

26 Carboxylic acids and their derivatives

KNOWLEDGE FOCUS

In this chapter you will answer questions on:

- the acidity of carboxylic acids

- oxidation of two carboxylic acids

- acyl chlorides.

EXAM SKILLS FOCUS

In this chapter you will:

- show that you understand the 'compare' command word and answer 'compare' questions.

Some questions – usually 'describe' and/or 'explain' questions – ask you to 'compare' something. This is often used in questions relating to trends in physical properties or reactivity. These questions often ask you to rank compounds or elements in some way, so it is important to ensure you use comparatives (such as 'larger', 'weaker' and 'more likely') when answering such questions and do not simply describe individual phenomena.

26.1 The acidity of carboxylic acids

1 a i Write an equation to show the reaction between ethanoic acid solution and sodium hydroxide solution. Include state symbols.

  ii Write the ionic equation for this reaction.

b i The pK_a values of some carboxylic acids are shown in the table. Describe and fully explain the relative acidities of these acids.

Name	pK_a
trichloroethanoic acid, CCl_3COOH	0.66
dichloroethanoic acid, $CHCl_2COOH$	1.35
chloroethanoic acid, $CH_2ClCOOH$	2.87
ethanoic acid, CH_3COOH	4.76

  ii Using the table above, calculate the pH of a $0.1\,mol\,dm^{-3}$ solution of trichloroethanoic acid.

  iii State the assumptions made in your calculation.

c Suggest a value for the pK_a of fluoroethanoic acid, CH_2FCOOH, explaining your choice.

2 a The pK_a values of ethanol, ethanoic acid and phenol are shown in the table. Compare these values. Explain your reasoning. [6]

Name	pK_a
ethanol, CH_3CH_2OH	15.5
phenol, C_6H_5OH	9.99
ethanoic acid, CH_3COOH	4.76

b Write a chemical equation for the reaction between phenol and sodium metal. [1]

c Calculate the pH of the solution formed when $100\,cm^3$ of $0.5\,mol\,dm^{-3}$ ethanoic acid solution is mixed with $75\,cm^3$ of $0.25\,mol\,dm^{-3}$ sodium hydroxide solution. [5]

[Total: 12]

《 RECALL AND CONNECT 1 《

The relative acidity of carboxylic acids is explained by the *inductive effect*. Bonds may be strengthened or weakened, and intermediates stabilised or destabilised, by positive and negative induction.

a   What is the difference between positive and negative induction?

b   Which types of groups produce a positive inductive effect? Give examples.

c   How does the inductive effect account for the formation of major and minor products in electrophilic addition reactions?

26.2 Oxidation of two carboxylic acids

1   a   Give the chemical formulae of some oxidising agents that methanoic acid can reduce.

   b   Give the chemical formulae of some oxidising agents that ethanedioic acid can reduce.

   c   Using [O] to represent the oxidising agent:

   i   Write a general equation for the oxidation of methanoic acid.

   ii   Write a general equation for the oxidation of ethanedioic acid.

   d   Write the half-equation for the oxidation of ethanedioic acid under acidic conditions. What is the oxidation number change for carbon in this reaction?

2   The table shows the results of carrying out some chemical tests on three organic compounds, methanoic acid (CH_2O_2), ethanedioic acid ($C_2H_2O_4$) and ethane-1,2-diol ($C_2H_6O_2$).

✓ indicates a positive test, ✗ indicates no observed reaction.

Test	Reagents	CH_2O_2	$C_2H_2O_4$	$C_2H_6O_2$	Observations
1		✓	✗	✗	
2		✓	✓	✓	
3		✓	✓	✗	

Copy and complete the table to show the reagents, conditions and observations.   **[Total: 4]**

26.3 Acyl chlorides

1 **a** **i** Draw the displayed formula for ethanoyl chloride.

   ii Draw the skeletal formula for butanoyl chloride.

  b Name the isomer of propanoyl chloride that gives a positive test with Fehling's reagent and exists as enantiomers.

  c Using structural formulae, write a balanced chemical equation for the hydrolysis of propanoyl chloride.

  d Draw the mechanism for the reaction between ethanol and ethanoyl chloride. Include all relevant curly arrows, lone pairs of electrons, charges and partial charges. What is the name of the organic product?

  e Devise a synthetic route to prepare propanamide from propanol that uses an acyl chloride. You should include the structures of any intermediate compounds as well as the necessary reagents and conditions.

  f Explain how ethanol, ethanoic acid and ethanoyl chloride could be distinguished using a simple, non-chemical test.

2 Compare the relative ease of hydrolysis of chlorobenzene, chloroethane and ethanoyl chloride. Explain your reasoning.   **[Total: 6]**

≪ RECALL AND CONNECT 2 ≪

Halogenoalkanes also undergo hydrolysis. Considering the following four halogenoalkanes, $C(CH_3)_3I$, CH_3CH_2F, $CH_3CHBrCH_2CH_3$ and $CH_3CHClCH_2CH_3$:

a What is the order of increasing rate of hydrolysis?

b What is the explanation for this order?

UNDERSTAND THIS TERM

- acyl chloride

REFLECTION

Carboxylic acids and acyl chlorides are useful building blocks in organic chemistry because they can be used to make many other functional groups. To see the connections between carboxylic acids, acyl chlorides and other functional groups, try constructing reaction flowcharts that show any necessary reagents and conditions over the reaction arrows. You can also add the reaction type and mechanism type to help you remember these. To test your understanding, you can make versions of the flowcharts that omit the chemical structures or the reagents/conditions – how confident are you that you could fill in the missing information?

SELF-ASSESSMENT CHECKLIST

Let's revisit the Knowledge focus and Exam skills focus for this chapter.

Decide how confident you are with each statement.

Now I can:	Show it	Needs more work	Almost there	Confident to move on
explain the relative acidity of carboxylic acids and chlorine-substituted ethanoic acids	Write a detailed explanation to the explain the pK_a values of ethanoic acid, chloroethanoic acid, and trichloroethanoic acid.			
describe how some carboxylic acids, such as methanoic acid and ethanedioic acid, can be further oxidised	Write chemical equations to show oxidation of methanoic and ethanedioic acid, including any observations.			
describe the reactions of carboxylic acids in the preparation of acyl chlorides	Construct a reaction flowchart starting from a named carboxylic acid, showing the different reagents and conditions to turn it into an acyl chloride.			
describe the hydrolysis of acyl chlorides	Write a chemical equation for a named acyl chloride showing its hydrolysis reaction. Write down any key observations.			
describe the reactions of acyl chlorides with alcohols, phenols, ammonia, and primary or secondary amines	Construct a reaction flowchart starting from an acyl chloride showing the different functional groups that can be obtained. Include necessary reagents and conditions.			
explain the relative ease of hydrolysis of acyl chlorides, alkyl chlorides (chloroalkanes) and aryl chlorides (chloroarenes)	Write a detailed explanation of the relative rates of hydrolysis of ethanoyl chloride, chloroethane and chlorobenzene.			

CONTINUED

Now I can:	Show it	Needs more work	Almost there	Confident to move on
describe the condensation (addition–elimination) mechanism for the reactions of acyl chlorides	Draw the curly arrow mechanism for the reaction between an acyl chloride and a nucleophile, showing relevant dipoles and lone pairs.			
use comparatives to identify or comment on similarities and/or differences where necessary	Find a question that requires a comparison and first state the trend or ranking order, then make a list of the key factors that explain your choice. Remember to include comparative words and phrases.			

27 Organic nitrogen compounds

EXAM SKILLS FOCUS

In this chapter you will:

- show that you understand the 'identify' command word and answer 'identify' questions.

'Identify' can be used in a similar way to 'state', in which case you will be required to give the correct name of something, or you may be required to recognise the correct choice or choices from a selection of possible answers. You have answered questions using the 'identify' command word in Chapter 2. When asked to identify a certain number of choices, you should be careful not to provide more responses than requested, otherwise you may have marks deducted for incorrect responses (this is known as the 'list principle').

Identify	name, select or recognise

Amines and amino acids undergo acid–base chemistry.

a   What are the definitions of Brønsted–Lowry acids and bases?

b   What is the definition of a conjugate acid–base pair?

c   In the equation shown, can you identify the conjugate acid–base pairs?

$$CH_3CH_2NH_2 + H_2SO_4 \rightarrow CH_3CH_2NH_3^+ + HSO_4^-$$

27.1 Amines

1   a   Give the systematic names for the amines shown in Figure 27.1.

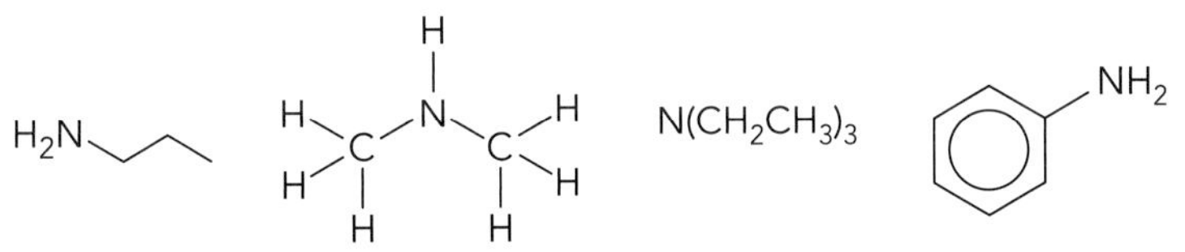

Figure 27.1: Structures of some amines

b   Classify the amines in Figure 27.1 as primary, secondary or tertiary.

c   Using skeletal formulae, draw the structures of:

   i   dibutylamine

   ii N,N-dimethylpropylamine.

2   This question is about the weak Brønsted–Lowry bases ammonia, ethylamine and phenylamine.

a   State what is meant by the term weak Brønsted–Lowry bases.   [2]

b   Write a chemical equation, including state symbols, to show ethylamine acting as a weak base in water.   [1]

   The pH values of $1\,mol\,dm^{-3}$ solutions of ammonia, ethylamine and phenylamine at 25 °C are shown in the table.

Compound	pH of $1.0\,mol\,dm^{-3}$ solution at 25 °C
ammonia	11.6
ethylamine	12.3
phenylamine	9.4

c   Explain why it is important to state the temperature when reporting pH values of weak bases.   [1]

d   Describe the relative basicities of these compounds and identify the bonding principles that account for their different base strengths.   [5]

[Total: 9]

27.2 Formation of amines

1 a Write balanced chemical equations, using structural formulae, to show how the named amine could be made from the specified reactants. State any necessary conditions.

    i   Propylamine, from ammonia and a chloroalkane.

    ii   Dimethylamine, from a primary amine and a bromoalkane.

    iii   Tributylamine, from a secondary amine and a chloroalkane.

b Devise a two-step synthesis of 1-pentylamine from 1-chlorobutane. Show the intermediate compound and give any necessary reagents and conditions.

c Write an equation, using [H] to represent the reducing agent, to show the products formed when N-methylpropanamide, $CH_3CH_2CONHCH_3$, is reduced using $LiAlH_4$. State any necessary conditions.

d In the synthesis of 1-hexylamine from 1-bromohexane and ammonia, a water-soluble by-product with a molecular mass of 433.9 was obtained. The infrared spectrum of this by-product did not have a peak at $3300–3500\,cm^{-1}$. Suggest the identity of this by-product and explain how it could be formed.

> **UNDERSTAND THESE TERMS**
> - coupling reaction
> - diazotisation
> - azo dyes

2 The synthesis of 2,4,6-tribromophenylamine from benzene is shown in Figure 27.2:

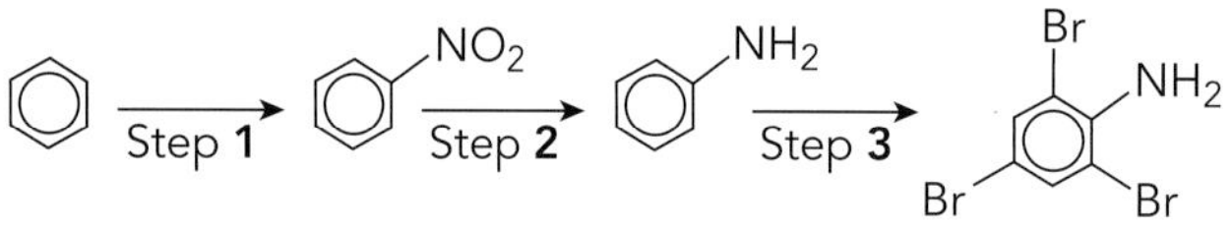

Figure 27.2

a State the reagents and conditions for step **1**. [2]

b Write an equation to show formation of the electrophile in step **1**. [1]

c Draw the mechanism for the reaction in step **1**. [3]

d State the reagents and conditions needed for step **2** and write a balanced chemical equation for this reaction. [3]

e State the reagents and conditions needed for step **3** and name the mechanism. [2]

f Explain why bromine reacts at the 2, 4 and 6 positions of the benzene ring in step **3**. [2]

[Total: 13]

3 Sudan red G is a red-orange azo dye that was formerly used as food colorant. The synthesis of Sudan red G from methoxybenzene is shown in Figure 27.3.

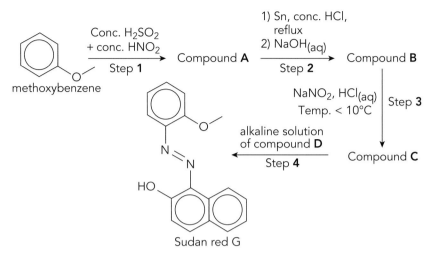

Figure 27.3

a Circle the functional group that identifies Sudan red G as an azo dye. [1]

b Give the molecular formula for Sudan red G. [1]

c Draw the structures of compounds **A**, **B**, **C** and **D**, ensuring the functional group in compound **C** is clearly displayed. [4]

d State the names of the reagents used in step **3** and write an equation to show formation of the reactive species involved. [2]

e Name the type of reaction occurring in step **3**. [1]

f Explain why the temperature must be kept less than 10 °C in step **3**. [1]

g State the role of compound **C** in step **4**. [1]

[Total: 11]

27.3 Amino acids

1 Some data for three amino acids are shown in the table.

Name	Structure	Isoelectric point (pI)
threonine	$CH_3CH(OH)CH(NH_2)CO_2H$	6.53
lysine	$H_2N(CH_2)_4CH(NH_2)CO_2H$	9.74
aspartic acid	$HO_2CCH_2CH(NH_2)CO_2H$	2.87

a Give the systematic name for threonine.

b Draw the displayed formulae of:

   i   threonine at its isoelectric point

   ii lysine at pH 3

   iii aspartic acid at pH 10.

    c   2-Nitrobutan-1-ol is an isomer of threonine. It is a colourless liquid at room temperature, whereas threonine is a white crystalline solid.

        i   Draw the skeletal formula of 2-nitrobutan-1-ol.

        ii Explain why threonine is a solid at room temperature, whereas 2-nitrobutan-1-ol is a liquid.

    d Draw the compounds formed when threonine is:

        i   reacted with ethanoyl chloride in the presence of a base

        ii refluxed with propanoic acid in the presence of an acid catalyst.

27.4 Peptides

1 Two naturally occurring amino acids are valine and glutamine. Their formulae are shown in Figure 27.4.

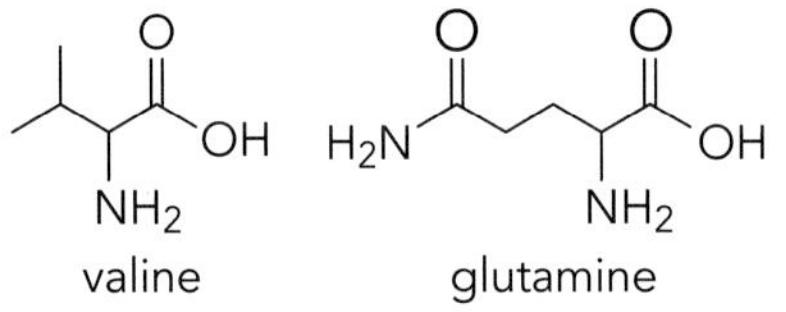

Figure 27.4: Structures of valine and glutamine

    a **i**   Draw the structure of the dipeptide formed when two molecules of valine undergo condensation.

        ii Using molecular formulae, write a balanced chemical equation for this reaction.

    b Draw structures of the two different dipeptides that could be formed when valine and glutamine undergo a condensation reaction together.

2 Naturally occurring amino acids can be represented by a three-letter code and peptides are often written using this code. An example is the tripeptide Ser-Ala-Gly shown in Figure 27.5, made from the amino acids serine, alanine and glycine.

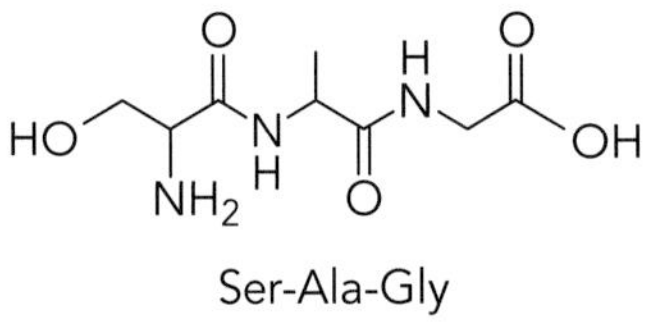

Ser-Ala-Gly

Figure 27.5

    a Draw the displayed formula of the amino acid serine.   [1]

    b Draw 3D structures to show both enantiomers of the amino acid alanine.   [2]

c   Using skeletal formula, draw the tripeptide Ala-Gly-Ser.   [1]

d   Under certain conditions, two molecules of serine can react via condensation to form a cyclic compound with a relative formula mass of molecular weight of 174. Suggest the structure of this compound.   [1]

[Total: 5]

27.5 Reactions of the amides

1   a   Identify an acyl chloride and an amine that could be used to make the following amides and write a balanced chemical equation for each reaction.   [2]

   i   *N*-Methylethanamide.

   ii   *N,N*-Dibutylpropanamide.

   b   Draw the products formed when *N,N*-diethylmethanamide is hydrolysed using aqueous sodium hydroxide solution.   [2]

[Total: 4]

2   a   The pH of a $1.0 \, mol \, dm^{-3}$ solution of triethylamine is 12.4, while that of a dilute solution of ethanamide is 7.6. Explain the difference between these values. You should refer to relevant bonding principles in your answer.   [5]

   b   *N*-Phenylethanamide used to be marketed as the analgesic and antipyretic (fever-reducing) drug 'Antifebrin' until it was found to be toxic to the liver and kidneys.

   i   Draw the displayed formula of *N*-phenylethanamide.   [1]

   ii   Identify an acyl chloride and an amine that could be used to prepare *N*-phenylethanamide.   [2]

   iii State what would be observed in this reaction.   [1]

   iv   The pH of a $1.0 \, mol \, dm^{-3}$ solution of *N*-phenylethanamide is 7.15. Compare this value with that of ethanamide.   [2]

[Total: 11]

27.6 Electrophoresis

1   a   Draw a labelled diagram of the apparatus used to carry out paper or gel electrophoresis of a mixture of amino acids.

   b   Explain how this apparatus can be used to measure the isoelectric point of an amino acid.

UNDERSTAND
THIS TERM

• electrophoresis

2   The structures of the amino acids leucine (Leu), phenylalanine (Phe) and lysine (Lys) are shown in Figure 27.6. A mixture of these amino acids was subjected to electrophoresis using a buffer of pH 8.

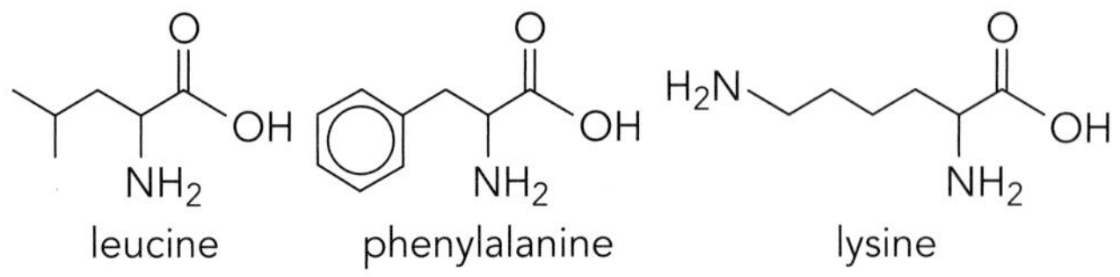

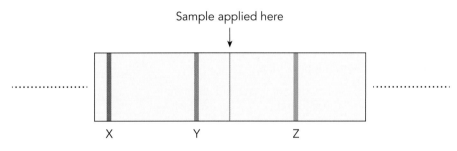

leucine   phenylalanine   lysine

Figure 27.6

a   Calculate the relative molecular mass of the tripeptide Leu-Phe-Lys.   [2]

b   The isoelectric point (p*I*) of lysine is 9.74.

   i   Explain how this value could be determined using electrophoresis.   [2]

   ii   Draw the structure of lysine at pH 8. Explain your answer.   [2]

c   State two factors that affect the rate at which amino acids move in electrophoresis.   [2]

d   Figure 27.7 shows the electropherogram at the end of the experiment.

Sample applied here

X   Y   Z

Figure 27.7

   i   Label the electrodes and their polarities in the space provided.   [1]

   ii   Identify the species responsible for the bands X, Y and Z. Explain your answer.   [4]

[Total: 13]

REFLECTION

How did you find the 'identify' questions in this chapter? Were you careful not to provide more responses than requested? How confident are you that you understand what is required from questions containing this command word?

≪ RECALL AND CONNECT 2 ≪

Electrophoresis of amino acids is carried out using buffer solutions.

a   Can you remember the definition of a buffer solution?

b   What is the equation used to calculate $[H^+]$ in a buffer?

c   What is the pH of a buffer solution that contains 0.02 mol of sodium propanoate and 0.05 mol of propanoic acid ($K_a = 1.35 \times 10^{-5}$).

REFLECTION

Memorising organic chemistry content can be daunting. Each functional group has its own structure that you need to recognise from different formulae types; its own reactions, complete with reagents, conditions and often a reaction mechanism; and also its own set of naming rules. You will need to devise an effective method for organising and then retaining all of this information. Some effective ways to learn organic chemistry include mind maps, concept maps and flowcharts. Can you think of any others?

SELF-ASSESSMENT CHECKLIST

Let's revisit the Knowledge focus and Exam skills focus for this chapter.

Decide how confident you are with each statement.

Now I can:	Show it	Needs more work	Almost there	Confident to move on
describe the formation of alkyl amines (by the reaction of ammonia with halogenoalkanes or the reduction of amides with $LiAlH_4$ or the reduction of nitriles with $LiAlH_4$ or H_2/Ni)	Construct a reaction flowchart showing the different reagents and conditions that can be used to prepare amines.			
describe the formation of phenylamine (by the reduction of nitrobenzene with tin/concentrated HCl, followed by NaOH(aq))	Write a chemical equation for the reduction of nitrobenzene using Sn/HCl.			
describe and explain the basicity of amines and the relative basicities of ammonia, ethylamine and phenylamine	Write an explanation to compare the strengths of these bases that includes the important bonding concepts.			

CONTINUED

Now I can:	Show it	Needs more work	Almost there	Confident to move on
describe the reaction of phenylamine with aqueous bromine	Write a chemical equation for the reaction between phenylamine and aqueous bromine, explaining the relative reactivity compared to benzene and the substitution pattern observed.			
describe the reaction of phenylamine with nitric(III) acid to give the diazonium salt and phenol, followed by the coupling of benzenediazonium chloride and phenol to make a dye	Write equations to illustrate formation of the given azo dye, including all necessary reagents and conditions and label the diazotisation and coupling reaction.			
identify the azo group and describe the formation of other azo dyes	Write equations to show the formation of some other azo dyes, and circle the azo group in each one.			
describe the formation of amides from the reaction between R^1NH_2 and R^2COCl, and the hydrolysis of amides by aqueous alkali or acid	Write general equations using R groups to show the reagents needed to prepare primary, secondary and tertiary amides, then show the hydrolysis products under acidic and basic conditions.			
explain why amides are weaker bases than amines	Draw the structures of ethanamide and ethylamine, and label them to show the factors affecting the availability of the nitrogen lone pair.			
describe the acid/base properties of amino acids and the formation of zwitterions, including the isoelectric point	Draw the structures of several amino acids at pH values equal to, above and below their isoelectric points.			
describe the formation of amide (peptide bonds) between amino acids to give dipeptides and tripeptides	Write chemical equations showing the formation of dipeptides and tripeptides from different amino acids.			

CONTINUED

Now I can:	Show it	Needs more work	Almost there	Confident to move on
describe simply the process of electrophoresis and the effect of pH, using peptides and amino acids as examples	Sketch electropherograms for three chosen amino acids in buffers at pH 3, 8 and 11.			
show that I understand the 'identify' command word and answer 'identify' questions	Write an 'identify' question involving organic nitrogen compounds, complete with mark scheme.			

Exam practice 7

This section contains past paper questions from previous Cambridge exams which draw together your knowledge on a range of topics that you have covered up to this point. These questions give you the opportunity to test your knowledge and understanding. Additional past paper practice questions can be found in the accompanying digital material.

The following question has an example student response and commentary provided. Work through the question first, then compare your answer to the sample response and commentary. Are your answers different to the sample responses?

1   Compound **M** is made from 1,3 dimethylbenzene in a two step synthesis.

a   Draw the structure of **L**.   [1]

b   Suggest reactants and conditions for each step of this synthesis.   [2]

c   Write an equation for step **2**.   [1]

d   A student investigates a possible synthesis of **M** directly from benzene using $COCl_2$ in the presence of an $AlCl_3$ catalyst.

Benzene initially reacts with $COCl_2$ as shown.

reaction 1 $COCl_2 + AlCl_3 \rightarrow AlCl_4^- + Cl{-}\overset{+}{C}{=}O$

reaction 2 $C_6H_6 + Cl{-}\overset{+}{C}{=}O \rightarrow C_6H_5COCl + H^+$

Reaction 2 is the electrophilic substitution of $Cl{-}\overset{+}{C}{=}O$ for H^+ in benzene.

Suggest a mechanism for reaction 2.   [3]

[Total: 7]

Adapted from Cambridge International AS & A Level Chemistry (9701) Paper 42 Q5b March 2021

Example student response	Commentary
a	This is correct. The carboxylic acid functional groups do not need to be drawn out but, as long as they are correct, then it does not matter which form is shown. *This answer is awarded 1 out of 1 mark.*
b First step $KMnO_4/H^+$ Second step PCl_5	The reagents given are correct; however, the question asked for reagents *and* conditions and the student has missed out a key condition of step 1. *This answer is awarded 1 out of 2 marks.*
c $C_8H_6O_4 + 2PCl_5 \rightarrow C_8H_4O_2Cl_2 + 2POCl_3 + 2HCl$	This is correct. Other equations are possible for reactions with $SOCl_2$ or PCl_3. *This answer is awarded 1 out of 1 mark.*
d	The student has shown a reasonable understanding of the mechanism; however, their cation intermediate is not accurate and, overall, the process does not represent a balanced chemical reaction. *This answer is awarded 1 out of 3 marks.*

2 Now that you have read the sample response, rewrite your answer to any part of question **1** where you did not score highly. Use the commentary as a guide. Write equations for the alternative reactions in part **c**.

The following question has an example student response and commentary provided. Work through the question first, then compare your answer to the sample response and commentary. Are your answers different to the sample responses? How are they different?

3 The three substances shown all have some acidic properties.

propanoic acid   propan-1-ol   phenol

a Write an equation for the reaction between propan-1-ol and sodium metal. [1]

b i Give the order of the relative acidities of propanoic acid, propan-1-ol and phenol, stating the most acidic first. [1]

  ii Explain your answer to **i**. [2]

c Methanoic acid, HCO_2H, has a similar acid strength to propanoic acid.

Describe a chemical test to distinguish between these two acids. Name the acid which gives a positive result in this test and describe the observations that would be made. [2]

[Total: 6]

Cambridge International AS & A Level Chemistry (9701) Paper 41 Q7a–c June 2018

Example student response	Commentary
a $C_3H_7OH + Na \rightarrow C_3H_7ONa + \frac{1}{2}H_2$	This is the correct equation. *This answer is awarded 1 out of 1 mark.*
b **i** Propanoic acid > phenol > propan-1-ol	This is the correct order of acidity. *This answer is awarded 1 out of 1 mark.*
ii The $C_3H_7O^-$ ion is destabilised because the $C_3H_7^-$ group has a positive inductive effect. In $C_6H_5O^-$, however, the lone pair on oxygen is delocalised into the ring, stabilising the negative charge.	A good response in which the student has correctly identified the relevant species and explained their stabilities. *This answer is awarded 2 out of 2 marks.*
c Methanoic acid reduces Tollens' reagent and gives a silver mirror.	An accurate description of the test and the result. *This answer is awarded 2 out of 2 marks.*

Now you have read the commentary to the previous question, here is a similar question which you should attempt. Use the information from the previous response and commentary to guide you as you answer.

4   Compound **R** is a weak diprotic (dibasic) acid which is very soluble in water.

     a   A solution of **R** was prepared which contained 1.25 g of **R** in 250 cm³ of solution.

         When 25.0 cm³ of this solution was titrated with 0.100 mol dm⁻³ NaOH, 21.6 cm³ of the alkali were needed for complete reaction.

         i   Using the formula H_2X to represent **R**, construct a balanced equation for the reaction between H_2X and NaOH.   [1]

         ii   Use the data above to calculate the amount, in moles, of OH^- ions used in the titration.   [1]

         iii   Use your answers to **i** and **ii** to calculate the amount, in moles, of **R** present in 25.0 cm³ of solution.   [1]

         iv   Calculate the amount, in moles, of **R** present in 250 cm³ of solution.   [1]

         v   Calculate the M_r of **R**.   [1]

     b   Three possible structures for **R** are shown below.

S	T	U
$HO_2CCH=CHCO_2H$	$HO_2CCH(OH)CH_2CO_2H$	$HO_2CCH(OH)CH(OH)CO_2H$

         i   Calculate the M_r of each of these acids.   [1]

         ii   Deduce which of the structures, **S**, **T** or **U**, correctly represents the structure of the acid, **R**.   [1]

         It is possible to convert **S**, **T**, or **U** into one another.

c State the reagent(s) and essential conditions that would be used for the following conversions.

   S into **T** [2]

   S into **U** [2]

   T into **S** [1]

d Give the structural formula of the organic product formed in **each** of the following reactions.

   T reacting with an excess of Na [1]

   U reacting with an excess of Na_2CO_3 [1]

e The acid **S** shows stereoisomerism. Draw structures to show this isomerism.

   Label each isomer. [2]

f When one of the isomers of **S** is heated at 110 °C in the absence of air, a cyclic compound **V**, with molecular formula $C_4H_2O_3$, is formed.

   The other isomer of **S** does not react at this temperature.

   Suggest the displayed formula of **V**. [2]

   [Total: 18]

Cambridge International AS & A Level Chemistry (9701) Paper 22 Q4 November 2013

The following question has an example student response and commentary provided. Work through the question first, then compare your answer to the sample response and commentary. Are your answers different to the sample responses?

5 a The amino acid tyrosine can be synthesised from phenol by the route shown.

   i Name the mechanism occurring in the following steps.

      step 1

      step 2 [2]

   ii What *type of reaction* is occurring in step 3? [1]

iii Suggest reagents and conditions for each of the following steps.

step 1

step 2

step 3

step 5   [5]

iv Draw the structures of the products of the reactions of tyrosine with an **excess** of each of the following reagents:

- with NaOH(aq)
- with HCl(aq)
- with Br$_2$(aq)   [4]

b   The dipeptide phe-tyr has the following structure.

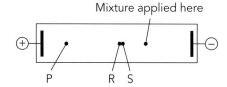

A mixture of this dipeptide (phe-tyr) and its two constituent amino acids (phe and tyr) was subjected to electrophoresis in a buffer at pH 12. At the end of the experiment the following results were seen. Spots **R** and **S** remained very close together.

Mixture applied here

P   R S

The three spots are due to the three species phe, tyr and phe-tyr.

i   Which species is responsible for spot **P**? Explain your answer.   [2]

ii Suggest why the other two species give spots **R** and **S** that are so close together.   [1]

[Total: 15]

Cambridge International AS & A Level Chemistry (9701) Paper 42 Q8 June 2017

Example student response	Commentary
a i Step 1: acylation. Step 2: addition.	Acylation is a reaction type, not the name of a mechanism. Addition is correct, but not specific enough – the *type* of addition must be specified. *This answer is awarded 0 out of 2 marks.*
ii Hydrolysis.	This is correct. *This answer is awarded 1 out of 1 mark.*
iii CH_3CHO and $AlCl_3$ for step 1. NaCN in ethanol for step 2. H_2SO_4 for step 3. Excess NH_3 for step 5.	Step 1 is a Friedel–Crafts alkylation, requiring a catalyst such as $AlCl_3$ and R–X (X = Cl, Br, I). CH_3CHO is not correct. Step 2: A source of H^+ is also needed. Step 3: This is acid hydrolysis, H_2SO_4 is correct. Step 5: This requires sealed tube condition (i.e., heat and pressure), not just excess NH_3. *This answer is awarded 2 out of 5 marks.*
iv with NaOH(aq) with HCl(aq) with Br_2(aq)	With NaOH, the student has overlooked the acidity of phenols, but correctly shown that the $-NH_3^+$ would be deprotonated. The structure with HCl is correct. With Br_2(aq), the student has not considered the directing effect of the –OH group on the benzene ring. *This answer is awarded 1 out of 4 marks.*
b i Spot P is tyr because it has a –2 charge and is lighter than phe and phe-tyr.	This is correct. *This answer is awarded 2 out of 2 marks.*
ii R and S must be phe and phe-tyr. These are close together because phe has a –1 charge and is about half as heavy as phe-tyr, which has a –2 charge.	The student has correctly identified that R and S have similar mass-to-charge ratios. *This answer is awarded 1 out of 1 mark.*

6   Now write an improved answer to the parts of question **5** where you lost marks.
Use the commentary to guide you.

28 Polymerisation

The 'deduce' command word usually requires you to work out the identity of a chemical species from information provided in the question or from information that becomes available by solving other parts of the question. Deducing the different chemical structures related to polymers is a common exam question and, in fact, the syllabus makes reference to the need to deduce the repeat units for both addition and condensation polymers. You may also be asked to do the reverse – deduce the structure of monomers from a given repeat unit or polymer structure.

Deduce	conclude from available information

28.1 Condensation polymerisation

1 Terylene is a polyester that can be made from the monomers benzene-1,4-dicarboxylic acid and ethane-1,2-diol.

   a Draw the structures of these monomers.

   b Draw two repeat units of Terylene, clearly showing the ester functional group.

   c Write a balanced equation, using structural formulae, to show formation of the polymer Terylene from these monomers.

   d Give the structure of an alternative monomer that could react with ethane-1,2-diol to produce Terylene.

2 The amino acids cysteine (Cys), valine (Val) and alanine (Ala) are shown in Figure 28.1.

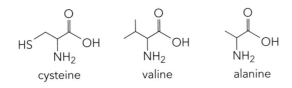

cysteine   valine   alanine

Figure 28.1

   a Deduce the structure of the tripeptide Val-Ala-Cys. [2]

   b Circle an amide functional group on your structure in part **a**. [1]

   c Explain why valine and alanine are considered non-polar amino acids. [1]

   [Total: 4]

28.2 Synthetic polyamides

1   a   Write a chemical equation, using displayed formulae, to show formation of nylon-4,4 from a suitable diamine and a dioyl chloride.

    b   Give the systematic names for the diamine and dioyl chloride used.

    c   What properties of nylons make them useful materials for synthetic fabrics?

> **UNDERSTAND THIS TERM**
> - polyamide

2   Kevlar is a synthetic polyamide that is widely used as a component in body armour and bullet-proof vests. It can be made from the monomers benzene-1,4-dioyl chloride and 1,4-diaminobenzene.

    a   Draw the structure of benzene-1,4-dioyl chloride.   [1]

    b   Draw the repeat unit of the polymer Kevlar.   [1]

    c   i   Deduce the structure of a single monomer containing an acyl chloride functional group that could be used to produce Kevlar.   [1]

        ii   Suggest why this monomer might not be suitable for making Kevlar.   [1]

    d   State and explain the properties of Kevlar that make it suitable for use in protective clothing.   [3]

    [Total: 7]

28.3 Biochemical polyamides

1   a   Describe fully how proteins are formed from amino acids.

    b   What is the mechanism associated with the reaction that forms proteins?

    c   What is meant by the primary structure of a protein?

> **UNDERSTAND THESE TERMS**
> - amino acid residue
> - polyester

2   The structure of the artificial sweetener aspartame is shown in Figure 28.2. Aspartame is the methyl ester of the dipeptide made from aspartic acid and phenylalanine. Aspartame is 2,000 times sweeter than table sugar, sucrose.

    a   Explain what is meant by the term dipeptide.   [1]

    b   Deduce the molecular formula of aspartame.   [1]

    c   Give the systematic name for aspartic acid.   [1]

    d   Draw the structure of the three organic products formed when aspartame is refluxed with dilute aqueous sodium hydroxide.   [3]

    [Total: 6]

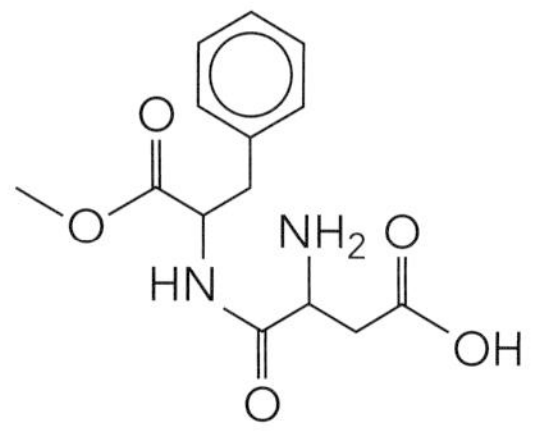

Figure 28.2

28.4 Degradable polymers

1   a   Addition polymers, such as poly(ethene), pose a significant environmental hazard because they do not biodegrade. Explain the reason for this.

    b   Chemists have designed polymers that incorporate starch granules into the polymer structure. How does this improve the biodegradability of such polymers?

2 In *ring-opening polymerisation*, cyclic monomers are converted into chain polymers. The monomer caprolactone undergoes ring-opening polymerisation to form poly(caproplactone), which has biomedical applications, including as implants and controlled-release drugs. The structure of caprolactone is shown in Figure 28.3.

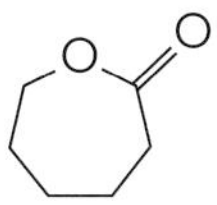

Figure 28.3

a Draw the structure of poly(caprolactone). [1]

b Poly(caprolactone) is an example of a photodegradable polymer.

    i Explain what is meant by the term photodegradable. [1]

    ii Explain why poly(caprolactone) is photodegradable. [2]

c Heating caprolactone with ammonia converts it to caprolactam and one other product. Caprolactam is an important monomer that also undergoes ring-opening polymerisation to form nylon-6.

    i Write an equation, using molecular formulae, for the reaction between caprolactone and ammonia. State symbols are not required. [1]

    ii Deduce the structure of caprolactam. [1]

[Total: 6]

28.5 Polymer deductions

1 **a** Two monomers have the chemical structure $HO_2C–(CH_2)_8–CO_2H$ and $H_2N–(CH_2)_6–NH_2$.

    i Give the systematic name for $H_2N–(CH_2)_6–NH_2$.

    ii State the type of polymer the two monomers would form.

    iii Deduce the structure of the polymer.

b The structure of two monomers is shown in Figure 28.4.

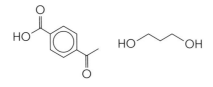

Figure 28.4: Structures of two monomers

    i Give the systematic names for these monomers.

    ii State the type of polymer the two monomers would form.

    iii Deduce the structure of the polymer.

c   Vectran is a synthetic fibre that contains varying ratios of its constituent monomers. Its structure is shown in Figure 28.5.

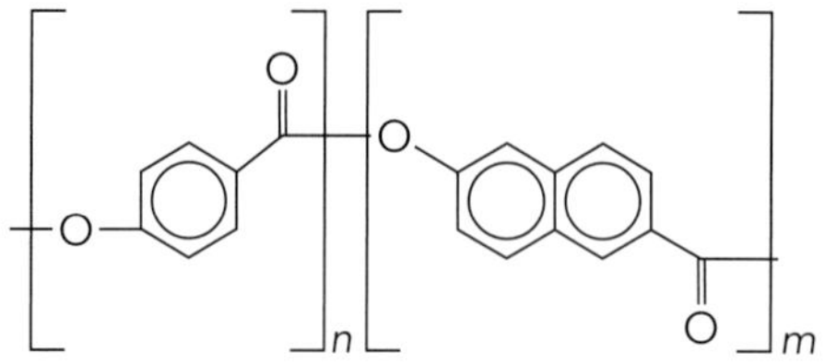

Figure 28.5: The structure of Vectran

i   What type of polymer is Vectran?

ii   Deduce the structures of the two monomers used to make Vectran.

2   A research chemist attempted to polymerise aspartic acid, $HOOCCH_2CH(NH_2)COOH$. Instead of obtaining a condensation polymer, they obtained a compound X that had a molecular ion peak at $m/e = 230$ in its mass spectrum and which was found to contain 41.7% carbon, 4.4% hydrogen, 12.2% nitrogen and 41.7% oxygen by mass.

a   Determine the empirical and molecular formula of compound X.   [3]

b   Write a chemical equation to show the formation of compound X from aspartic acid.   [1]

c   Deduce the structure of compound X.   [1]

[Total: 5]

≪ RECALL AND CONNECT 2 ≪

Acyl chlorides are reactive compounds that can be used to prepare polyesters and polyamides.

a   Which three reagents can be used to prepare acyl chlorides from carboxylic acids?

b   What reaction occurs between acyl chlorides and water, and what is observed?

c   What is the mechanism when acyl chlorides react with alcohols or amides?

REFLECTION

When creating your study plan, set SMART goals to keep your exam preparation focused. SMART stands for:

- Specific: make your goal a specific task or objective.

- Measurable: ensure you have a way to measure progress.

- Achievable: ensure your goal is achievable.

- Relevant: make sure your goal is connected to your long-term objective.

- Timed: set a time limit on achieving your goal.

'Tonight, I will study chemistry for two hours' is not a SMART goal.
A better goal is 'To improve my understanding of condensation polymers, I will spend an hour reviewing the relevant chemical reactions and structures, and will then answer five multiple choice and five long-answer questions, keeping track of my score.'

Do you feel confident that you could write a SMART goal about how you could improve your answers to 'deduce' questions?

SELF-ASSESSMENT CHECKLIST

Let's revisit the Knowledge focus and Exam skills focus for this chapter.

Decide how confident you are with each statement.

Now I can:	Show it	Needs more work	Almost there	Confident to move on
describe the characteristics of condensation polymerisation in polyesters and polyamides	Write a chemical equation for a reaction forming a polyester or polyamide and use it to explain why the reaction is a condensation.			
describe how polyesters are formed from a diol and a dicarboxylic acid or a dioyl chloride	Write chemical reactions using structural formulae to show the formation of a common polyester from these monomers.			
describe how polyesters are formed from a hydroxycarboxylic acid	Write chemical equations using structural formulae for the formation of a common polyester from a hydroxycarboxylic acid.			

CONTINUED

Now I can:	Show it	Needs more work	Almost there	Confident to move on
describe how polyamides are formed from a diamine and a dicarboxylic acid or a dioyl chloride	Draw the structure of a named polyamide and show the different monomer combinations that could form it.			
describe how polyamides are formed from amino acids	Practise drawing different polyamides starting from some of the common amino acids.			
deduce repeat units, identify monomer(s) and predict the type of polymerisation reaction that produces a given section of a polymer molecule	Look up the structures of some common polymers (such as Kevlar, Terylene, Nomex, Sorona and different nylons) and identify suitable monomers and reaction types that could form them.			
recognise that polyalkenes are chemically inert and therefore non-biodegradable but that polyesters and polyamides are biodegradable, either by acidic hydrolysis, alkaline hydrolysis or by action of light	Explain the properties of polyalkenes and condensation polymers that make them react differently in hydrolysis reactions and towards light.			
show that I understand the 'deduce' command word and answer questions that require me to make deductions from information provided	Complete some questions that require you to deduce repeat units or monomers and try to develop a strategy to quickly find the right structure.			

29 Organic Synthesis

Organic synthesis is a topic that sums up all the organic chemistry you have learned in the course. It is about connecting all the different functional groups you have studied in organic chemistry and how they can be transformed into each other. The whole of organic synthesis is a huge web of connected reactions. In this chapter you will bring all this knowledge together to answer questions on organic synthesis. The Exam skills chapter at the end of this book has more support and suggestions for how to learn to recognise and use synoptic links between topics.

29.1 Chirality in pharmaceutical synthesis

1 What is a chiral carbon atom?

2 Describe the relationship between the physical, chemical and biological properties of enantiomers. **[Total: 3]**

29.2 Preparing pure enantiomers for use as drugs

1 Give two methods of optical resolution.

2 Describe why enzymes make good chiral catalysts. **[Total: 3]**

« RECALL AND CONNECT 1 «

What element is present in all Brønsted–Lowry acids?

29.3 Synthetic routes

1 How do research chemists approach the design of synthetic routes for target molecules?

2 Sometimes, the starting compound from a raw material does not have enough carbon atoms in its molecules to make the desired product. Write general equations for reactions that add carbon atoms to:

a a halogenoalkane (RBr) [2]

b benzene. [3]

Include any relevant reaction conditions. **[Total: 5]**

UNDERSTAND THESE TERMS

- enantiomers
- chiral centres
- polarised light
- optically active mixtures
- racemic mixtures

REFLECTION

This is a big, over-arching topic that brings together all the organic chemistry in the course. It can be easy to become overwhelmed by all the transformations, reagents and conditions. How well have you been able to recall the individual parts? Can you chunk the knowledge into smaller pieces to allow you to be more efficient with your learning?

SELF-ASSESSMENT CHECKLIST

Let's revisit the Knowledge focus and Exam skills focus for this chapter.

Decide how confident you are with each statement.

Now I can:	Show it	Needs more work	Almost there	Confident to move on
explain the meaning of: • enantiomers • chiral centres • polarised light • optically active mixtures • racemic mixtures	Give the meanings of the terms: • enantiomers • chiral centres • polarised light • optically active mixtures • racemic mixtures Illustrate your explanations with examples.			
state reasons why the synthetic preparation of drug molecules often requires the production of a single optical isomer	Give two reasons why drug molecules are often needed as single enantiomers.			
for an organic molecule containing several functional groups: • identify organic functional groups using key reactions • predict properties and reactions	Draw a revision map of the organic chemistry transformations from this course. Use the following molecules as your starting point: • propene • 1-chlorobutane • methylbenzene.			
devise multi-stage synthetic routes to prepare organic molecules using key reactions	Add multi-stage synthetic routes to your revision maps from above.			
analyse a given synthetic route in terms of type of reaction and reagents used for each one of its steps and possible by-products	Annotate your revision maps from above with the types of reaction and mechanisms. Add detail on any side reactions.			

CONTINUED

Now I can:	Show it	Needs more work	Almost there	Confident to move on
understand that organic synthesis connects all the organic chemistry I have covered	Choose a synthetic route from the maps you have written for this chapter. From memory, add in the key connections, reagents and conditions, types of reaction and mechanism, including side reactions.			

30 Analytical chemistry

KNOWLEDGE FOCUS

In this chapter you will answer questions on:

- general principles of chromatography
- thin-layer chromatography
- gas–liquid chromatography
- proton nuclear magnetic resonance
- carbon-13 NMR spectroscopy.

EXAM SKILLS FOCUS

In this chapter you will:

- show that you understand the 'predict' command word and answer questions that require you to make predictions.

Making and testing predictions is central to experimental sciences, so you will certainly be required to make predictions of some sort in the exam. 'Predict' questions require you to deduce possible outcomes based on data provided, which sometimes needs to be combined with your own knowledge. Because you may have to use different types of data from different sources and apply your understanding in unfamiliar situations, 'predict' questions can be challenging. A good example of this is predicting the appearance of NMR spectra.

| Predict | suggest what may happen based on available information |

30.1 General principles of chromatography

UNDERSTAND THESE TERMS

- mobile phase
- stationary phase
- R_f value

1 Explain the general principles involved in the separation of soluble compounds by chromatography, using paper chromatography as an example. In your answer, you should make reference to the following terms: *mobile phase, stationary phase, polarity, retention factor, solvent front, partition.*

2 A class uses paper chromatography to investigate the separation of some polar food dyes by a non-polar solvent. The names of the dyes, together with their R_f values, are shown in the table.

Food dye	R_f value
Fast green FCF	0.25
Brilliant blue FCF	0.48
Allura red AC	0.75
Sunset yellow FCF	0.88

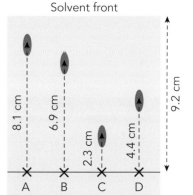

Solvent front

Figure 30.1

Figure 30.1 shows the paper chromatogram obtained by one group of students.

a Identify the dyes A, B, C and D. Show your working. [2]

b State and explain which of the dyes is the most polar. [2]

Another group of students analysed a food colouring 'Z' that is known to be a mixture of dyes. The paper chromatogram the students obtained is shown in Figure 30.2.

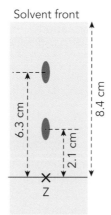

Solvent front

Figure 30.2

c   Identify the dyes from the table above that are present in the food colouring Z.   [1]
d   Suggest why different solvent fronts were measured even though each group
used the same solvent and the temperature in the lab did not change.   [1]

[Total: 6]

30.2 Thin-layer chromatography

1   a   Outline the principles behind the use of thin-layer chromatography (TLC)
to separate and identify compounds.

b   Describe the main difference between the stationary phases in paper
chromatography and TLC.

c   What are some of the advantages of TLC over paper chromatography?

d   Why can TLC be classed as adsorption or partition chromatography?

e   How could a research chemist use TLC to monitor the progress of a reaction?

2   A tripeptide was hydrolysed and the amino acids obtained were analysed
using thin-layer chromatography (TLC). The TLC plate obtained is shown
in Figure 30.3.

a   Give the name of a suitable reagent that would hydrolyse the tripeptide.   [1]

b   The TLC plate was sprayed with the chemical ninhydrin.
Explain why this was done.   [1]

The table shows some amino acids and their R_f values.

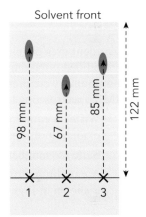

Figure 30.3

Name	Structure	R_f value
glutamine (Glu)		0.15
serine (Ser)		0.33
asparagine (Asn)		0.55
proline (Pro)		0.70
isoleucine (Ile)		0.80

c   Give the names of the functional groups present in asparagine.   [1]

d   Using data from the table, identify the amino acids present in the
     tripeptide. Show your working.   [3]

e   Calculate the mass of the tripeptide.   [2]

f   Draw the dipeptide Pro-Asn.   [1]

[Total: 9]

30.3 Gas–liquid chromatography

1 **a** Explain, with the aid of a simple labelled diagram, how a gas-
            chromatography (GC) machine is able to separate compounds.

     b How can compounds be identified using GC?

     c What are some of the limitations of GC?

     d Explain how the amount of a substance present in a mixture can
            be determined using quantitative GC.

     e What are the requirements for quantitative GC to be accurate?

> **UNDERSTAND THIS TERM**
>
> • retention time

2 A student uses gas chromatography (GC) to investigate the oxidation of ethanol
     by acidified potassium dichromate under reflux conditions. Three volatile organic
     compounds were present in the reaction mixture, which were shown by proton
     NMR spectroscopy to be ethanol, ethanal and ethanoic acid.

     a Write an equation, using [O] to represent the oxidising agent, for the
            oxidation of ethanol to ethanal.   [1]

     b State the number of peaks in the proton NMR spectrum of ethanol.   [1]

     A gas chromatogram of the reaction mixture near the start of the reaction
     is shown in Figure 30.4.

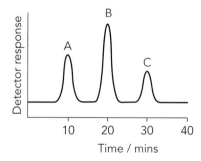

Figure 30.4

     c Identify components A, B and C in the gas chromatogram, explaining
            your answer.   [2]

     The peak areas for each component are shown in the table.

Peak	A	B	C
Area / mm²	55	95	40

d Calculate the percentage of B in the mixture.   [1]

e Predict how the appearance of the chromatogram would differ if the
reaction had been carried out under distillation conditions instead.   [2]

f Suggest how GC could be used to check when the reaction was complete.   [1]

[Total: 8]

30.4 Proton nuclear magnetic resonance

≪ RECALL AND CONNECT 2 ≪

Chemical shift values for proton and carbon-13 NMR spectroscopy will be
provided in the exam, but mass spectrometry fragment ions will not be – what
are the important, common fragment ions often seen in mass spectrometry
that help with structure determination?

**UNDERSTAND
THESE TERMS**

- NMR
- TMS
- splitting pattern

1 **a** What properties of tetramethylsilane (TMS) make it suitable for NMR?

b What is the 'n+1 rule' in proton NMR spectroscopy and how is it useful
in determining structures of organic compounds?

c For each of the compounds i-v in Figure 30.5, construct a table to show
the number of protons, splitting pattern and predicted chemical shifts (δ)
for each proton environment.

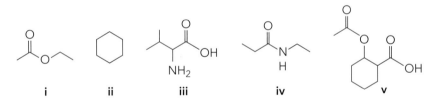

| i | ii | iii | iv | v |

Figure 30.5: Compounds for proton NMR prediction

As an example, the table shows the predicted proton NMR data for ethanol,
CH_3CH_2OH.

Proton environment	Number of protons	Splitting pattern	Chemical shift (δ)
$CH_3–$	3	triplet	0.9–1.7
$–CH_2–$	2	quartet	3.2–4.0
$–OH$	1	singlet	0.5–6.0

2   a   Chloroform is the trivial name for the common organic solvent
        trichloromethane, $CHCl_3$. In NMR spectroscopy, compounds are often
        dissolved in the solvent **deuterochloroform**, which has the formula $CDCl_3$.
        Explain why $CDCl_3$ is used.   [2]

    b   The structure and proton NMR spectrum of the anti-inflammatory drug
        naproxen is shown in Figure 30.6.

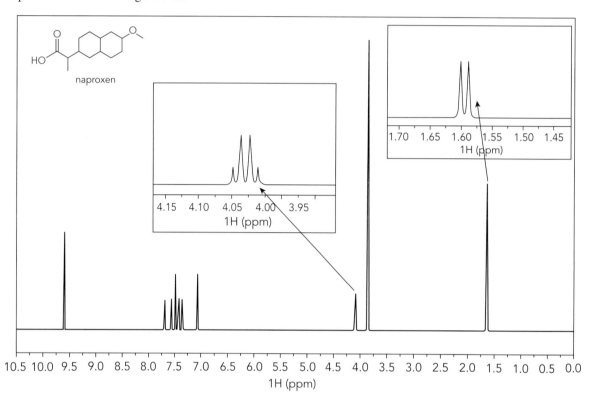

Figure 30.6

    i   Name the splitting patterns at δ 1.6 and 4.0.   [1]
    ii   The relative peak area of the peaks at 9.6 and 1.6 is 1 : 3, respectively.
         Identify the protons in the proton NMR spectrum of naproxen that
         produce peaks at the following chemical shifts:
         δ 9.5
         δ 7.0
         δ 3.8   [3]
    iii Predict the number of peaks in the carbon-13 NMR spectrum
         of naproxen.   [1]

                                                          [Total: 7]

REFLECTION

How challenging did you find the two 'predict' questions in this chapter?
Were you confident in applying your understanding of the NMR spectra
to the contexts given in the questions in order to make your predictions?

30.5 Carbon-13 NMR spectroscopy

1   Several organic compounds are shown in Figure 30.7. How many carbon-13 NMR environments do these compounds have in their spectra?

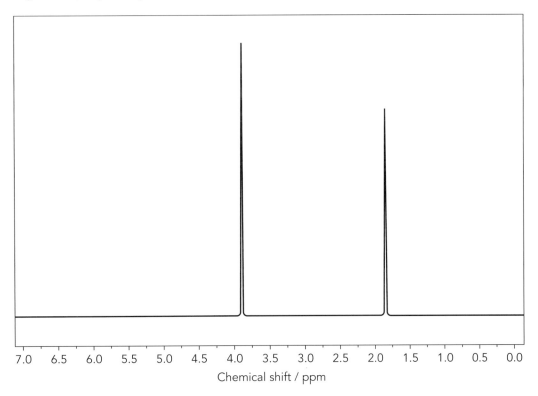

Figure 30.7: Compounds for carbon-13 NMR prediction

2   Compound **X** was analysed and found to contain 29.8% carbon, 4.4% hydrogen and 65.9% chlorine by mass. Its mass spectrum showed a molecular ion peak at $m/e = 161.5$, together with peaks at $m/e = 146.5$ and $m/e = 15$. The proton and carbon-13 NMR spectra of compound **X** are shown in Figures 30.8 and Figure 30.9, respectively.

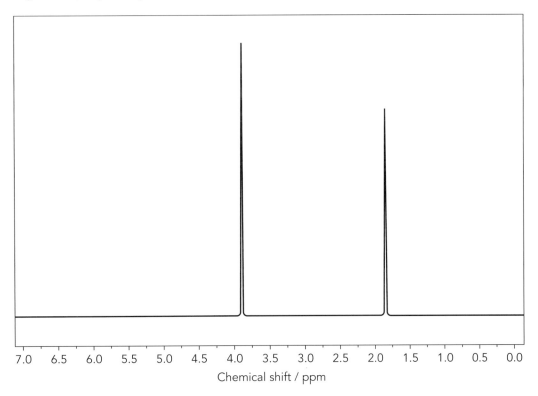

Figure 30.8

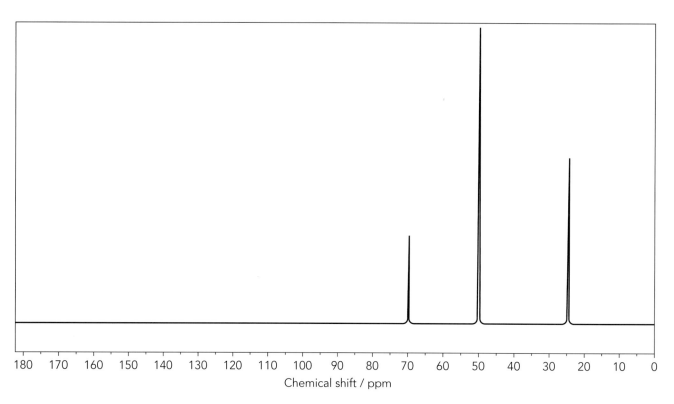

180 170 160 150 140 130 120 110 100 90 80 70 60 50 40 30 20 10 0
Chemical shift / ppm

Figure 30.9

a   Determine the molecular formula of compound **X**.   [3]

b   Identify the species responsible for the peaks at *m/e* = 146.5 and
     m/e = 15 in the mass spectrum of compound **X**.   [2]

c i   Identify the protons in the proton NMR spectrum of compound **X**
        that produce peaks at the following chemical shifts:

        δ 3.9

        δ 1.8   [2]

   ii   State what can be concluded from the splitting patterns for these
        two peaks.   [1]

d   Identify the carbons in the carbon-13 NMR spectrum of compound **X**
     that produce peaks at the following chemical shifts:

     δ 27

     δ 50

     δ 69   [3]

e   Hence, deduce the structure of compound **X**.   [1]

                                                                              [Total: 12]

REFLECTION

NMR spectroscopy has a reputation for being a challenging topic.
An important step towards mastering NMR questions is realising that they are mostly about applying a set of rules logically to determine a structure. There is very little theory that you need to recall. It can therefore be viewed more as a 'skills' topic as opposed to, for example, periodicity in Period 3, which requires recall of lots of factual information like equations. This means practice is essential when it comes to NMR. The phrase 'use it or lose it' strongly applies when it comes to the skill of interpreting NMR data.
You should therefore set aside time in your study programme to practise solving NMR problems. This will help reduce the time it takes you to determine structures by making you more familiar with the characteristic patterns seen in NMR spectra.

SELF-ASSESSMENT CHECKLIST

Let's revisit the Knowledge focus and Exam skills focus for this chapter.

Decide how confident you are with each statement.

Now I can:	Show it	Needs more work	Almost there	Confident to move on
explain and use the term R_f value in thin-layer chromatography	Create a labelled diagram of a TLC plate that contains several separated compounds and show how the R_f value is calculated for each component.			
explain and use retention time in gas–liquid chromatography and interpret gas–liquid chromatograms to find the percentage composition of a mixture	Sketch a labelled chromatogram for three separated components and show an example calculation of how the amount of each can be determined from peak area.			
analyse a carbon-13 NMR spectrum of a simple molecule to deduce the different environments of the carbon atoms present and the possible structures for the molecule	Look up the carbon-13 NMR spectra of some simple alkanes, cycloalkanes, alkenes, halogenoalkanes and alcohols, and assign each peak based on its chemical shift.			

CONTINUED

Now I can:	Show it	Needs more work	Almost there	Confident to move on
predict the number of peaks in a carbon-13 NMR spectrum for a given molecule	Draw the structures of 2-methylbutane, 2-methylpropan-1-ol, propyl methanoate and 1-iodo-2-methylpropane, then predict how many carbon-13 environments each has.			
analyse and interpret a proton NMR spectrum of a simple molecule to deduce the different types of proton present, the relative numbers of each type of proton present, the number of equivalent protons adjacent to a given proton, and the possible structures for the molecule	Look up the proton NMR spectra of some simple branched alkanes, branched halogenoalkanes, esters, amines and amides, and fully assign each peak to the protons in the structure.			
predict the chemical shifts (δ) and splitting patterns of the signals in an NMR spectrum, given the molecule	Sketch the proton NMR spectra of bromoethane, 2-propanol, ethyl ethanoate, 3-methylbutan-2-one and 4-methylphenol.			
in obtaining an NMR spectrum, describe the use of tetramethylsilane, TMS, as the standard for chemical shift measurements and the need for deuterated solvents, e.g., $CDCl_3$	Write a description of the properties of TMS that make it suitable for use as the NMR standard and why a compound would be dissolved in $CDCl_3$ not $CHCl_3$ for NMR analysis.			
describe the identification of O–H and N–H protons by proton exchange using D_2O	Sketch the proton NMR spectra of 2-hydroxypropanoic acid and 2-aminoethanoic acid. Label the peaks on the spectra that would disappear with D_2O and explain why.			

CONTINUED

Now I can:	Show it	Needs more work	Almost there	Confident to move on
understand the 'predict' command word and answer questions that require me to make predictions	Practise answering different types of predict questions and ensure you are able to justify your predictions.			

Exam practice 8

This section contains past paper questions from previous Cambridge exams which draw together your knowledge on a range of topics that you have covered up to this point. These questions give you the opportunity to test your knowledge and understanding. Additional past paper practice questions can be found in the accompanying digital material.

The following question has an example student response and commentary provided. Work through the question first, then compare your answer to the sample response and commentary. Are your answers different to the sample responses?

1   Polymers consist of monomers joined by either addition or condensation reactions.

   a   Name an example of a synthetic addition polymer and a synthetic condensation polymer.   [2]

   b   Addition polymers are long-term pollutants in the environment but condensation polymers are often biodegradable.

      i   What *type of reaction* occurs when condensation polymers biodegrade?   [1]

      ii   Identify **two** functional groups that could undergo this type of reaction.   [1]

   c   Petroleum is a non-renewable resource from which a wide range of useful polymers is currently produced. Current polymer research is looking at renewable plant material as a potential source of monomers.

      Two monomers obtained from plants are shown.

$$CH_3CH(OH)COOH \qquad HOCH_2COOH$$

      Draw the displayed formula of the repeat unit of a polymer using **both** monomers.   [2]

   d   Monomers obtained from plant sources do not usually form addition polymers. Suggest why this is.   [1]

   e   The diagrams show sections of two polymers **Y** and **Z**.

i   What would be the main force between the chains in each polymer?   [1]

ii   Which is likely to be the more hydrophilic of these two polymers?
      Explain your answer.   [2]

[Total: 10]

Cambridge International AS & A Level Chemistry (9701) Paper 42 Q8
June 2014

Example student response		Commentary
a	Addition polymer: polyethene. Condensation polymer: nylon.	Both polymers are correct. *This answer is awarded 2 out of 2 marks.*
b **i**	Elimination.	This is not correct. Polymers degrade by hydrolysis (or nucleophilic substitution). *This answer is awarded 0 out of 1 mark.*
ii	Ester and amide bonds.	The correct functional groups are identified. *This answer is awarded 1 out of 1 mark.*

c	H O O
	 | || ||
	—O—C—C—O—C—
	     |
	     CH₃
		The student hasn't shown a correct ester linkage (they've drawn an anhydride).
		This answer is awarded 0 out of 2 marks.

d	Plants don't make alkenes.	This is correct; plant materials don't usually contain unsaturated hydrocarbons. *This answer is awarded 1 out of 1 mark.*
e **i**	London forces in Y. Hydrogen bonding in Z.	Both answers are correct. *This answer is awarded 1 out of 1 mark.*
ii	Z, because it will hydrogen bond to water molecules.	This is the correct explanation for why Z is more hydrophilic. *This answer is awarded 2 out of 2 marks.*

Now you have read the commentary to the previous question, here is a similar question which you should attempt. Use the information from the previous response and commentary to guide you as you answer.

2 **a** Polyvinyl acetate, PVA, is a useful adhesive for gluing together articles made from wood, paper or cardboard. The monomer of PVA is ethenyl ethanoate, **B**.

B

PVA is formed from **B** by the process of addition polymerisation.

i   Draw a section of the PVA molecule containing at least 2 monomer molecules, and identify clearly the repeat unit. [2]

The ester **B** can be hydrolysed in the usual way, according to the following equation.

ii   Use this information to suggest a possible structure for **C** and draw it in the box above.

When substance **C** is extracted from the product mixture, it is found that it does **not** decolourise $Br_2(aq)$, but it **does** form a pale yellow precipitate with alkaline aqueous iodine. [1]

iii Suggest a structure for **C** that fits this new information. [1]

iv Suggest a confirmatory test for the functional group in the structure you have drawn in **iii**. Your answer should include the reagent you would use and the observation you would make. [2]

b   The following diagram represents a section of another polymer.

i   On the above formula draw brackets, [ ], around the atoms that make up the repeat unit of this polymer. [1]

ii   Name the functional group in polymer **D**. [1]

iii Suggest and draw the structure of the monomer, **E**, that could form this polymer. [1]

iv What *type of polymerisation* is involved in making polymer **D** from its monomer? [1]

v   What is the relationship between the repeat unit of polymer **D** and the repeat unit of PVA? [1]

c   Monomer **E** exists as two stereoisomers. Heating either isomer with Al_2O_3 gives a mixture of two unsaturated carboxylic acids **F** and **G**, which are stereoisomers of each other.

i   Name the *type of stereoisomerism* shown by compound **E**. [1]

ii   Suggest structures for **F** and **G**, and name the type of
stereoisomerism they show.   [3]

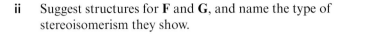

[Total: 15]

*Cambridge International AS & A Level Chemistry (9701) Paper 42 Q4
June 2011*

The following question has an example student response and commentary provided.
Work through the question first, then compare your answer to the sample response
and commentary. Are your answers different to the sample responses?

3   Procaine is used as an anaesthetic in medicine. It can be synthesised from
methylbenzene in five steps as shown in Fig. 3.1.

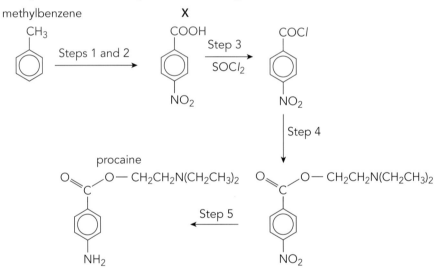

Fig. 3.1

a   i   Name all the functional groups present in procaine.   [1]

ii   A molecule of procaine has 13 carbon atoms.
State the number of carbon atoms that are sp, sp^2 and sp^3 hybridised
in procaine.   [1]

b   State why procaine can act as a base.   [1]

c   Compound **X** can be synthesised in two steps from methylbenzene.

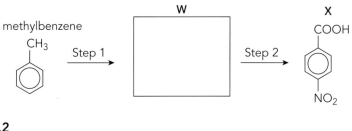

Fig. 3.2

i   Draw the structure of compound **W** in the box provided.   [1]

ii State the reagents and conditions for step 1 and step 2.   [2]

d   Procaine is synthesised in three steps from **X**.

Suggest the reagents and conditions for step 4 and for step 5
in Fig. 3.1.   [3]

[Total: 9]

Adapted from Cambridge International AS & A Level Chemistry (9701)
Paper 41 Q7a,c,d,e June 2022

Example student response	Commentary
a i Amine and ester.	The student has correctly identified the two functional groups at a basic level. They have made a very common mistake as they have considered the amine group attached to the benzene ring as a simple amine group like the one on the side chain. However, this amine group is specifically a phenylamine, not just 'amine', and this needed to be stated alongside the other groups to get the mark. *This answer is awarded 0 out of 1 mark.*
ii There are 7 sp^2 carbons and 6 sp^3 carbon atoms.	The student has counted the types of hybrid carbon atoms in the molecule. However, the question specifically asked for the number of each type of hybrid carbon atom (sp, sp^2 and sp^3) and the student has not given the number of sp carbon atoms, so doesn't get the mark. *This answer is awarded 0 out of 1 mark.*
b There is a lone pair, which can accept a proton.	This answer is correct but not quite complete. The student must also state which atom the lone pair is on to get the mark. *This answer is awarded 0 out of 1 mark.*
c i CH_3 ... NO_2	This answer is correct. *This answer is awarded 1 out of 1 mark.*

Example student response	Commentary
ii Step 1: a mixture of concentrated nitric acid and sulfuric acid. Step 2: hot potassium manganate (VII).	This answer is completely correct. Either correct names or formulae would get the marks here. *This answer is awarded 2 out of 2 marks.*
d Step 4: $HOCH_2CH_2N(CH_2CH_3)_2$ Step 5: Sn and HCl.	This answer is correct; however, the student has missed out the conditions needed for the reduction with Sn and HCl, so loses a mark. *This answer is awarded 2 out of 3 marks.*

4 Now that you have read the sample response, rewrite your answer to any part of question **3** where you did not score highly. Use the commentary as a guide.

The following question has an example student response and commentary provided. Work through the question first, then compare your answer to the sample response and commentary. Are your answers different to the sample responses? How are they different? What information does this give you about your understanding of the topic?

5 a Ethanoic acid, CH_3CO_2H, and trichloroethanoic acid, CCl_3CO_2H, are both carboxylic acids.

Ethanoic acid can be used to make ethanamide, CH_3CONH_2.

Place these three compounds in order of acidity, starting with the **least** acidic.

Explain your answer. [3]

b Methanoic acid, HCO_2H, and ethanedioic acid, HO_2CCO_2H, are two other carboxylic acids.

i State which, if any, of ethanoic acid, methanoic acid and ethanedioic acid will react with Fehling's reagent. [1]

ii State which, if any, of ethanoic acid, methanoic acid and ethanedioic acid will react with warm acidified manganate(VII) ions. [1]

c Ethanamide can be made from ethanoic acid in a two-step synthesis.

$$\text{ethanoic acid} \xrightarrow{\text{step 1}} A \xrightarrow{\text{step 2}} \text{ethanamide}$$

i Compound **A** contains chlorine.

Give the structural formula and name of **A**. [2]

ii Suggest suitable reagents for steps 1 and 2. [2]

d Compound **A** can also be used to make the amide $CH_3CONHC_2H_5$.

The proton NMR spectrum of the amide $CH_3CONHC_2H_5$ in the solvent $CDCl_3$ is shown.

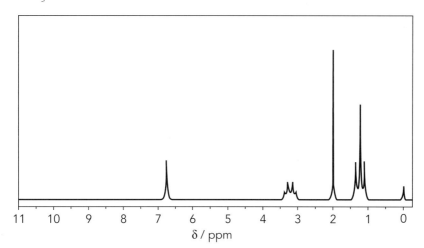

δ / ppm

i Explain why $CDCl_3$ is used as a solvent instead of $CHCl_3$. [1]

ii Complete the diagram with the chemical shifts, δ, of the protons labelled in the $CH_3CONHC_2H_5$ molecule.

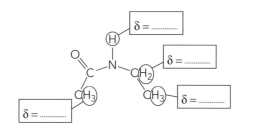

[2]

iii State and explain how the proton NMR spectrum of the amide $CH_3CONHC_2H_5$ differs when dissolved in D_2O rather than $CDCl_3$. [2]

e The mass spectrum of the amide $CH_3CONHC_2H_5$ includes a fragment ion with m/e value of 58.

Give the molecular formula of this fragment ion. [1]

f The amide undergoes the following reaction to produce diethylamine.

$$CH_3CONHC_2H_5 \xrightarrow{\text{reagent } \textbf{B}} C_2H_5NHC_2H_5$$
diethylamine

i Identify reagent **B**. [1]

ii State the number of different absorptions in the carbon-13 NMR spectrum of diethylamine. [1]

[Total: 17]

Cambridge International AS & A Level Chemistry (9701) Paper 42 Q6 November 2020

		Example student response	Commentary
a		Ethanamide is least acidic, then ethanoic acid, then trichloroethanoic acid. In ethanamide, there are no acidic groups, and it has a pH of around 7 (it's neutral). Trichloroethanoic acid is strongest because the electronegative Cl atom weakens the OH bond and stabilises the conjugate base anion.	This is the correct ranking and the student has accurately explained the relative acidities in terms of structure and bonding. *This answer is awarded 3 out of 3 marks.*
b	i	Methanoic acid reacts.	This is correct, like aldehydes, methanoic acid also reduces Fehling's reagent. *This answer is awarded 1 out of 1 mark.*
	ii	Methanoic acid and ethanedioic acid both react.	Both correct as both compounds are oxidised by warming with acidified MnO_4^-. *This answer is awarded 1 out of 1 mark.*
c	i	CH_3COCl, which is ethanoic chloride.	Correct structure, but acyl chlorides are named by adding the suffix -oyl to the parent alkane, hence this should be ethanoyl chloride. *This answer is awarded 1 out of 2 marks.*
	ii	In step 1, use Cl_2. In step 2, use methylamine.	Neither reagent is correct. Step 1 requires PCl_3, PCl_5 or $SOCl_2$ to convert the carboxylic acid to an acyl chloride, followed by a condensation reaction with ammonia in step 2. *This answer is awarded 0 out of 2 marks.*
d	i	D doesn't give a peak in NMR.	The student is correct; deuterium does not give a peak in proton NMR. *This answer is awarded 1 out of 1 mark.*
	ii	(structure with assignments: H $\delta = 6.5-7.0$; CH_2 $\delta = 3-3.5$; CH_3 $\delta = 1-1.5$; CH_3 $\delta = 1.9-2.1$)	All of these protons have been correctly assigned based on the spectrum. *This answer is awarded 2 out of 2 marks.*
	iii	The peak around 6.5–7 would disappear because H is exchanged by D.	This is correct. Labile protons (O–H and N–H) are exchanged by deuterium when D_2O is added. *This answer is awarded 2 out of 2 marks.*
e		The M_r is 87 so an m/e of 58 means loss of 29, which is ethyl. This leaves CH_3CONH^+ as the fragment.	The fragment ion identity has been correctly deduced by considering the mass lost from the molecular ion – this is a good approach. *This answer is awarded 1 out of 1 mark.*
f	i	$NaBH_4$ could be used.	This is incorrect. $LiAlH_4$ is required to reduce an amide. *This answer is awarded 0 out of 1 mark.*
	ii	Two environments.	This is correct, both carbons in the CH_3CH_2– groups are unique. *This answer is awarded 1 out of 1 mark.*

Now you have read the commentary to the previous question, here is a similar question which you should attempt. Use the information from the previous response and commentary to guide you as you answer.

6 **a** Describe what is meant by a racemic mixture. [1]

b Asparagine (Fig. 6.1) is an amino acid that contains a chiral carbon atom and displays stereoisomerism.

Separate samples of asparagine are dissolved in $CDCl_3$ and analysed using carbon-13 and proton (^1H) NMR spectroscopy.

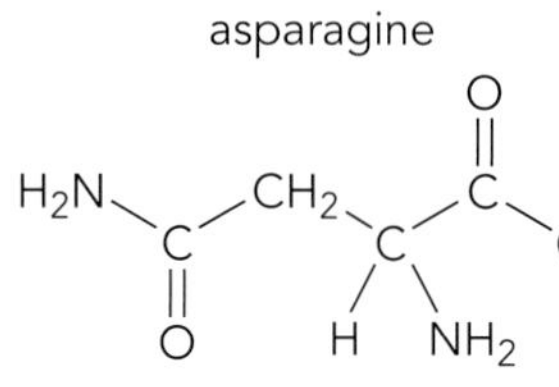

asparagine

Fig. 6.1

Predict the number of peaks seen in the carbon-13 and proton (^1H) NMR spectra of asparagine. [1]

c The isoelectric point of asparagine, asn, is at pH 5.4.

i Describe the meaning of the term isoelectric point. [1]

ii Draw the structure of asparagine at pH 1.0. [1]

d Asparagine can polymerise to form poly(asparagine).

Draw the structure of poly(asparagine), showing **two** repeat units. The peptide linkage should be shown displayed. [2]

e The isoelectric point of lysine, lys, (Fig. 6.2) is at pH 9.8.

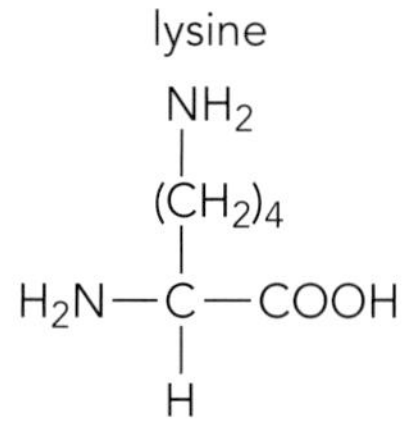

lysine

Fig. 6.2

A mixture of the dipeptide lys-asn and its two constituent amino acids, asparagine and lysine, is analysed by electrophoresis using a buffer at pH 5.0. The results obtained are shown in Fig. 6.3.

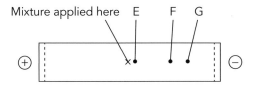

Fig. 6.3

Suggest identities for the species responsible for spots **E**, **F** and **G**. Explain your answers. [3]

f Thin-layer and gas–liquid chromatography can be used to analyse mixtures of substances.

Each type of chromatography makes use of a stationary phase and a mobile phase.

i Complete the table with an example of each of these.

	stationary phase	mobile phase
thin-layer chromatography		✕
gas-liquid chromatography	✕	

[1]

ii An unknown amino acid is analysed using thin-layer chromatography. Two chromatographs of the unknown amino acid and four reference amino acids, **P**, **Q**, **R** and **S**, are obtained using two different solvents (Fig. 6.4).

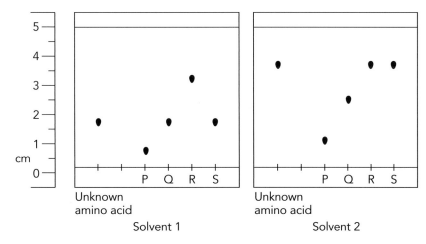

Fig. 6.4

Identify the unknown amino acid. Justify your answer. [1]

g A mixture containing three organic compounds is analysed by gas chromatography and mass spectrometry. The gas chromatogram is shown in Fig. 6.5.

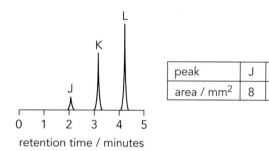

peak	J	K	L
area / mm^2	8	44	58

Fig. 6.5

The area underneath each peak is proportional to the mass of the respective compound in the mixture.

The concentration of **K** in the mixture is 5.52×10^{-2} g dm^{-3}.

Calculate the concentration, in mol dm^{-3}, of compound **L** in the mixture.

[M_r: **L**, 116] [1]

[Total: 12]

Cambridge International AS & A Level Chemistry (9701) Paper 41 Q6 June 2022

Practical skills for A Level

Paper 5 consists of two or more questions on experimental planning, data analysis, conclusions and evaluation. Paper 5 may seem less time pressured than the other papers, but it still needs careful time management. This is because the paper consists of short-answer questions alongside questions requiring apparatus diagrams, data tables and graphs to be drawn. These tasks, particularly if you are not practised at them, can easily take longer than the question time limit. It is very important to do timed practice of questions involving data analysis and graphing. As you answer the exam skills questions in this chapter, pay attention to the time it takes you to answer each one and consider whether your time could be better managed. In the exam, note the total marks available for each of the questions and ensure you divide your time between them accordingly.

P2.1 Introduction

1   What do the following important practical terms mean?

   a   Range

   b   Interval

   c   Anomalous result

   d   Precise results

   e   Accurate results

P2.2 Planning

《 RECALL AND CONNECT 1 《

What is the difference between random and systematic errors?

1   For each of the following investigations, identify the independent variable, dependent variables and any control variables:

   a   How does the acid concentration affect the rate of reaction between calcium carbonate and hydrochloric acid?

   $$CaCO_3(s) + 2HCl(aq) \rightarrow CaCl_2(aq) + CO_2(g) + H_2O(l)$$

   b   How does the structure of the alkanes hexane, 2-methylpentane, 2,3-dimethylbutane and 2,2-dimethylbutane affect their enthalpies of combustion?

   c   What is the effect of temperature on the equilibrium constant for the acid catalysed reaction between ethanol and propanoic acid?

   $$CH_3CH_2OH(l) + CH_3CH_2COOH(aq) \rightarrow CH_3CH_2COOCH_2CH_3(aq) + H_2O(l)$$

2   Suggest suitable experimental techniques, apparatus, reagents and any hazards for the following investigations:

   a   Which metals apart from iron can catalyse the peroxodisulfate–iodine reaction?

   $$S_2O_8{}^{2-}(aq) + 2Fe^{2+}(aq) \rightarrow 2SO_4{}^{2-}(aq) + 2Fe^{3+}(aq)$$
   $$2Fe^{3+}(aq) + 2I^-(aq) \rightarrow 2Fe^{2+}(aq) + I_2(aq)$$
   Overall reaction: $S_2O_8{}^{2-}(aq) + 2I^-(aq) \rightarrow 2SO_4{}^{2-}(aq) + I_2(aq)$

   b   Is the enthalpy of neutralisation of sodium hydroxide by acids different with strong and weak acids?

   $$HA(aq) + NaOH(aq) \rightarrow NaA(aq) + H_2O(l)$$

   c   What is the percentage of iron(II) in an iron tablet?

3   For the following investigations, predict the likely trends and sketch a graph of your prediction. You should ensure your prediction is fully explained.

   a   How does the enthalpy of combustion of the linear C_1–C_6 alkanes relate to the number of carbon atoms?

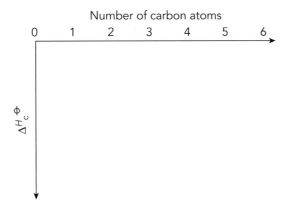

Figure P2.1: Enthalpy of combustion of the linear C_1–C_6 alkanes

   b   How does the concentration of manganate(VII) ions change over the course of their reaction with ethanedioate?

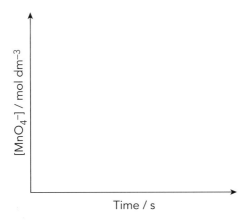

Figure P2.2: Concentration of manganate(VII) ions

c How does the enthalpy of solution of Group 1 metal fluorides vary down the group? When comparing Group 1 metal fluorides, changes in $\Delta H^{\ominus}_{latt}$ are more significant than changes in $\Delta H^{\ominus}_{hyd}$.

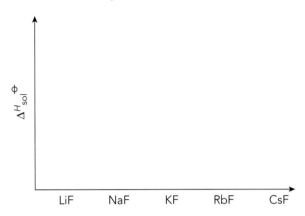

Figure P2.3: Enthalpy of solution of Group 1 metal fluorides

d In a displacement reaction, a more reactive metal displaces a less reactive metal with the release of heat energy. A group of students plan an experiment to investigate the relationship between metal reactivity and the enthalpy change of displacement reactions. The metals chosen are shown in the table, along with their standard electrode potentials.

Equilibria	$E^{\ominus}$ / V
$Ag^+(aq) + e^- \rightarrow Ag(s)$	+0.80
$Cr^{3+}(aq) + 3e^- \rightarrow Cr(s)$	−0.74
$Cu^{2+}(aq) + 2e^- \rightarrow Cu(s)$	+0.34
$Mg^{2+}(aq) + 2e^- \rightarrow Mg(s)$	−2.37
$Mn^{2+}(aq) + 2e^- \rightarrow Mn(s)$	−1.18
$Sn^{2+}(aq) + 2e^- \rightarrow Sn(s)$	−0.14

In the experiment, an excess of each metal was added to dilute copper(II) sulfate solution and the enthalpy change of the displacement reaction was calculated from measurements of the temperature change.

i Predict the relationship between metal reactivity and the enthalpy change for the displacement reaction.

ii Sketch a graph to illustrate your prediction. You will need to label the x-axis. Ensure you explain the appearance of your graph.

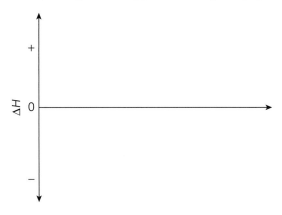

Figure P2.4

4 In this question, you will need to describe some common experimental procedures.

a Describe how a student could prepare $250.0\,cm^3$ of a standard solution of sodium hydroxide ($M_r = 40\,g\,mol^{-1}$). The concentration of the standard solution should be $1.00\,mol\,dm^{-3}$ to the nearest three significant figures. Your answer should include the names and capacities of any apparatus used. Sodium hydroxide is a solid and must be weighed (a balance is available).

b Describe how a titration would be carried out to determine the concentration of ammonia solution using hydrochloric acid as the standard and methyl orange as the indicator. Methyl orange appears orange at the endpoint. You should only describe the apparatus and method, you do not need to specify quantities.

c Describe how the enthalpy change for the reaction of magnesium powder with dilute sulfuric acid could be determined using a simple calorimeter consisting of an insulated beaker with a lid. You should only describe the apparatus and method, you do not need to specify quantities.

5 Halogenoalkanes undergo hydrolysis to produce alcohols:

$$RX(aq) + H_2O(l) \rightarrow ROH(aq) + HX(aq)$$

You are to plan an experiment to investigate the rate of hydrolysis of chloroalkanes, bromoalkanes and iodoalkanes, and of primary, secondary and tertiary bromoalkanes.

a Using your knowledge of the relationship between halogenoalkane structure and their reactivity towards nucleophilic substitution, predict the relationship between:

i the rate of hydrolysis and the type of halogenoalkane (i.e., chloroalkanes versus bromoalkanes versus iodoalkanes) [1]

ii the rate of hydrolysis and halogenoalkane structure (i.e., primary versus secondary versus tertiary). [1]

b   Design a laboratory experiment that you would use to investigate your predictions. You are provided with the following reagents:

- silver nitrate solution

- ethanol (b.p. 78 °C)

- 1-chloropentane (b.p. 108 °C)

- 1-bromopentane (b.p. 130 °C)

- 2-bromopentane (b.p. 117 °C)

- 2-bromo-2-methylbutane (b.p. 107 °C)

- 1-iodopentane (b.p. 157 °C)

Your plan should give a step-by-step description of the method, including:

- a list of the apparatus you would use

- how you would measure the dependent variable

- how you would control other variables

- appropriate quantities to use in the experiment.   [5]

c   State and explain the role of ethanol in the experiment.   [2]

d   Water acts as nucleophile in this reaction. Explain what is meant by the term *nucleophile*.   [1]

e   Suggest why sodium hydroxide could not be used in the experiment as an alternative nucleophile.   [1]

f   Draw a table that you could use to record all of the data from the experiment. Explain how you would use the data to confirm or reject your predictions.   [3]

[Total: 14]

P2.3 Analysis, conclusions and evaluation

1   Hess's law is used to calculate enthalpy changes for reactions that cannot easily be carried out. A student plans to use calorimetry to determine the enthalpy change, ΔH_r, for the decomposition of calcium carbonate:

$$CaCO_3(s) \rightarrow CaO(s) + CO_2(g)$$

This enthalpy change can be calculated indirectly using ΔH_1 and ΔH_2 for the reactions, as shown:

$$CaCO_3(s) + 2HCl(aq) \rightarrow CaCl_2(aq) + H_2O(l) + CO_2(g) \qquad \Delta H_1$$

$$CaO(s) + 2HCl(aq) \rightarrow CaCl_2(aq) + H_2O(l) \qquad \Delta H_2 = -126\,kJ\,mol^{-1}$$

In order to determine ΔH_1, the student used the procedure outlined as follows:

- 50.0 cm³ of 2.0 mol dm⁻³ hydrochloric acid was added to a polystyrene cup and its temperature measured.

- 4.10 g of calcium carbonate was added, the mixture was stirred and the temperature recorded at regular intervals.

The student's data is shown in the table.

Time / s	Temperature / °C
0	21.5
5	21.5
10	21.5
15	26.5
20	26.9
25	26.8
30	26.7
35	26.6
40	26.5
45	26.4
50	26.3
55	26.2
60	26.1
65	26.0
70	25.9

a   State Hess's law. [1]

b   Suggest why the enthalpy change for the decomposition of calcium carbonate cannot be measured directly. [1]

c   Show that the acid used in the experiment is in excess. [2]

d   Plot the student's data and use the graph to determine the maximum temperature reached. [3]

e   Calculate the enthalpy change for the reaction of calcium carbonate and hydrochloric acid to three significant figures. The specific heat capacity of the solution is $4.18\,J\,g^{-1}\,K^{-1}$. [2]

f   Draw a Hess cycle to show how the enthalpy change for the decomposition of calcium carbonate (ΔH_r) can be calculated from ΔH_1 and ΔH_2. [1]

g   Hence, calculate a value for ΔH_r. [2]

h   Suggest one way that the accuracy of the experiment could be improved without making any equipment modifications. Explain your answer. [2]

[Total: 14]

2   A group of students decided to determine the standard molar gas volume (V_{molar}) by measuring the volume of carbon dioxide produced when different masses of calcium carbonate are reacted with ethanoic acid. The chemical equation for the reaction is:

$$CaCO_3(s) + 2CH_3COOH(aq) \rightarrow Ca(CH_3COO)_2(aq) + CO_2(g) + H_2O(l)$$

The apparatus used is shown in Figure P2.5:

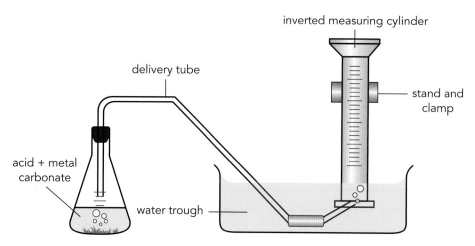

Figure P2.5

A description of the procedure from one of the student's laboratory notebooks is as follows:

'50 cm³ of 1 mol dm⁻³ ethanoic acid was added to a conical flask fitted with a bung and delivery tube. 0.100 g of powdered calcium carbonate was accurately weighed. The bung on the conical flask was removed and the calcium carbonate added, taking care to quickly replace the bung. When the reaction was complete, the total volume of gas collected in the measuring cylinder was recorded. The experiment was repeated four times, increasing the amount of calcium carbonate each time up to 0.300 g.'

a   Write the ionic equation for the reaction between calcium carbonate and ethanoic acid, including state symbols. [1]

b   Suggest why ethanoic acid was chosen in the experiment. [2]

c   A student suggested that the acid should be first titrated to accurately determine its concentration. Explain whether you agree with this suggestion. [1]

d   Explain how the students could determine when the reaction was complete. [1]

e   Give two random errors that would arise in this experiment. [2]

f Show that, for the students' experiment, the molar gas volume, V_{molar}, may be calculated using the equation:

$$V_{molar} = (V/m) \times 100.1$$

where V is the volume of CO_2 collected and m is the mass of calcium carbonate. [1]

g The students' results are shown in the table.

	Experiment number				
	1	2	3	4	5
mass of sample bottle + calcium carbonate / g	14.336	14.142	14.499	14.445	14.549
mass of sample bottle / g	14.235	13.994	14.301	14.187	14.239
mass of calcium carbonate used / g	0.101	0.148	0.198	0.258	0.310
volume of carbon dioxide collected / cm³	7	14	22	48	65

Using the students' data and the equation given in part **f**, calculate V_{molar}, recording your answers in the table. [1]

	Experiment				
	1	2	3	4	5
V_{molar} / dm³					

h A typical value for V_{molar} is 24.8 dm³. Using this value, calculate the percentage error in the students' results, recording your answers in the table. [1]

	Experiment				
	1	2	3	4	5
% Error					

i **i** State the trend shown in the percentage errors you have calculated. [1]

   ii Suggest an explanation for this trend. [1]

j Figure P2.6 shows a different method for measuring the molar gas volume. List two reasons why this method would lead to a more accurate value for the molar gas volume. [2]

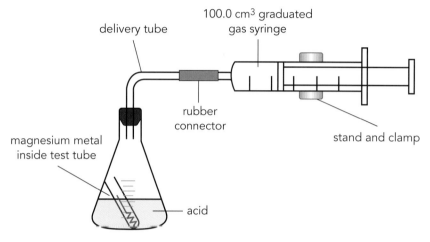

Figure P2.6

[Total: 14]

3 Hydrogen peroxide undergoes catalytic decomposition by iodide in acidic conditions. The equation for the reaction is:

$$H_2O_2(aq) + 2I^-(aq) + 2H^+(aq) \rightarrow I_2(aq) + 2H_2O(l)$$

A student investigates the rate of this reaction using the initial rates method. In each experiment, the same total volume was used. The student's results are shown in the table.

Experiment	$[H_2O_2(aq)]$ / mol dm^{-3}	$[I^-(aq)]$ / mol dm^{-3}	$[H^+(aq)]$ / mol dm^{-3}	Initial rate / mol dm^{-3} s^{-1}
1	0.05000	0.05000	0.00100	3.75×10^{-3}
2	0.10000	0.05000	0.00100	7.50×10^{-3}
3	0.15000	0.15000	0.00100	3.38×10^{-2}
4	0.25000	0.30000	0.00100	1.13×10^{-1}
5	0.25000	0.30000	0.01000	1.13×10^{-1}

a Use the student's data to deduce the rate equation for this reaction, explaining fully how you arrived at your conclusions. [4]

b Calculate the rate constant for this reaction and its units, giving your answer to two significant figures. [2]

In order to determine the activation energy, the rate constant for the reaction between hydrogen peroxide and iodide ions was determined at five different temperatures. The results are shown in the table.

Temperature (T) / K	1 / T / K⁻¹	Rate constant, k	ln k
293		5.83×10^{-5}	
303		1.67×10^{-4}	
313		5.26×10^{-4}	
323		1.36×10^{-3}	
333		3.77×10^{-3}	

c   Complete the missing values in the table, giving your answers to three significant figures. [2]

The relationship between rate constant, k, and temperature, T, is given by the Arrhenius equation:

$$\ln k = \frac{-E_a}{RT} + \ln A$$

where E_a is the activation energy and R is the gas constant, $8.31\,\mathrm{J\,K^{-1}\,mol^{-1}}$.

d   Plot a graph of ln k against $1/T$. [3]

e   Using your graph and the Arrhenius equation, calculate a value for the activation energy, E_a. Give your answer in kJ mol⁻¹ to three significant figures. [3]

[Total: 14]

≪ RECALL AND CONNECT 2 ≪

Practical questions often involve chemical tests.
How do you test for the following?

a NO_2^-(aq)   c SO_4^{2-}(aq)   e Mn^{2+}(aq)

b Br^-(aq)   d I_2(aq)

REFLECTION

The possibility of questions on unfamiliar experiments makes Paper 5 a daunting prospect for many students. What approach will you use to prepare for Paper 5? You should certainly ensure you know all the required apparatus and practical techniques, and how to draw accurate diagrams of apparatus. It is also important to understand sources of random and systematic error as questions might ask you to identify these and assess their impact. Working through lots of Paper 5 questions and studying both the mark schemes and examiner reports is recommended. This will expose you to a far wider range of experiments and help you to prepare for the unknown. Finally, don't overlook the basics – not knowing the formulae of ions, how to balance equations or use significant figures cost students too many marks each year.

SELF-ASSESSMENT CHECKLIST

Let's revisit the Knowledge focus and Exam skills focus for this chapter.

Decide how confident you are with each statement.

Now I can:	Show it	Needs more work	Almost there	Confident to move on
define the problem and identify a suitable experimental approach to solve it	Answer several Paper 5 'planning' questions and list the dependent, independent and control variables, and write a hypothesis that can be tested experimentally.			
Develop a reliable and safe method	Make notes on the apparatus and methods used for standard laboratory experiments, including making standard solutions, titrations and measuring enthalpy changes, rate constants, equilibrium constants and $E^{\ominus}$.			
record, present and analyse data	Practise tabulating and graphing data taken from Paper 5 investigations in different ways so that important findings and trends are highlighted.			
draw conclusions from data	Use scientific principles to explain data and conclusions from Paper 5 investigations.			
evaluate data and conclusions drawn from it	Calculate percentage uncertainties, suggest improvements, identify anomalous data and assess whether conclusions are adequately supported by the data.			
practice time management in order to effectively manage distribution of my time across the whole of Paper 5	Work through different types of Paper 5 questions, then attempt full, timed papers to get used to completing exams under timed conditions.			

> Acknowledgements

The authors and publishers acknowledge the following sources of copyright material and are grateful for the permissions granted. While every effort has been made, it has not always been possible to identify the sources of all the material used, or to trace all copyright holders. If any omissions are brought to our notice, we will be happy to include the appropriate acknowledgements on reprinting.

Cambridge International copyright material in this publication is reproduced under licence and remains the intellectual property of Cambridge Assessment International Education.

Cambridge Assessment International Education bears no responsibility for the example answers to questions taken from its past question papers which are contained in this publication.

Thanks to the following for permission to reproduce images:

Cover image: *cybrain/Getty Images*